Duncan and Marjorie Phillips and America's First Museum of Modern Art

Dr. Pamela Carter-Birken

Foreword by
Dr. Steven A. Burr

Series on the History of Art

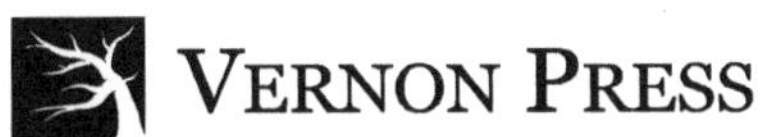

www.vernonpress.com

In the Americas:
Vernon Press
1000 N West Street, Suite 1200
Wilmington, Delaware, 19801
United States

In the rest of the world:
Vernon Press
C/Sancti Espiritu 17,
Malaga, 29006
Spain

Series on the History of Art

Library of Congress Control Number: 2021931488

ISBN: 978-1-64889-327-8

Also available:

978-1-64889-212-7 [Hardback, Premium Color]; 978-1-64889-107-6 [Hardback, B&W]

978-1-64889-326-1 [Paperback, Premium Color]; 978-1-64889-260-8 [PDF, E-Book]

Cover design by Vernon Press. Cover image: Duncan and Marjorie Phillips with son Laughlin, early 1930s. The Phillips Collection Archives. Background image designed by aopsan / Freepik.

Table of Contents

List of Figures

For Mum and Dad

Acknowledgments

Thanks to all who helped this book become reality, through knowledge and support.

At The Phillips Collection: Karen Schneider, Michele DeShazo, Vivian Djen, Elsa Smithgall, and Hayley Barton. Karen and Michele, it would not have been possible without your expertise. At Vernon Press: Ellisa Anslow, Victoria Echegaray, Marianna Pascariello, Javier Rodriquez, and Argiris Legatos.

Staff at: National Gallery of Art, Archives of American Art, Smithsonian American Art Museum, Schomburg Center for Research in Black Culture, Amistad Research Center, Fisk University, Philadelphia Museum of Art, Museum of Modern Art, Metropolitan Museum of Art, Art Institute of Chicago, Whitney Museum of American Art, Tate Modern, Baltimore Museum of Art, Century Club, David Kordansky Gallery, Artists Rights Society, and Library of Congress.

Thanks also to: Michael J. Collins, Percy North, Anne Ridder, Kate Hooten, Lynne Heneson, Lyn Kukral, Jill Bartholomew, Judy Johnston, James W. Hill, Kenneth J. Wolfe, Marsha Semmel, Rakia Faber, Carole Sargent, Suzanne Wright, Paul Richard, and Sam Gilliam.

A special note of appreciation to my family for their encouragement: Rick, Billie, Don, Kathy, Marty, Mark, Dawn, Greg, Chris, Jordan, and Nova. My husband, fiction writer Richard Birken, inspired me with the quality of his own work. He creates worlds so vivid that readers are left wondering about his characters long after the stories end.

Foreword by Steven A. Burr - In Dialogue with Art: The Phillips Collection as Interpretive Paradise

"If the world were clear, art would not exist."[1] With this claim, from his 1942 essay *Le myth de sisyphe*, Albert Camus contends that art is necessary for us, at least in part, precisely for its capacity to allow us to better understand the world and our place therein. Because human existence in the world is characterized by its absurdity, there is no absolute way in which finite human beings can ever attain ultimate certainty or truth in the world or realize an enduring reconciliation with the world. Yet through art, Camus contends, the individual can achieve some measure of understanding, meaning, and harmony in the world. Art acknowledges the meaning that is absent in an absurd world, while depicting that world in a new way which, although not necessarily a present or future reality, still stands as a real and meaningful *possibility*. Thus the unity that art is intended to portray, although not presented as a Truth, is no less meaningful by being 'merely' a possibility. As Camus explains, art must hold at its center a recognition of the world as it is and as it is experienced, without illusion. Yet at the same time, art must likewise propose aspects of existence which, although not necessary or inevitable, are also not necessarily precluded from being so. Thus, in his 1951 essay *L'homme révolté*, Camus concludes that "art, in a sense, is a revolt against everything fleeting and unfinished in the world."[2]

Camus' contention that art, both as an endeavor and as an object to be engaged, may be rightly understood as a particular manner of engaging the world toward a greater understanding of its reality and meaning, was neither new nor original in the middle of the twentieth century. Variations of this way of thinking, although perhaps without Camus' unique Absurdist perspective, can be seen throughout the history of Western thought. In his Socratic dialogue *Phaedrus* (ca. 370 BCE), Plato suggested that the experience of particular beauty, more than the experience of any other kind of quality, most nearly approaches the experience of Absolute Beauty in that, in order for any particular entity to be beautiful, it must possess some degree of absolute beauty; the beauty of any particular object is illuminated by the radiance of Absolute Beauty which it possesses; thus, in contemplating a beautiful object, one thereby approaches through contemplation the "higher" reality (the Truth) of Absolute Beauty. Plato was not here suggesting that, through the beauty of art, one could fully know the Truth of Absolute Beauty; as finite beings who are fundamentally limited by the physical aspects of our existence, such knowledge is not possible. However, what the encounter with the beauty of art *can* reveal is the *possibility* of the existence of such Truth. As Hans-Georg Gadamer explains:

> The important message that [Plato] has to teach is that...however unexpected our encounter with art may be, it gives us an assurance that the truth does not lie far off and inaccessible to us, but can be encountered in the disorder of reality with all its imperfections, evils, errors, extremes, and fateful confusions. The ontological function of the beautiful is to bridge the chasm between the ideal and the real.[3]

It is through the experience of beauty that one is able to most fully glimpse Beauty as an Absolute (and thus as Truth) and perhaps finally achieve a union (or even a re-union) with the Absolute (Truth). Art is, in this light, the most suitable means for a human engagement with the Eternal and the Divine. In Gadamer's terms, it is the *hermeneutic experience* with art, a particular manner of engagement that is constituted in and as a dialogical question and answer between the viewer and the work of art, which allows the viewer to embark upon the path toward the realization of the Truth of art. Through the hermeneutic experience, an open dialogue is formed and perpetuated in the reciprocity of question and answer as both the individual engaging in the act of interpretation and the 'object' to be interpreted address each other in question and in response.[4] Surely Marjorie and Duncan Phillips shared the preceding understanding of art's capacity to contain profound meanings, as well as the necessity of a certain way of viewing art—as a dialogical endeavor, an ongoing *conversation*—to allow for the full emergence of these meanings. Whether either Marjorie or Duncan would have articulated this understanding in exactly these terms, the fact remains that, through their creation of The Phillips Collection in Washington, D.C., in 1921, they established the perfect environment for exactly this manner of hermeneutic engagement with specific works of art.

* * *

Dr. Carter-Birken emphasizes throughout the present work that, with the establishment of the collection, Duncan and Marjorie were driven by their desire to foster the optimal conditions for the personal exploration of art. As Carter-Birken explains, Duncan's job—his ultimate *mission*—was to "continually present his collection with the maximum potential for meaningful encounters by members of the public." With this intention, Duncan and Marjorie were guided by the fundamental presumption that what matters most in the experience with art is the manner in which each individual viewer relates to each individual work, and vice-versa. Citing his 1931 text *The Artist Sees Differently,* Carter-Birken notes Duncan's contention that the experience of beauty is necessarily subjective. Yes, the artist may have a specific idea or sense that she wishes to create with any particular work of art, and yes, that particular idea *may* be received by the viewer in more or less the way in which the artist intended. But this is not to say that this is the *only* manner in which meaning may be transmitted, from artist to viewer, through the work of art. In fact, not only is this very often *not* how the transmission of meaning occurs, there is perhaps greater value in a different manner of engagement, one which depends as much on the viewer as on the work itself. The individual *conversation* with a work of art—the give and take fostered wholly through the viewer's openness to experiencing the work and the reciprocal openness of the work itself to be interpreted in different, perhaps unintended ways—this is precisely the experience with art that Marjorie and Duncan Phillips sought to create; what's more, as Dr. Carter-Birken so aptly and ably demonstrates over the pages that follow and as the enduring legacy of The Phillips Collection attests, they were wildly successful in this effort.

To fully demonstrate the depth and breadth of this success, Dr. Carter-Birken chooses here to focus on six specific artists who were key to the foundation and structure of the collection: Pierre Bonnard, Arthur Dove, Georgia O'Keeffe, John Marin, Jacob Lawrence, and Mark Rothko. With a full chapter devoted to each artist, Carter-Birken situates each artist both historically and thematically and provides a comprehensive account of how each came to be associated with the collection and with Marjorie and Duncan themselves; these accounts, which often reveal the immense overlap in sentiment and sensibility between the artists and the collection founders, beautifully reveal precisely why each artist, and her or his specific works, resonated so profoundly with Marjorie and Duncan. To augment these accounts, Dr. Carter-Birken also includes sensitive, evocative descriptions of several of the artists' works; at times, these descriptions attain the status of poetry, of art itself. Each description is itself an encounter with a work of art, engaged by and expressed from an individual, subjective experience. In this manner, Dr. Carter-Birken presents unique encounters with the work of art, of precisely the same style and quality that Marjorie and Duncan hoped to foster with their creation of the collection; just as the collection was intended to inspire contemplation, conversation, and collaboration between the work and the viewer, here we see, through each moving description, a perfect example of this dialogical relationship in action. This, then, is the twofold value and profundity of the present text—it clearly and concisely articulates the artistic principles held by Marjorie and Duncan Phillips which would ultimately inform and structure the collection, while simultaneously, and *beautifully*, demonstrating the kinds of encounters with art that the collection was intended to foster. Imperative to the collection was the generosity that Marjorie and Duncan showed, welcoming and engaging artist, artwork, and viewer. In the same fashion, the present text is a similar act of generosity, equally engaging the collection (and its creators), the artists, the works, and the viewer-reader.

* * *

Duncan Phillips' work *The Artist Sees Differently* shares many of the same principles as John Dewey's landmark text *Art as Experience*, the publication of which followed Phillips' text by three years. As Dr. Carter-Birken notes (see Chapter 1, p. xxvi), in Phillips' own copy of Dewey's work, the following line was both underlined and recopied by Phillips: "For to perceive, a beholder must create his own experience." And although Phillips would have encountered these exact words more than a decade after the opening of the collection, there is perhaps no better way to describe the motivations and means which guided Duncan and Marjorie. To initiate the experience, Marjorie and Duncan selected examples of Modern works of art which they believed had something urgent and profound, if also ambiguous, to say to the viewer. At the same time, however, they did not limit the works on display to just these works of Modern art; to create a broader context for engagement, pre-Modern art was also included and highlighted in the collection, borne of the Phillips' desire to demonstrate the links traversing the history of art to the Modern, to provide a ground to inform the conversation between viewer and artwork and from which the conversation between the two could grow (see, e.g., Chapter Two, p. 15-27). Yet, although Marjorie and Duncan felt it important to establish such historical threads and influences to better elucidate the meanings of the Modern works (or rather, to better allow the Modern works to present their meanings), they intentionally avoided definitive explanations of the works they chose to display; just as the presence of historical precursors could potentially inspire new directions of conversation, so this avoidance of 'sanctioned' interpretation would better allow each viewer to engage the work on its terms and on one's *own* terms, toward an individual, *personal* determination of the meaning of the work for oneself. Here again, we see the Phillips' intentional commitment to creating the perfect conditions for a unique engagement between an individual viewer and a work of art, as equals, in a *relationship* toward the determination of meaning.

Underlying the experience of meaningful, reciprocal dialogue in general, and the dialogical relationship envisioned and established by the collection, is the fundamental commitment to *openness*. In 1931, Duncan contended that the "collector or critic who adventures in modern art is wise if he…simply advocates tolerance and respectful study of the many different ways of seeing and painting" (see Chapter 3, p. 15). The manner in which specific works were presented as part of the collection, in the presence of precursor works but without explicit, prescribed interpretation, as discussed above, was only the first step in fostering the kind of openness to experiencing art which would ultimately define The

Phillips Collection and set it apart from other museums of Modern art that would follow. Recognizing that the conversation between viewer and art could never be static, and similarly acknowledging that experiences with and meanings of works could change over time, Marjorie and Duncan regularly changed the structure of specific exhibits, re-arranging the works themselves, moving works into and out of different collections to inspire new conversations between the works themselves and the viewer; as Duncan himself explicitly stated in 1926, "[the] arrangements are for the purpose of contrast and analogy" (see Chapter 3, p. 16). This contrast is *critical*; it is the separation, the *difference*, which demands, perhaps even presupposes, the relationship that will develop between viewer and work and the communion that will occur between the two in a resolution toward an understanding of meaning.

Here now perhaps can be seen the full brilliance of the values and intentions that guided Marjorie and Duncan in the creation of the collection: Not only did they foster the ideal conditions to invite a personal, subjective exploration of, and conversation with, each work of art for the individual viewer, but they constantly reshaped the terms of that conversation to encourage questioning on the part of the viewer, not just of what a particular work might mean but also of what the viewer herself has decided that the work means, an ongoing and evolving hermeneutic exploration of the work, of oneself, and of the relationship between the two, directed not toward an ultimate, final 'truth' but rather toward a myriad of potential meanings to be discovered and explored. Although it is essential that each work of art be allowed to present itself without commentary, it is equally essential that each work be allowed to present itself in proximity to other works, be they precursor or contemporary works. *This is the brilliance of The Phillips Collection*—the combination of a profound openness, guided by the insistence on allowing each work to present itself on its own terms, juxtaposed with other works as partners in a dynamic dialogue that compels the viewer not only to *question*, but to *continue* to question, the possible meanings presented in any given work. It is perhaps only through a constant—and constantly renewed—re-arranging and re-examining the work of art, seeing each work again and again, seeing each work *differently*, that the viewer can not only more fully experience the meaning of a particular work but also the greater meaning of 'Art' itself. What's more, this unique perspective on art, emphasizing openness, patience, and tolerance, can equally and profitably be applied on broader terms, in times increasingly defined by the wonder and diversity of humanity but equally undermined by the forces of marginalization and polarization, as we seek to be not just better viewers of art but also better participants in culture and in society—in short, to be better human beings.

Steven A. Burr,
Loyola University Maryland

Notes

[1] Albert Camus, *The Myth of Sisyphus and Other Essays*, trans. Justin O'Brien (New York: Alfred A. Knopf, 1955), 98.
[2] Albert Camus, from "Create Dangerously," a lecture originally delivered at the University of Uppsala in December 1957; published in Albert Camus, *Resistance, Rebellion, and Death*, trans. Justin O'Brien (New York: Alfred A. Knopf, 1961), 265.
[3] Hans-Georg Gadamer, "The Relevance of the Beautiful," in *The Relevance of the Beautiful and Other Essays* (Cambridge: Cambridge University Press, 1986). This is a translation of the 1977 essay *Die Aktualität des Schönen*, which itself was a revised version of a lecture entitled "Art as Play, Symbol, and Festival" (delivered 1974, published 1975), 15.
[4] Hans-Georg Gadamer, *Truth and Method*, second edition, translation revised by Joel Weinsheimer and Donald G. Marshall (New York: Continuum, 1989, 2004), 363.

Introduction: Trusting the Viewer

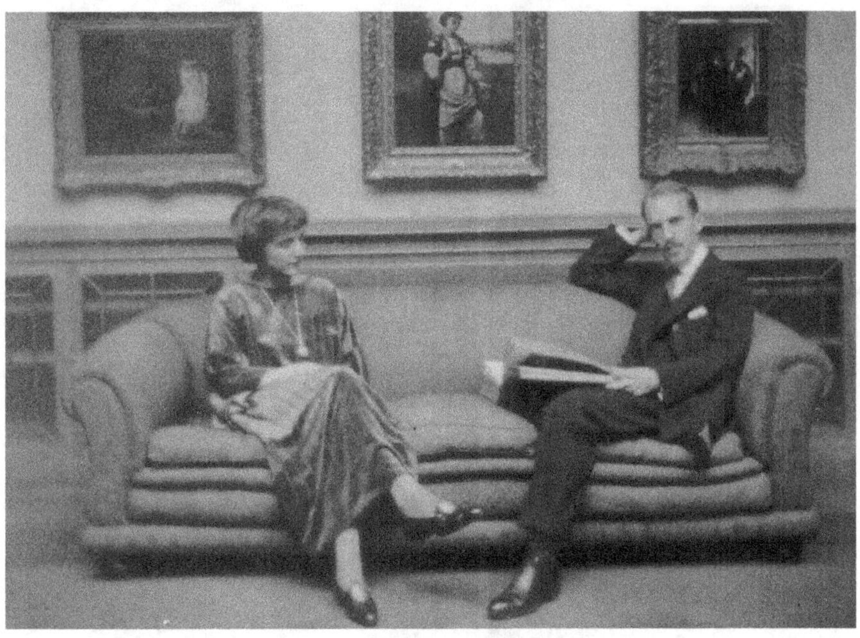

Image I. 1. Marjorie Acker Phillips and Duncan Phillips, ca. 1922. They met and married in 1921, the year they opened America's first museum of modern art. The Phillips Collection Archives.

He was born to privilege and sought the world of art through collecting and writing. She lived at the center of that world – a working artist encouraged by the famous artists in her extended family. Together, Duncan Phillips and Marjorie Acker Phillips founded The Phillips Collection in Washington, D.C., the first museum of modern art in America. It opened in the autumn of 1921, a few weeks after they wed. Located within the mansion his parents built at the end of the nineteenth century, The Phillips Collection predates New York City's Museum of Modern Art (MoMA) by eight years and its Whitney Museum of American Art by nine.

For the most part, Duncan took the lead in developing the couple's art collection and showcasing it. Marjorie, by her own adamant choice, kept space and time to paint. Duncan considered Marjorie a partner in the museum even though she was not directly involved in all purchasing and presentation decisions. To him, her influence was omnipresent.

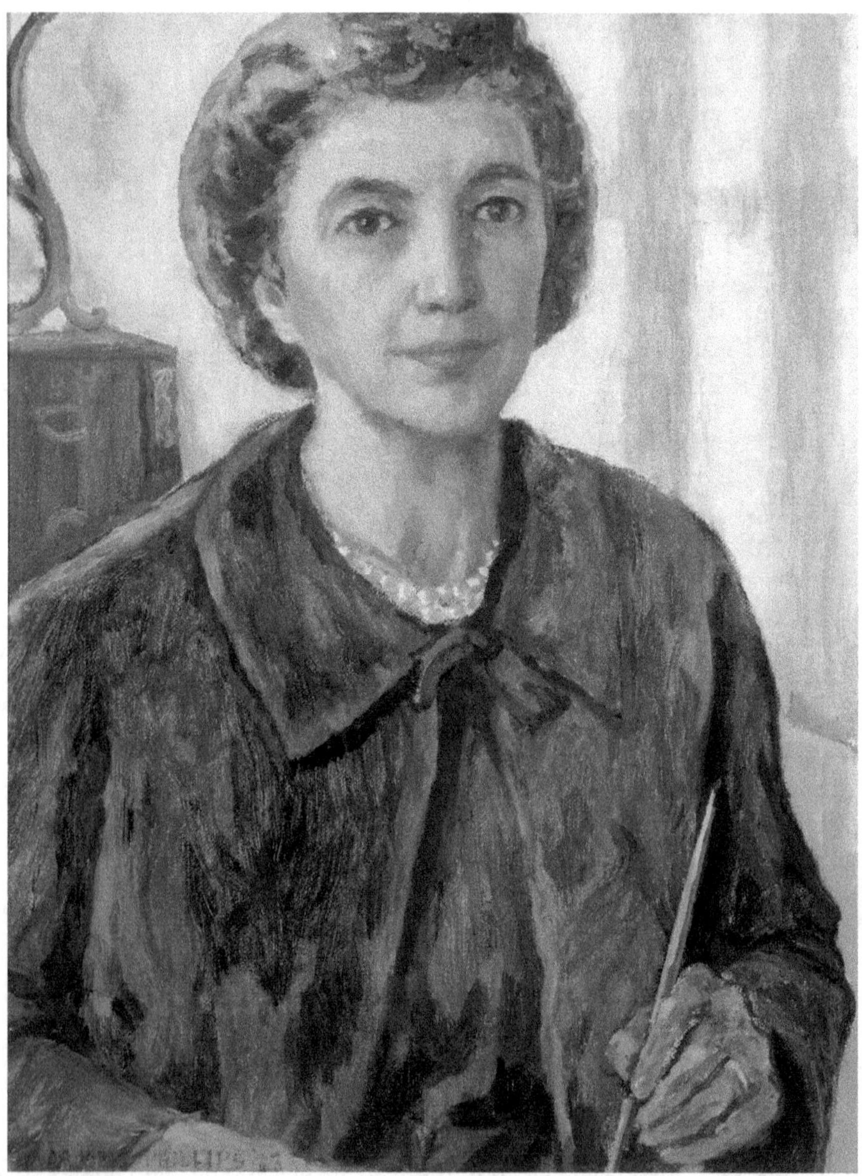

Image I. 2. Marjorie Phillips, Self-Portrait, 1963, Oil on canvas 16 x 12 in.; 40.64 x 30.48 cm. The Phillips Collection: Gift of the artist, 1984. Paintings, 1539, American.

Although Duncan's writings on artists and art history were widely published, he chose not to provide much instruction for visitors to the museum. As curator of its rooms, he employed several methods of helping visitors interact with art without asserting how they should respond to any particular work. While Phillips blazed the trail with a museum of modern art, he intentionally did not collect only modern works; he believed viewers should be provided with links to art of the past. Another Phillips practice was to place works by American and European painters in the same vicinity, no matter the art's era. Phillips's other methods of prompting independent thinking included in-depth collecting of certain artists and changing the juxtaposition of paintings on gallery walls. Additionally, he believed the homelike atmosphere of The Phillips Collection was more conducive to personal reflection of art than a traditional marble-halls institution. Over and over, he wrote that he and Marjorie wanted the people who came through the doors to enjoy themselves. Yet, he also encouraged viewers to move beyond their comfort zones when considering the piece of art before them. Each of Duncan's tenents for operating The Phillips Collection contributed to his overarching goal of providing optimal conditions for personal exploration of art.

Duncan Phillips worked his entire adult life not at a bank or a law firm or as the patriarch of a corporation. Thanks to money made by his mother's father in the steel industry and from his father's glass manufacturing business, he could devote himself to sharing art. To Phillips, his job was to continually present his and Marjorie's collection with the maximum potential for meaningful encounters by members of the public. Importantly, his life's work of assisting both artists and viewers extended far beyond his own museum. Phillips was a prolific writer of books, articles, essays, speeches, exhibition material, and letters. Through them he reached a national, and sometimes, international audience. His published writing and speaking engagements undeniably expanded his influence on modern art beyond the walls of The Phillips Collection. So, too, did his service as a trustee for the National Gallery of Art and MoMA. He was also called upon to lead a regional committee of the Public Works of Art Program during the Great Depression, and then as World War II was ending, to chair a group of renowned modern art experts in determining which nineteenth and twentieth-century works of American art would be selected for a post-war exhibition in London.

Phillips was passionate about the power of the artist to create something unique and the power of the viewer to experience it personally. His advocacy for individual encounters with works of art can be seen in many of his writings. In fact, Phillips published twice on the subject before philosopher and education reformer John Dewey released his book *Art as Experience* in 1934. Still in print, Dewey's *Art as Experience,* which covers architecture, sculpture, painting, music, and literature, remains on the required reading lists in many college courses on education and art history, among others. In Phillips's 1931 book *The Artist Sees Differently* he considered it essential for viewers to understand that beauty is subjective. An artist communicates through his or her work, but a viewer perceives the work in his or her individual way. Phillips took the individual encounter further in a 1931 article for *The American Magazine of Art* when he wrote that a particular work of art can be received by the same viewer differently when revisited. Both points –art is interpreted independently, and a viewer's reaction to the same piece of art can change – are exactly what Dewey would espouse. Phillips, a life-long learner, admired Dr. Dewey, even supplying the venue for Dewey's Washington, D.C. lecture "The Philosophy of the Arts." The headline in the *Washington Post* for its review of the 1938 lecture summarized the main theme of the event as "Let Art Do Things to You, Dewey Urges."[1]

Today, nearly all art museum directors and curators adhere to the Phillips-Dewey approach of avoiding too much instruction for people visiting their permanent collections and temporary exhibitions. Through much of the first half of the twentieth century, however, arts intelligentsia prescribed the tamping down of a viewer's individualized reaction to a work of art, and set forth rules to be followed. British art critics Clive Bell and Roger Fry, and later, American art critic Clement Greenberg championed formalism, the position that a picture should be met solely on its structural elements such as line, shape, color, and texture. Bell and Fry were members of London's culturally elite Bloomsbury Group, remembered mostly for Bell's sister-in-law, author Virginia Woolf. Without question, the protean figure in art criticism in the United States at mid-century was Greenberg. His dogma of formalism became the primary impetus for dialogue about art on American college campuses from the late 1940s into the 1960s.

For Duncan Phillips, formalism was too limiting. It did not allow for the imaginative participation of the viewer, crucial to his concept of art appreciation because it can further an individual approach to art. The Phillips Collection Archives maintains his personal copy of a first edition of Dewey's *Art as Experience*. In it, Phillips underlined numerous passages or made notes in the margins. By way of emphasis, he both underlined and copied in his own hand these words from Dewey: "For to perceive, a beholder must create his own experience."[2]

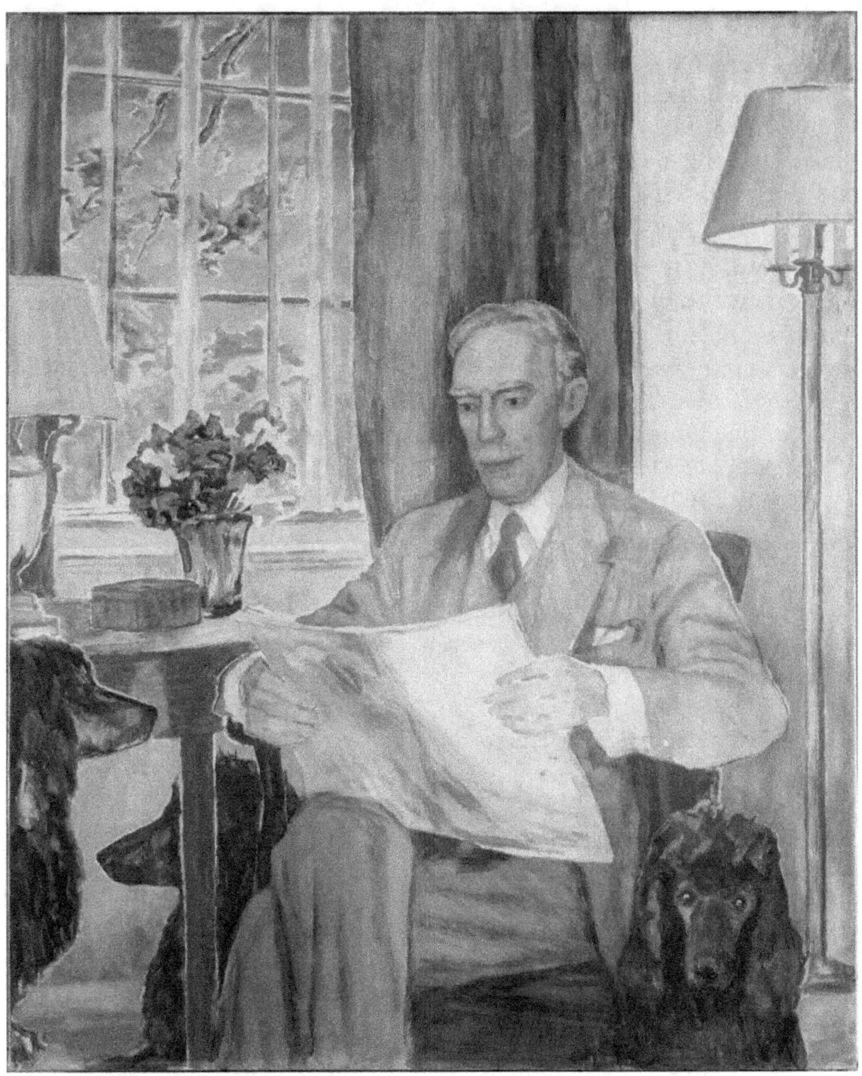

Image I. 3. Marjorie Phillips, *Duncan Phillips with the Dogs C'Est Tout, Ami and Babette*, 1975, Oil on canvas 40 x 32 in.; 101.6 x 81.28 cm. The Phillips Collection: Gift of the artist, 1984. Paintings, 1497, American.

To aid the beholder in deriving personal enrichment from art, Duncan and Marjorie Phillips purchased works by scores of artists from different places and different times. Among the most renowned are: Pierre-Auguste Renoir's *Luncheon of the Boating Party*, an Impressionist masterwork of weekend leisure; thirty panels of Jacob Lawrence's sixty-panel *The Migration Series*, a stirring account of African Americans moving from the agrarian South to the industrial North; and four deeply abstract color-soaked canvases by Mark Rothko. Art lovers the world over come to The Phillips Collection to see paintings by Renoir, Lawrence, Rothko, and many others, including works by Paul Klee, Georges Braque, Honoré Daumier, Stuart Davis, Milton Avery, Vincent van Gogh, Edgar Degas, John Sloan, Edward Hopper, Winslow Homer, and Albert Pinkham Ryder.

Several artists admired by Duncan Phillips offer important pipelines into art history, especially connections to romanticism, which he prized over purely classical art. Two of his favorite romantic painters were the fifteenth-century Italian Giorgione, about whom he authored the book *The Leadership of Giorgione* (American Federation of Arts, 1937), and the nineteenth-century American Ryder. A fine accolade from Phillips to a modern artist was a comparison to one or the other. Although he often conveyed the significance of Giorgione and Ryder to romanticism, it represents only a small portion of his writing and public speaking.

While Duncan Phillips avoided telling viewers what to think about particular works of art, he sometimes deemed it valuable to articulate to his audience pertinent connections within the history of art. He would share such insights with readers of his books and articles as well as attendees at his gallery talks and slide presentations. Certainly, Duncan could have held forth on any of the artists in his and Marjorie's collection. But six particular artists stand out for their stark individualism as creators and as igniters of viewers' imaginations: Pierre Bonnard, Arthur Dove, Georgia O'Keeffe, John Marin, Lawrence, and Rothko. Works by the six artists solidify the Phillips-Dewey stance that there is no right way to feel about a piece of art. Duncan Phillips did, however, offer specific thoughts on how they encourage viewer participation. Technical skills come into play, of course, as well as each painter's artistic vision, but the thing that sets the six apart is their savvy in inviting the viewer in. As examples, he wrote of Bonnard, "who with his brush opens a window on flowers dreaming in the sun"[3] and of Dove, "who is especially sensitive to light absorbed and light refracted."[4] Phillips felt O'Keeffe possessed the ability to coax contemplation from viewers by challenging them. He wrote that a blue petunia she painted "will cause blue to become an emotional experience in and for itself."[5] Perhaps most dramatically, he wrote of Marin, "whose far-away islands call to our imagination from the blur of the near and from the world that cannot hold us."[6] Washington, D.C. artist Lou Stovall said it best about Lawrence. In an essay based on a lecture he delivered at The Phillips Collection about collaborating with Lawrence, Stovall wrote: "The triumph of the human spirit is to rise above limitations, to create a sense of order, a place of well-being, and an attitude of possibilities."[7] As for Rothko, who shared with Phillips an unshakable commitment to a viewer's personal encounter with art, he could have been speaking for them both when he told a reporter for *Life* magazine: "A painting is not a picture of an experience; it is an experience."[8]

Not only did Duncan Phillips feel that Bonnard, Dove, O'Keeffe, Marin, Lawrence, and Rothko were artists whose work provokes independent thought in viewers, he thought it imperative that viewers take responsibility for their own opinions. In an undated, handwritten essay, Phillips wrote "The capacity to decide for oneself is the only protection against the contagions of fashion in art."[9] When discussing viewer autonomy in his book *The Artist Sees Differently*, he wrote that "each of us makes his own beauty out of his inner consciousness."[10] A review of the book by Elizabeth Luther Cary, the first full-time art critic at the *New York Times*, pointed out Phillips's knack for energizing others toward self-reliant ideas about art. "An exuberance of appreciation of his subject carry [*sic*] the reader into a state of mind to think for himself," Cary wrote in 1931.[11]

Carrying the viewer into a state of mind to think for herself remained Duncan Phillips's leitmotif throughout his life. He died in 1966 at age seventy-nine, and although he spoke publicly many times, recordings of his lectures, gallery talks, or radio and television interviews seemingly did not exist. Consolation could be found in the abundance of Phillips's writings, which survive. It turns out, so does an audio recording of Phillips during a presentation about his life with art. The recording arrived at The Phillips Collection in 2017, courtesy of Federal News Service. The audience, location, and precise date are unknown, but the presentation was delivered sometime in 1961. Phillips would have been seventy-five years old that year, and what may be most remarkable in his comments are their consistency with statements he had made decades earlier. In addition to returning to the importance of individualism in society and art, Phillips would again remark on continuity in art and how modern artists had not strayed from the past nearly as much as they might profess.

People who were privy to how Duncan Phillips interacted with visitors have recounted his respect for varying reactions to the art he had collected. Artist Willem de Looper, who worked at The Phillips Collection in several capacities, said his employer did not like to explain art in great detail. "He trusted the education of the viewer to enjoy things and learn things."[12] Marjorie Phillips agreed that while her husband would "go around talking" to visitors, "he wasn't trying to teach or implant anything."[13] She added that when Duncan was at the museum conversing about art, "he enjoyed what others said."[14]

Duncan Phillips could very much be described as old-school in his dress and manner. "That anyone still wore white gloves when coming out to dinner was deeply impressive to me," wrote art critic John Russell about breaking bread with Phillips in the 1960s.[15] Allene Talmey of *Vogue* studied Phillips for a 1955 feature story about the museum and its founders. She shared her observations with the magazine's readers: "Few realize the tall, almost translucent man, white-haired and white moustached, who darts with the nervous transitions of a hummingbird is Duncan Phillips."[16] Talmey wrote that Phillips "usually wears a gray suit, a small dark bow tie and he speaks as neatly as that tie – clearly, with pleasure."[17]

The voice was indeed clear. In the tape recording from 1961, Phillips, in both cadence and enunciation, brings to mind an anchor from an evening news broadcast. While not as polished as a network star, he nonetheless handled his remarks with finesse. Phillips knew how to modulate volume and pacing. The few times he started to falter, he drew upon the richness of his timbre. Beyond discussing art history and the history of The Phillips Collection, he took the opportunity to suggest to his audience two participatory guidelines he had proffered in the past. First, they allow themselves to enjoy art. Second, they broaden their horizons with the kind of art they are willing to contemplate. "It has been our wish to share our treasures with open-minded people," he said of himself and Marjorie. "They are welcome to feel at home with the pictures in an unpretentious domestic setting, which is at the same time physically restful and mentally stimulating."[18]

Part One of this book, *Foundations for Personal Art Encounters*, looks at the elements of Duncan and Marjorie's partnership. He would become the curator who developed innovative methods of presenting art that invite reflection, and the scholar who wrote and spoke about modern art. She would prove herself to be an accomplished painter as well as a thoughtful decision-maker for The Phillips Collection. Marjorie always gave credit to Duncan for the ongoing success of their museum, yet he stated many times that he could not have done it without her. In Part Two of this book, *Six Artists Through a Phillips Collection Lens*, connections between the Phillipses and the six are examined – and ideas about imaginative viewing of works of art are offered.

For Duncan Phillips, being open-minded meant "to be receptive, responsive, unprejudiced, and thoroughly alive."[19] For Marjorie Phillips, being thoroughly alive meant painting. When Marjorie became director of The Phillips Collection upon Duncan's death, not only did she honor his trust in the viewer, but she added the strength of her lifetime as an artist. "In painting," she said, "let there be surprise, mystery, indefiniteness."[20] Through their collection of works by Bonnard, Dove, O'Keeffe, Marin, Lawrence, and Rothko, the Phillipses increased the likelihood a viewer might experience one, two, or all three.

Notes

[1] "Let Art Do Things to You, Dewey Urges," *Washington Post*, November 14, 1938.
[2] Duncan Phillips, "Handwritten notes on 1934 Edition of John Dewey's *Art as Experience*," ca. 1934, The Phillips Collection Archives, Washington, D.C.
[3] D. Phillips, *The Artist Sees Differently* (New York: E. Weyhe, 1931), 128.
[4] D. Phillips, "Original American Painting of Today," *Formes*, January 1932, 198.
[5] D. Phillips, A Collection in the Making: A Survey of the Problems Involved in Collecting Pictures Together with Brief Estimates of the Painters in the Phillips Memorial Gallery (New York: E. Weyhe, 1926), 66.
[6] Ibid., 60.
[7] Lou Stovall, *The Art of Silkscreen Printmaking* (Washington, D.C.: Howard University Gallery of Art, 2001), 40.
[8] "Mark Rothko: Luminous Hues to Evoke Emotions and Mystery," *Life*, November 16, 1959, 83.
[9] D. Phillips, "Untitled Essay on Romantic Art, The Phillips Collection Archives, Washington, D.C., Unknown.
[10] D. Phillips, The Artist Sees Differently, 28.
[11] Elizabeth Luther Cary, "Various Ways to See and to Do in Art Reconciled," *New York Times*, June 14, 1931.
[12] Willem de Looper, interview by Donita M. Moorhus, 2005, The Phillips Collection Oral History Program, The Phillips Collection, Washington, D.C.
[13] Marjorie Phillips, interview by Paul Cummings, 27 June 1974, Archives of American Art Oral History Program, Archives of American Art, Washington, D.C.
[14] Ibid.
[15] John Russell, "The Eye of Duncan Phillips," *New York Times Book Review*, December 5, 1999.
[16] Allene Talmey, "The Unique Phillips Collection," *Vogue*, February 1, 1955, 40.
[17] Ibid.
[18] D. Phillips, transcript of 1961 lecture, audience and location unknown, audio recording and transcript provided by Federal News Service, Washington, D.C. to The Phillips Collection Archives.
[19] D. Phillips, "Modern Art and the Museum," *American Magazine of Art* 23 (October 1931): 275.
[20] M. Phillips, *Marjorie Phillips and her Paintings*, ed. Sylvia Partridge (New York: W.W. Norton, 1985), 117.

Part One: Foundations for Personal Art Encounters

"My gifted wife is my constant associate and mentor."

— Duncan Phillips

Chapter 1

The Phillips Memorial Art Gallery Opens

It was born of grief.

Best man Duncan Phillips stood at his brother's side when James Laughlin Phillips married Alice Conyngham Gifford on Nantucket in September 1917. The groom's father, Major Duncan Clinch Phillips, was not well enough to travel so he remained at the family's summer home in the Allegheny Mountains of Pennsylvania. Major Phillips, a veteran of the Union Army and a retired industrialist, died on the day of the wedding. Sadly, death would come again to the tight-knit family the following year.

"The Kaiser's armies were in retreat and World War I was winding down," wrote memoirist J. George Butler. "As the world was heaving a sigh of relief over the war's ending, another tragedy was waiting to strike mankind everywhere."[1] Butler was referring to the influenza pandemic of 1918, responsible for anywhere from twenty-million to fifty-million deaths worldwide. Within Washington, D.C., 35,000 people would become ill with the flu, and 3,000 would die from it. In October 1918, edition after edition of the *Washington Post* updated citizens on the health crisis that had necessitated the closing of schools and churches. Headlines included "Malady Spreads in City at Alarming Rate," "FLU Reaches Crest," and "Number of Deaths Went to New High Mark." One of the articles detailed the shortage of coffins and gravediggers in the city. The names of the dead were listed in the *Post* as near as possible to the date each individual succumbed; many were men and women in their twenties and thirties. James L. Phillips, at age thirty-four, became one of the influenza fatalities that October. He left behind his widow, Alice, and an infant son, Gifford. James died only thirteen months after his father, leaving Duncan and his mother with new and compounded grief.

The brothers had always been close. James, older by two years, delayed going away to Yale until Duncan was eligible to accompany him. At the university, Duncan studied literature, but he advocated for courses in art history. He felt so strongly about art appreciation education that he authored an article for *The Yale Literary Magazine* titled "The Need of Art at Yale." In the lengthy 1907 piece, the twenty-year-old argued that art history classes would bring beauty to the lives of "future citizens in this marvelous breathless modern world, so sadly stained in cities with excess of printer's ink and factory smoke."[2] After the brothers graduated college in 1908, they returned to live with their parents in the District of Columbia, where they pursued independent aspirations. James concentrated on a banking career and Duncan published poetry and articles on art. Duncan also became active in Washington, D.C.'s Reading Club, a group of young society people who counted Helen Taft among its members. During William Howard Taft's presidency, his daughter would sometimes host the club at the White House.

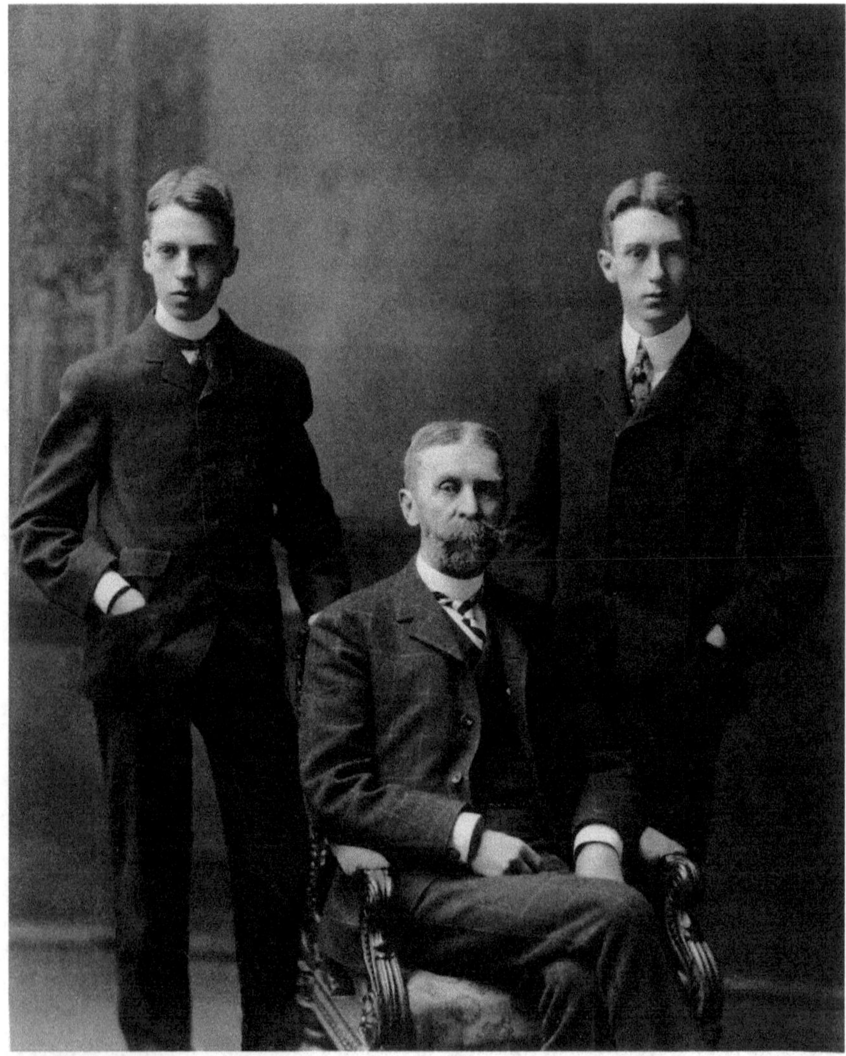

Image 1. 1. Left to right: Duncan Phillips, Major D. C. Phillips, and James Phillips, ca. 1900. The Phillips Collection Archives.

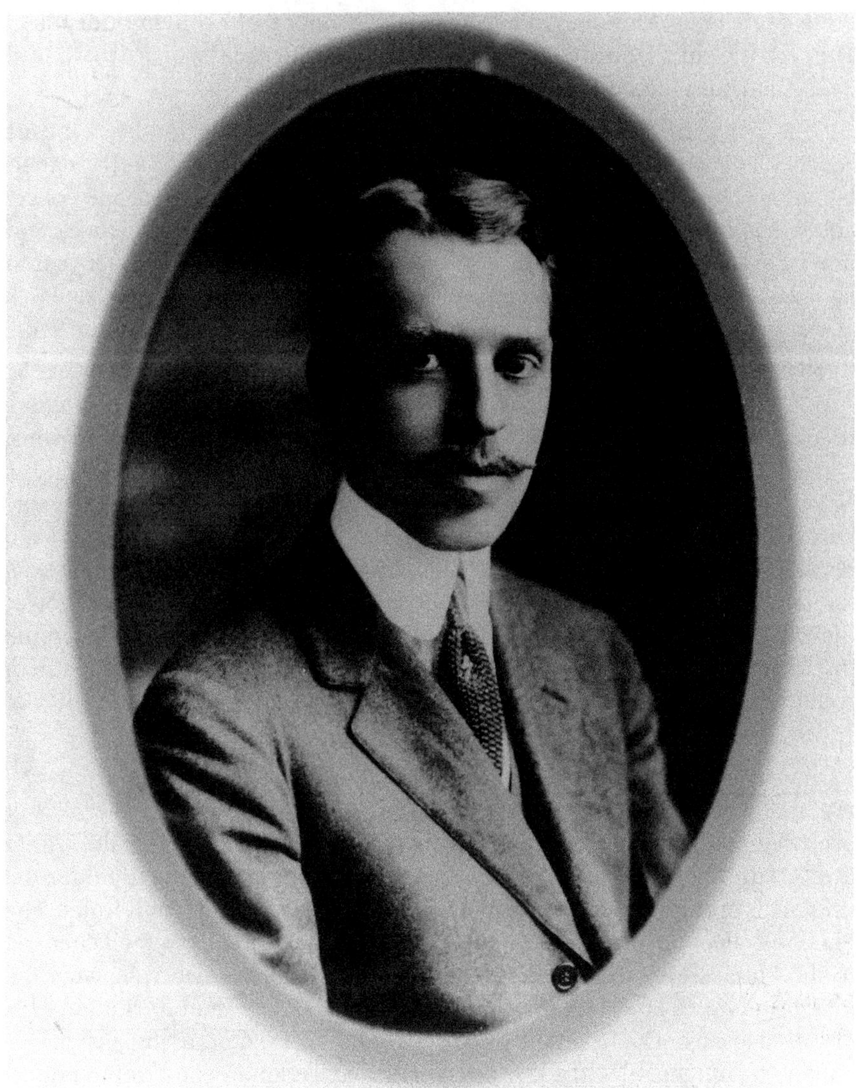

Image 1. 2. Duncan Phillips, ca. 1908. Duncan and his brother James graduated Yale University in 1908. The Phillips Collection Archives.

James and Duncan Phillips moved to New York City in 1914, and shared an apartment in Midtown Manhattan. Duncan, with his growing interest in culture, was elected to the Century Association, also known as the Century Club, a private club founded to promote art and literature. Members included: "Artists, Literary Men, Scientists, Physicians, Officers of the Army and Navy, members of the Bench and Bar, Engineers, Clergymen, Representatives of the

Press, Merchants, and men of leisure."[3] (It did not admit women until 1989.) Through the club, Duncan nurtured friendships with American artists Gifford Beal, Augustus Vincent Tack, and J. Alden Weir.

While living in New York, Duncan and James sought to fund a joint art collection. It was James, with his business background, who sent a letter to their father in 1916 requesting that he and Duncan be given an allowance to collect art. James suggested "a very small percentage of your annual income and mother's ... for buying pictures."[4] Specifically, he asked for $10,000 per year to be shared between the sons, citing collectors J.P. Morgan and Henry Clay Frick as examples to be followed. Although the Phillips family was not in the same league of wealth as Morgan and Frick, the art allowance was granted.

In 1917, when the United States entered World War I, the Phillips brothers tried to volunteer for military service, but were denied for physical reasons. Duncan wrote that he "made many unsuccessful efforts to get into the Army or Navy,"[5] but was ruled chronically under-weight. James was turned away because he had been weakened by two bouts of pneumonia. Each, however, participated in the war effort as civilians. James became an associate personnel director for the American Red Cross. Duncan put his energies into a position at the Division of Pictorial Publicity, "making use of war pictures to drive home the issues of the war to the American People."[6] Neither of the Phillips men could foresee the irony of James dying on the home front the year the war ended.

Duncan wrote about how deeply James's death affected him, and how he eventually found solace in art. "There was a time when sorrow all but overwhelmed me," he wrote, explaining that he turned to art "for the will to live."[7] With the cooperation of his mother, Duncan made plans to honor the lives of his brother and father by showing art within the grand family home. The Phillips Collection, first called the Phillips Memorial Art Gallery, then changed to the Phillips Memorial Gallery and later, The Phillips Gallery, became the manifestation of Duncan's grief. But it was much more than a tribute to his departed loved ones. His intent, he wrote, was to offer visitors a "joy-giving, life-enhancing influence."[8] In 1921, the year the collection opened to the public, the city's *Sunday Star* reported that "Washington is to have a new art gallery of a unique and impressive character established by Mrs. D.C. Phillips and her son Duncan Phillips, the well-known art writer and connoisseur."[9]

Mrs. D.C. Phillips was born Eliza Irwin Laughlin to Ann McCully Laughlin and James H. Laughlin in 1844. James, who immigrated from County Down, Ireland, became president of the First National Bank of Pittsburgh and co-founded Jones and Laughlin Steel, one of the largest steel and iron companies in the United States. Ann, whose ancestors were Scottish and Irish, was the great-granddaughter of an American Revolutionary War officer. Eliza came of debutante age during the Civil War but did not marry until she was in her late thirties. Not only was Eliza an heir to the Laughlin steel fortune, but her husband, Major Duncan Clinch Phillips (who even in his later years was referred to by his Army rank), became a millionaire by specializing in manufacturing glass for windows. Eliza Phillips, mother of James and Duncan, was an active member of the Daughters of the American Revolution and throughout her life donated money to charities with an emphasis on caring for the poor. When Eliza died at age eighty-four, the bulk of her estate went to Duncan but she also left notable sums for the Society for the Home of the Friendless in Pittsburgh and the Washington Home for Incurables.

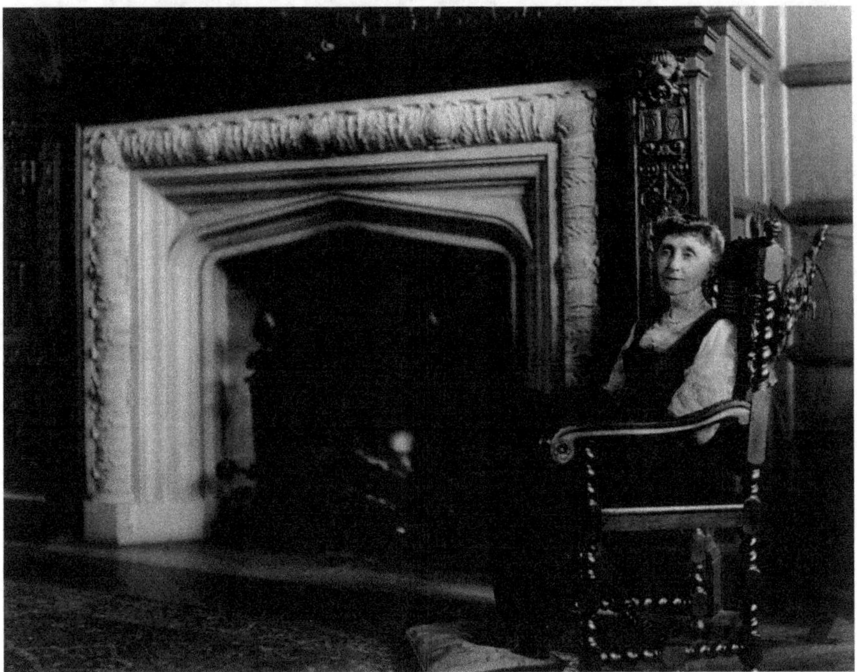

Image 1. 3. Eliza Laughlin Phillips, undated. Called "Mother Phillips" by her daughter-in-law Marjorie Phillips, she was known in the society pages as Mrs. D. C. Phillips. The Phillips Collection Archives.

Eliza and the major moved their family to Washington, D.C. in 1896, when James was twelve and Duncan ten. The next year, they built a Georgian Revival mansion in a section of the Dupont Circle neighborhood that would become known as Embassy Row. By all accounts, it was a happy home and certainly a lively period in the city's history. Bicycles were a popular mode of transportation for office workers, and according to more than one newspaper article, a blight on the downtown landscape. In the more residential areas of town, such as Dupont Circle, children fed sugar cubes to the horses who pulled ice-delivery wagons. Street vendors near the Phillips home announced fruit for sale, inventing melodic inflections to attract customers. It was here, some two decades after the home at 1600 21st Street, N.W. was first occupied by the Phillips family, that the Phillips Memorial Art Gallery opened.

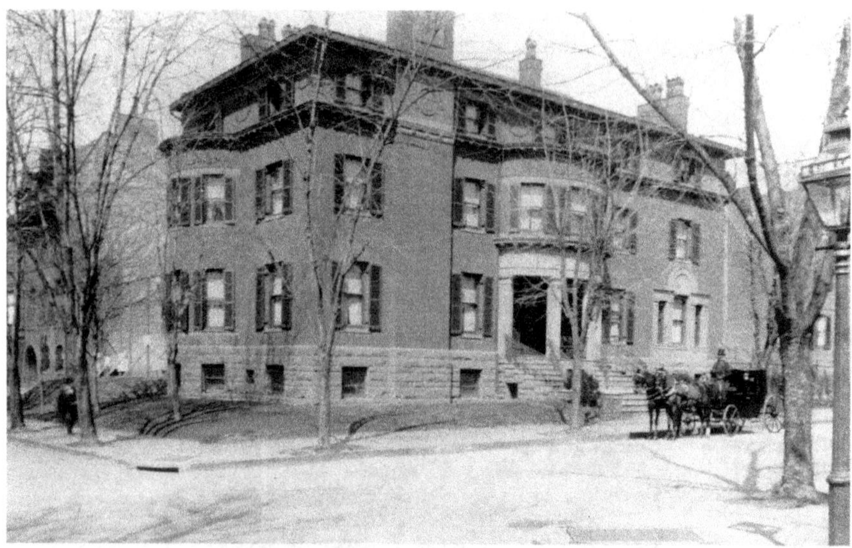

Image 1. 4. The Phillips home at 1600 21st Street, N.W., Washington, D.C., shown ca. 1900, became the location for the Phillips Memorial Art Gallery, later known as The Phillips Collection. The building remains an integral part of the museum and is often referred to by staff and visitors as "the house." The Phillips Collection Archives.

When the *Sunday Star* listed the hours the collection could be visited, the paper also shared Duncan Phillips's articulation that the gallery "will specialize in modern art" and "works by the masters of other days will be shown chiefly with the purpose of creating a better understanding of the works of artists of today."[10] The hours and the mission statement came from a letter Phillips sent Washington, D.C. newspapers, which served as a forerunner to a current-day press release. When Phillips published his book *A Collection in the Making*, the *Star's* "Notes of Arts and Artists" columnist reviewed it, noting that the memorial gallery was created "not merely to commemorate his father and brother … but also to create a beneficent force in the community where he lives."[11]

The 1920s: Meet, Marry, Start a Family and a Museum

"The 'Twentieth Century' begins after the First World War, that is to say, in the 'twenties'," wrote art historian Arnold Hauser in *The Social History of Art.*[12] The 1920s proved to be an important decade in the life of Duncan Phillips, personally and professionally. In January 1921, he met the painter Marjorie Acker, a niece of artists Gifford and Reynolds Beal. They married that same year. When she told of the first time they met, which was at an art exhibit at the Century Club, Marjorie wrote: "I knew. I knew that art had the same tremendous meaning for us both and that we would probably marry. I think Duncan knew too because he immediately began sending me books and flowers and all sorts of things."[13]

Just a few weeks after their autumn wedding, the Phillipses opened America's first museum of modern art. The Washington newspapers supported their endeavor with positive coverage, but Duncan longed for heightened public participation. "My father felt he needed one really great painting to attract crowds. He was disappointed with the numbers of people coming in,"[14] said Duncan and Marjorie's son Laughlin (Loc) Phillips, the museum's director from 1972 to 1992. Ticket sales did not factor into the motivation for a wider audience because admission to the Phillips Memorial Art Gallery was free.

Duncan Phillips envisioned a way to entice more members of the public to his and Marjorie's art collection, and he planned for it. Circa 1922, Phillips wrote in his journal that the number-one work of art he desired for their gallery was Pierre-Auguste Renoir's *Dejeuner des Canotiers*, the French title for *Luncheon of the Boating Party*. He even noted in the journal the name of the art dealer for the work, as he did for the other works of art on his list of desired acquisitions. In 1923, he and Marjorie lunched at the Paris home of Joseph Durand-Ruel, son of art dealer Paul Durand-Ruel. "Much to our delight, we were seated opposite that fabulous, incredibly entrancing, utterly alive and beguiling Renoir masterpiece." Marjorie recounted. "It was just thrilling, really dazzling to us."[15] Painted in 1880-81, it depicts the life of late-nineteenth-century Parisians who could take the train to the countryside for daytrips or weekends of boating or other recreational activities. The painting, famous for its charm and beauty long before the Phillipses bought it, features friends and acquaintances of the artist on a restaurant balcony overlooking the Seine River in Chatou, France. Within the picture are examples of portraiture, still life, and landscape. One of the most significant attributes of the painting is its invitation to viewers to imagine the conversations taking place among the members of the boating party.

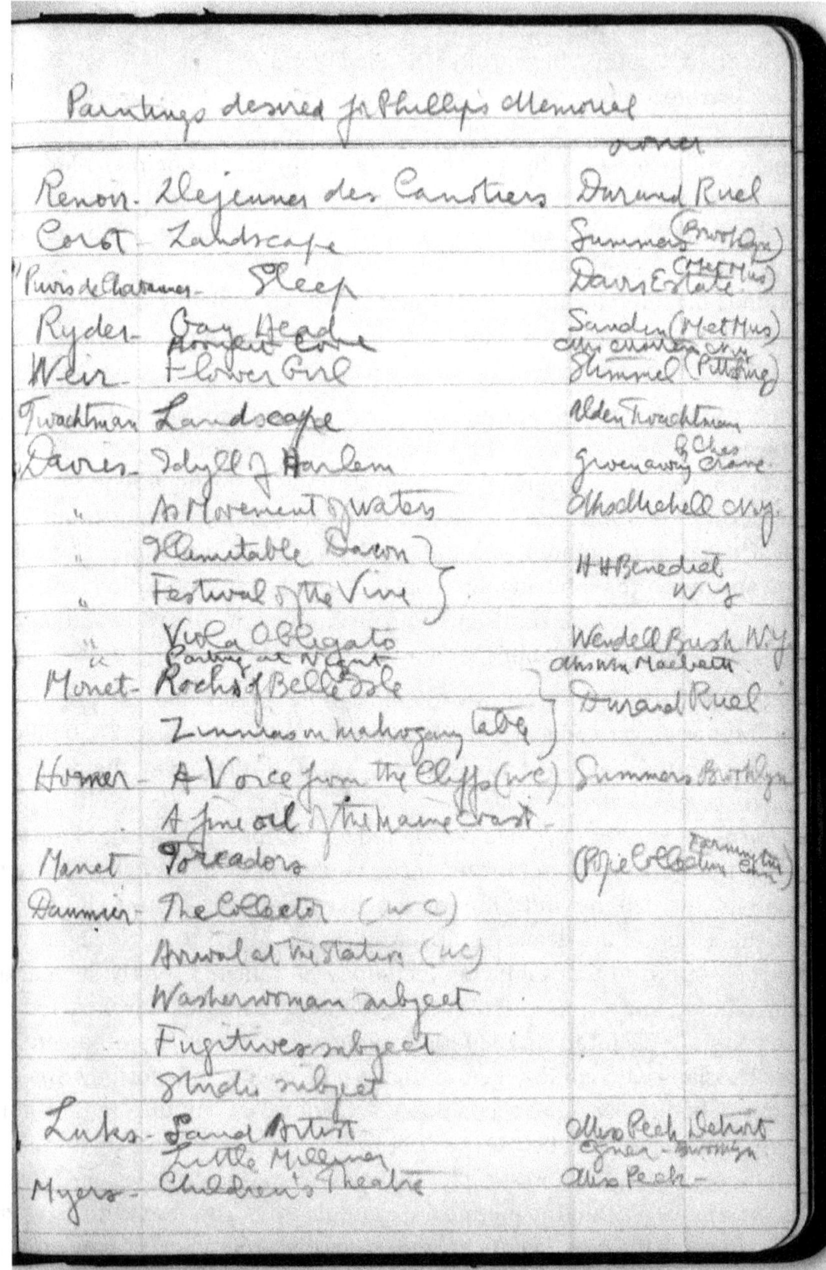

Paintings desired for Phillips Memorial

		owner
Renoir -	Dejeuner des Canotiers	Durand Ruel
Corot -	Landscape	Summers (Brooklyn)
Puvis de Chavannes -	Sleep	Davis Estate (Met Mus)
Ryder -	Gay Head / Moonlight Cove	Sanden (Met Mus)
Weir -	Flower Girl	Shimmel (Pittsburg)
Twachtman	Landscape	Alden Twachtman
Davies -	Idyll of Harlem	
"	Movement of water	Mitchell N.Y.
"	Illimitable Dawn	H H Benedict N.Y.
"	Festival of the Vine	H H Benedict N.Y.
"	Viola Obligato	Wendell Bush N.Y.
"	Parting at Night	Mrs Wm Macbeth
Monet -	Rocks of Belle Isle	Durand Ruel
	Zinnias on mahogany table	Durand Ruel
Homer -	A Voice from the Cliffs (WC)	Summers Brooklyn
	A fine oil of the Maine Coast	
Manet	Toreadors	(Pope Collection Farmington Conn)
Daumier -	The Collector (WC)	
	Arrival at the Station (WC)	
	Washerwoman subject	
	Fugitives subject	
	Studio subject	
Luks -	Sand Artist	Mrs Peck Detroit
	Little Milliner	Owner - Brooklyn
Myers -	Children's Theatre	Mrs Peck -

Image 1. 5. A page from a journal belonging to Duncan Phillips (ca. 1922), shows his wish-list of acquisitions. At the top, he wrote *Dejeuner des Canotiers,* translated as *Luncheon of the Boating* Party. The Phillips Collection Archives.

Duncan and Marjorie bought *Luncheon of the Boating Party* for their young museum and it remains, for many visitors, the touchstone of The Phillips Collection. However, the transaction for the painting was not without angst. While in Paris, Phillips wrote a long letter to Dwight Clark, the Phillips Memorial Gallery's treasurer, inquiring why recent cables had not been answered. Phillips had made the deal, he told Clark, but "Durand-Ruel has asked me not to breathe a word to any one over here, lest the news should reach someone able to start a newspaper campaign of protest against allowing so great a masterpiece of French painting to leave France."[16] In the letter, Phillips proclaimed the Renoir "finer than any Rubens – as fine as any Titian or Giorgione."[17] He revealed to Clark his ambition to affect viewers well beyond Washington, D.C. when he wrote that "people will travel thousands of miles to our house to see it."[18] Phillips also told Clark that he had secured additional paintings for the collection during the time abroad, and explained why: "The prices here are much lower than when they get to New York and we have to pay the American dealer's profits, so I have had to take advantage of this visit, even though we will feel the pinch next winter in New York."[19] There is no record of what caused the delay in Clark's response to his boss's cables, but Americans Duncan and Marjorie Phillips became the owners of the Renoir, paying what was then considered a high price for a single work of art: $125,000.

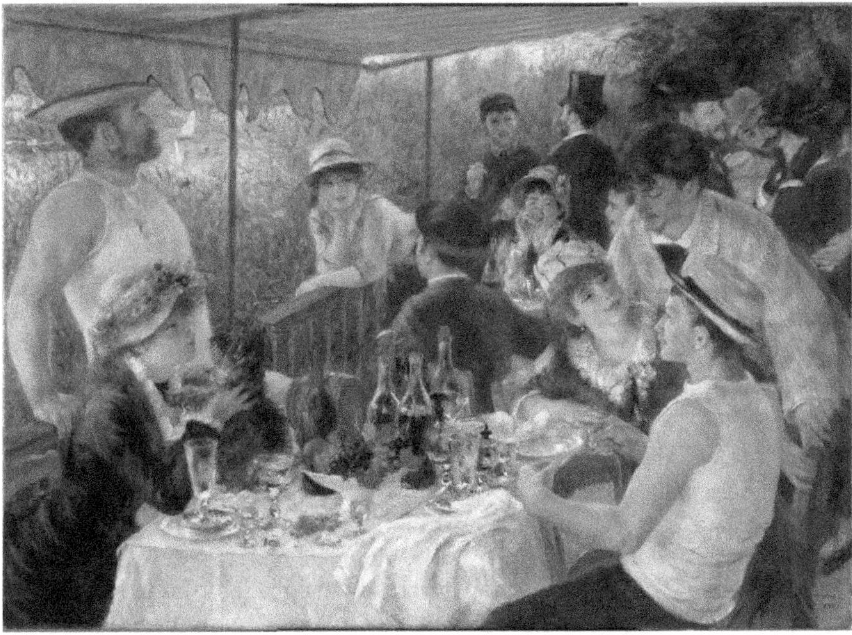

Image 1. 6. Pierre-Auguste Renoir, *Luncheon of the Boating Party,* 1880-81, Oil on canvas 511/4 x 691/8 in.; 130.2 x 175.6 cm. The Phillips Collection: Acquired 1923. Paintings, 1637, French.

Duncan Phillips realized his dream of bringing more visitors to The Phillips Collection with the purchase of Renoir's *Luncheon of the Boating Party.* However, he did not consider it the finest painting he and Marjorie owned. He believed that the greatest picture in their collection was Honoré Daumier's *The Uprising (L'Emeute),* likely depicting France's revolution of 1848, which caused the overthrow of Louis-Phillipe. In the painting, angry Parisians bunch together on a narrow street, grime visible on their faces. The picture's dominant figure wears a white shirt, his right fist raised and pumped. "This is not a mob, it is *the* mob," wrote art critic Frank Jewett Mather, whom Duncan quoted in an article describing his and Marjorie's 1925 acquisition of *The Uprising.* The work had been discovered rolled up in an attic and a few years later, when it became available for sale, Phillips wrote: "While the Louvre was deliberating, I cabled to have the picture shipped."[20]

The Phillipses were proud of acquiring both *The Uprising* and *Luncheon of the Boating Party.* Although Duncan thought of Renoir as "the great lover of life, for whom the visible world existed, filled to the brim and overflowing with rapture,"[21] he did not consider him unrivaled even among Impressionists. He said as much to one of his employees at The Phillips Collection. Arthur Hall Smith was hired by Phillips in 1959 to serve as a jack-of-all-trades at the museum. Smith, himself an artist, performed the duties of a curatorial assistant, lecturer, tour guide, and handyman. Of all the conversations Smith enjoyed with Duncan Phillips, one, in particular, stood out. "They had over some pink fireplace Monet's *The Cliffs at Dieppe [Val-Saint-Nicolas near Dieppe (Morning)],*" Smith said during an interview in his Paris studio. "One day when I was in the room with him, Mr. Phillips looked at it and toward the Renoir [*Luncheon of the Boating Party]* and back at the Monet. He said to me he thought the Monet was an equally great painting."[22]

Contemplation was one of Duncan Phillips's strengths. When composing his 1927 book *The Enchantment of Art,* Phillips, by then a father of two, included the passage "Art is a means of giving permanence to our moods and memories."[23] He may have been thinking of his and Marjorie's daughter when he wrote those words. Their son, Loc, would live a full, adventurous life as an Army intelligence officer in World War II, then for many years as a CIA analyst at stations around the globe. Before taking over the directorship of The Phillips Collection from his mother, Loc Phillips co-founded *Washingtonian* magazine. His sister Mary Marjorie was not as fortunate. Not long after her parents bought *The Luncheon of the Boating Party* – and when she had not yet celebrated her second birthday – Mary Marjorie contracted encephalitis. She lived with the family for a time after being diagnosed with the disease, which causes a swelling of the brain that can lead to developmental disabilities. Mary Marjorie, the first child born to Duncan and Marjorie Phillips, was eventually institutionalized. "A great tragedy for all," Marjorie Phillips wrote.[24]

The Phillips Collection was born in grief and it grew in grief. It survives as a world-class museum of American and European art.

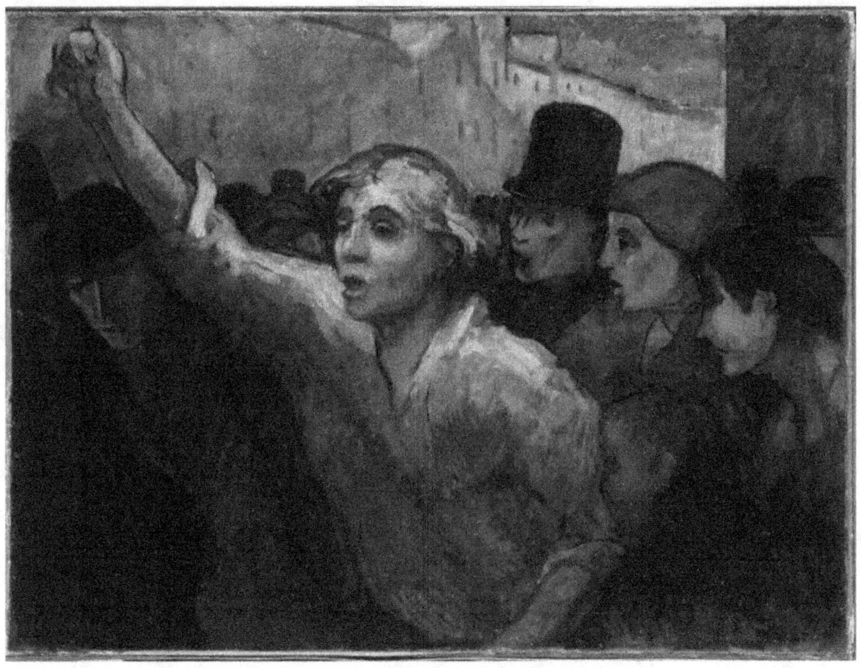

Image 1. 7. Honoré Daumier, *The Uprising*, 1848 or later, Oil on canvas 34 1/2 x 44 1/2 in.; 87.63 x 113.03 cm. The Phillips Collection: Acquired 1925, Paintings, 0384, French.

Notes

[1] George J. Butler, *Simpler Times: Stories of Early Twentieth Century Life* (Arlington, VA: Vandemere Press, 1997), 154.

[2] Duncan Phillips, "The Need of Art at Yale," *The Yale Literary Magazine* 72, no. 9 (1907): 361.

[3] Edwin G. Burrows and Mike Wallace, *Gotham: A History of New York City to 1898* (New York: Oxford University Press, 1999), 713.

[4] Marjorie Phillips, *Duncan Phillips and His Collection* (New York: W.W. Norton, 1982), 55.

[5] Ibid., 59.

[6] Ibid.

[7] D. Phillips, *A Collection in the Making: A Survey of the Problems Involved in Collecting Pictures Together with Brief Estimates of the Painters in the Phillips Memorial Gallery* (New York: E. Weyhe, 1926), 3.
[8] Ibid., 4.
[9] Leila Mechlin, "Washington is to Have a New Gallery of Art," *Washington Sunday Star,* January 2, 1921.
[10] Mechlin, "Notes of Art and Artists," *Washington Sunday Star,* February 5, 1922.
[11] Mechlin, "Notes of Art and Artists," *Washington Sunday Star,* January 16, 1927.
[12] Arnold Hauser, *The Social History of Art* (New York: Vintage Books, 1958), 226.
[13] M. Phillips, *Marjorie Phillips and Her Paintings* (New York: W.W. Norton, 1985), 14.
[14] "The Collector," *NewsHour with Jim Lehrer,* featuring Paul Solman interviewing Laughlin Phillips, aired December 23, 1999, on PBS.
[15] M. Phillips, *Duncan Phillips and His Collection,* 63.
[16] D. Phillips to Dwight Clark, 10 July 1923, The Phillips Collection Archives, Washington, D.C.
[17] Ibid.
[18] Ibid.
[19] Ibid.
[20] D. Phillips, "The Palette Knife: A Collection Still in the Making," *Creative Art* 4 (May 1929), 21.
[21] D. Phillips, transcript of a 1961 lecture, audience and location unknown, audio recording and transcript provided by Federal News Service, Washington, D.C. to The Phillips Collection Archives.
[22] Arthur Hall Smith, interview with the author, Paris, November 2007.
[23] D. Phillips, *The Enchantment of Art: As Part of the Enchantment of Experience Fifteen Years Later* (Washington, D.C.: Phillips Publications, 1927), 17.
[24] M. Phillips, *Duncan Phillips and His Collection,* 132.

Chapter 2

Supporting Many Methods of Seeing and Painting

"The Phillips Collection is based on a definite policy of supporting many methods of seeing and painting."[1] Duncan Phillips declared his and Marjorie's mantra of open-mindedness with instructions on exactly how he wanted those words to appear in print: "That sentence should always be in italics in anything written about us and our work."[2] Phillips never faltered in his message that there is no one way to experience art. He found his own point of view changing constantly and bade others to dismiss with preconceived notions about works of art. Phillips was addressing readers of the periodical *The American Magazine of Art* when he wrote that the "collector or critic who adventures in modern art is wise if he ... simply advocates tolerance and respectful study of the many different ways of seeing and painting."[3] What he could not abide was intolerance of varied points of view. Chastising the art establishment of the late 1920s, he wrote that "The usual concern of ultra conservative museum directors with public funds to spend and tradition-bound trustees standing over them is to avoid making mistakes."[4] He pointed out: "Having no boards to consult I have no such worry."[5] The art collector also stated that the only person he relied upon in making purchasing decisions was Marjorie Phillips. "My gifted wife is my constant associate and mentor. I have no other advisors and no agents among 'experts' or dealers."[6]

Art Encounters for the Many

In 1929's "Art and Understanding," Phillips explained that he had obtained permission to reprint a large section of novelist John Galsworthy's *Vague Thoughts on Art* in order "to convey more perfectly than lies within my power the philosophy which I cherish for my collection."[7] The author of *The Man of Property* and *The Forstye Saga* wrote of art: "It is the real cement of human life ... the great and universal refreshment. You may take it or leave it ... It is an uncapturable fugitive visiting our hearts at vagrant, sweet moments."[8] There is no denying the beauty and poignancy in Galsworthy's prose, yet Phillips need not have relied on the British writer to explain why he supported many methods of seeing and painting. At the beginning of "Art and Understanding," the collector expressed himself perfectly when he stated that "There is nothing beyond the comprehension of the average man in that incessant spiritual activity, almost as old as the human species, which we call art. The enriched capacity for living which art can give, not only to those who create, but also to those who contemplate, is, I like to think, a privilege of the many."[9] By creating optimal conditions for encountering art, Duncan and Marjorie Phillips and their privately-owned museum played an outsized role in assuring that viewing art could truly be a privilege of the many.

Different Parts of the World and Different Periods of Time

Phillips was not coy about his methods of collecting and displaying art. Five years after opening his art collection to the public, he discussed some of the factors he weighed in determining which works to purchase. "I bring together congenial spirits among the artists from different parts of the world and from different periods of time," he wrote in his book *A Collection in the Making.*[10] "I avoid the usual period rooms – the chronological sequence. ... My arrangements are for the purpose of contrast and analogy."[11] A few years after the book's publication, he explained his methods of combining time periods as well as "art foreign and American, of effort both representative and abstract" by stating that one of his goals was to present to museum visitors "the continuity of human thought and aspiration."[12] In fact, Phillips felt that one of his most significant contributions as a collector was to honor what he called "the continuity of tradition"[13] and to that end, he purchased masterworks by El Greco (1541-1614) and Goya (1746-1828). "I demonstrate the antiquity of modern ideas, or, if you prefer, the modernity of some of the old masters,"[14] Phillips wrote. He would often refer to his and Marjorie's collection as a "museum of modern art and its sources."

Phillips credited El Greco with pioneering Expressionism, lauding the Renaissance painter as "a hero of evolutionary progress in art."[15] Born on the island of Crete, Domenikos Theotokopoulus, better known as El Greco (the Greek), spent much of his life in Spain, after studying art in Venice under Titian. Phillips wrote that "Greco conceived of the human spirit as a flame,"[16] referring to the intensity the artist relayed in his paintings, and considered him "the earliest, and by far the most poignant Expressionist."[17] The collector saw Francisco Goya, native-born Spaniard and painter to the Spanish royal court in the late eighteenth century, as "a stepping stone between the Old Masters and the great Moderns."[18] Only a year after opening the Phillips Memorial Gallery, Duncan Phillips purchased El Greco's *The Repentant St. Peter.* When he subsequently bought a Goya depicting the same subject, also titled *The Repentant St. Peter,* Phillips compared the two oil paintings in a slide presentation. First, he projected a slide of the El Greco version, then told his audience: "El Greco's Repentant Peter was, as we have just seen, a grand old

Byzantine – a disembodied spirit soaring heavenwards, far above the mundane emotions of that simple fisherman the New Testament Peter."[19] Next, Phillips showed his audience a slide of Goya's Peter and narrated: "He is grubby, earth-bound, weather-beaten, strong and solid as a rock. One could well base a church on him for he is the human unit, the universal building block."[20]

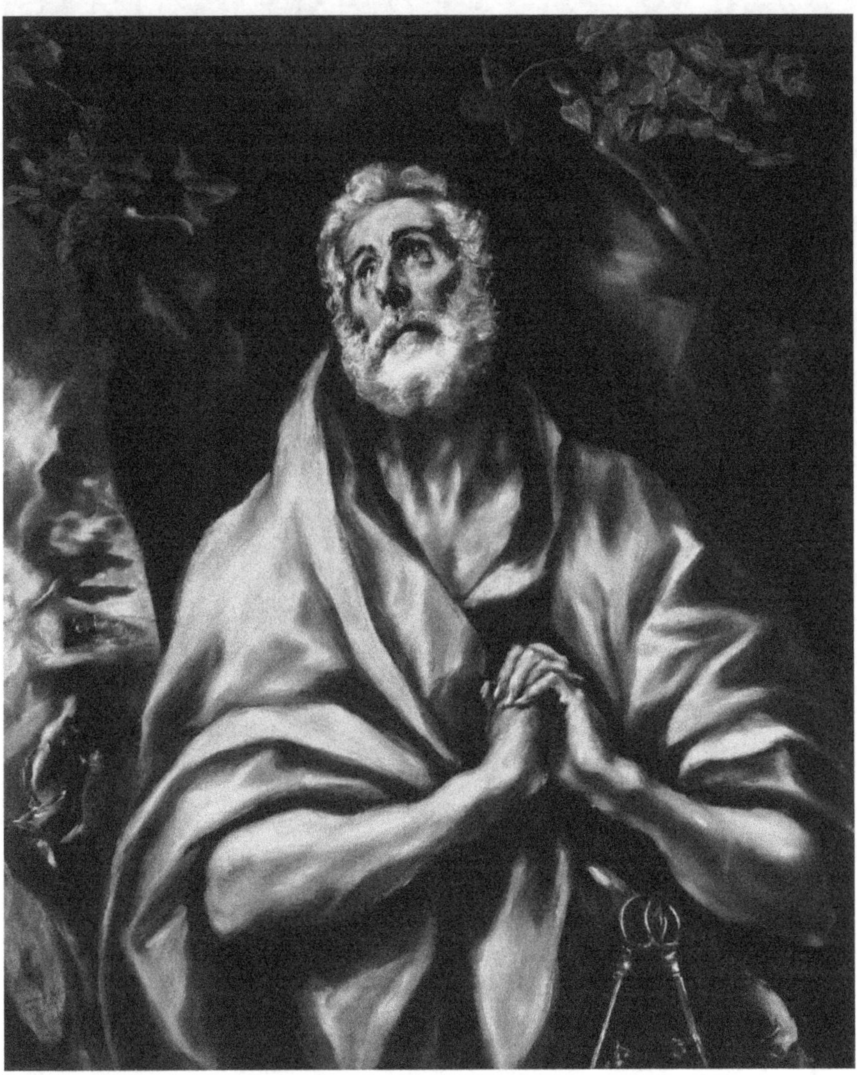

Image 2. 1. El Greco, *The Repentant St. Peter*, 1600-1605 or later,
Oil on canvas 36 7/8 x 29 5/8 in.; 93.7 x 75.2 cm. The Phillips Collection: Acquired 1922. Paintings, 0851, Spanish.

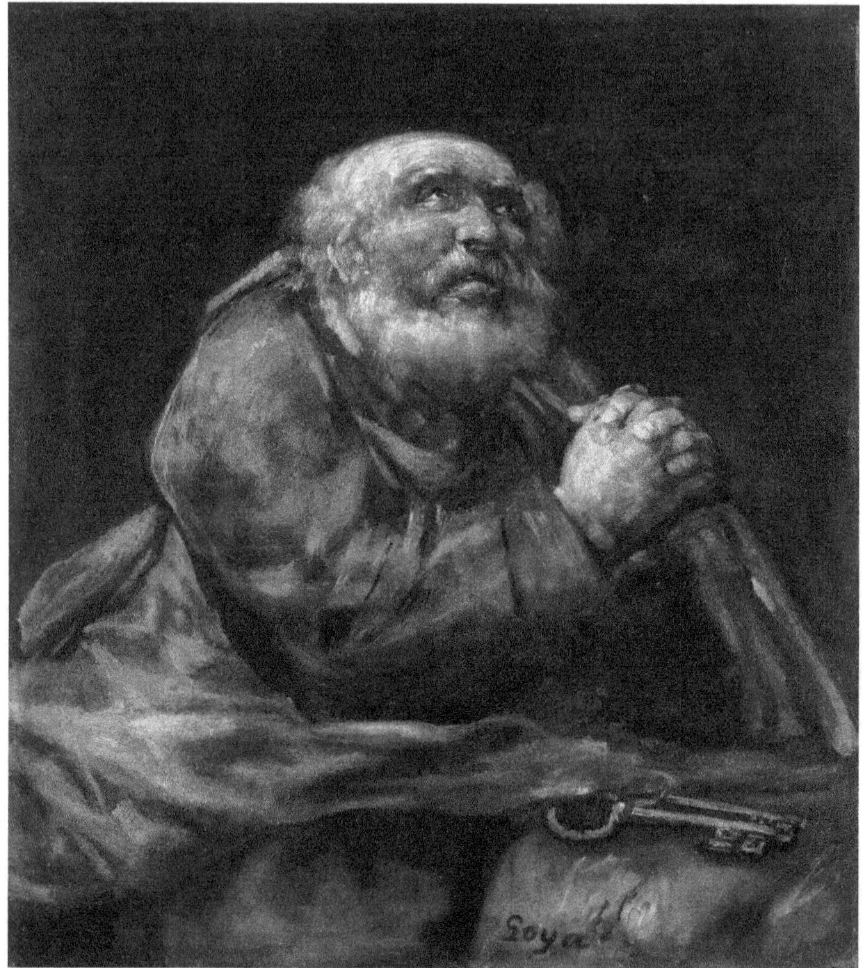

Image 2. 2. Francisco José de Goya, *The Repentant St. Peter*, ca. 1820-ca. 1824, Oil on canvas 28 3/4 x 25 1/4 in.; 73.025 x 64.135 cm. The Phillips Collection: Acquired 1936. Paintings, 0806, Spanish.

Phillips brought Goya's *The Repentant St. Peter* to his and Marjorie's museum to amplify the continuity of tradition for visitors, but the picture also had a profound effect on one of the twentieth century's greatest "Moderns" – the painter John Marin. For a 1948 issue of *Look*, the magazine surveyed dozens of art critics, museum directors and curators, asking them to rank the best contemporary painters in America. At the same time, the popular bi-weekly made an identical request of nearly fifty artists. When the responses from both groups were tallied, John Marin topped both lists.[21] Slightly more than ten years before *Look* crowned him the best painter in America, Marin had conveyed to

Duncan and Marjorie Phillips how moving it had been to see their Goya *The Repentant St. Peter.* "That Goya still haunts me," Marin wrote after spending time with the painting during one of his visits to Washington, D.C ., "It is not that it is just a good picture – there are many of those in the world – but it has all through it that which I find so lacking – that which I am striving so after – rhythm – and that to me hooks a picture right up with – music."[22]

Return Inward

A picture that would always haunt Duncan Phillips was Albert Pinkham Ryder's depiction of a night sky swept in yellow, titled *Moonlit Cove.* Phillips saw "a spiritual loneliness in the work of Ryder"[23] and wrote of *Moonlit Cove*: "Something is soon to happen in this black corner of the coast. We *know* this, although we find, dimly ... an empty deep-bottomed boat which casts its own shadow across the glistening, seething surf. The shape of the boat, the blackness of the shadow behind it, suggest a luxury of danger."[24] Such imaginative viewing added richness to Phillips's personal encounters with art, something he wished for others to experience.

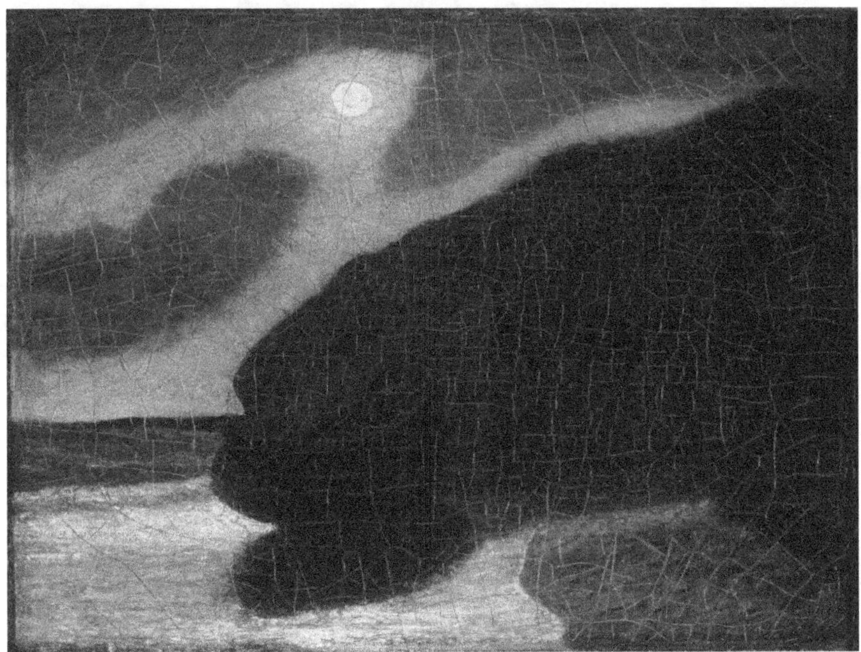

Image 2. 3. Albert Pinkham Ryder, *Moonlit Cove,* 1880s, Oil on canvas 14 1/8 x 17 1/8 in.; 35.8775 x 43.4975 cm.; Framed: 21 3/8 in. x 24 1/2 in. x 3 in.; 54.29 cm x 62.23 cm. x 7.62 cm. The Phillips Collection: Acquired 1924. Paintings, 1708, American.

Certainly, another artist who knew his way around a night sky was Vincent van Gogh. His most famous painting, *The Starry Night,* was acquired by MoMA, but Phillips would purchase other works by van Gogh for The Phillips Collection. He spaced his and Marjorie's acquisitions of Vincent's oils on canvas over many years, buying *Entrance to the Public Gardens in Arles* in 1930; *The Road Menders* in 1949; and *House at Auvers* in 1952. Van Gogh inspired Phillips to philosophize on how individualism is linked to creating art, and by implication, how it affects viewing art. He used the Dutch Expressionist's work to discuss the merits of romanticism over classicism and why it mattered for viewer freedom. Of romantic artists, Phillips wrote: "No matter how much he may explore the visible world and proclaim his naturalism there will always be the same return inward, the same driving need to invent his own unique method to be as identical as possible with himself."[25] With those words Phillips got to the core of his belief that art enhances the human experience. The "return inward" is the overarching reason he supported myriad painters and methods of painting. Moreover, it is why he supported many methods of seeing.

Critic as well as Collector

In arguing for unprejudiced encounters with paintings, Duncan Phillips would sometimes write or speak with a romantic flair about the artists whose work he collected. In a slide presentation, he remarked: "When with his brush, Bonnard opens a window on a park of midsummer trees it seems to be on a world undiscovered until he had called us to his side to see it with him."[26] When referring to "a world undiscovered," he could just as easily have been inviting a viewer to look at one of The Phillips Collection's paintings by Dove, O'Keeffe, Marin, Lawrence, or Rothko. Phillips's ability to communicate about art was noted over the years. "His writing shows him to be capable of considerable analysis," wrote Guy Pene du Bois of Phillips in 1923, adding "This is rare in a collector."[27] The *Washington Post* took the sentiment further in 1937, calling him "one of the foremost critics of art in this country."[28] The accolades for his art criticism continued well into the mid-twentieth century. An article about Phillips in a 1955 issue of the magazine *Arts,* conveyed the premise that "In America we have not had many great collectors who at the same time have been articulate or eloquent in critical discourse."[29] The anonymous author of the *Arts* piece concluded that Phillips was one of the rare exceptions. Arthur Hall Smith agreed that his former employer communicated eloquently in his writing about art. "His diction when he wrote his art criticism was almost Edwardian," Smith said of Phillips. "He had that elevated Yale-educated turn-of-the-century vocabulary. Of course, what became his art criticism was the collection itself."[30]

"Mr. Phillips is Doing a Great Deal to Awaken Interest in Art"

Smith was right. What Duncan Phillips collected did indeed become a form of critiquing art. So, too, did his presentation of it. Phillips wrote that his idea was not to show all the works at once "but in ever-varied and purposeful exhibitions … changed so that the walls of the various rooms reveal interesting transformations."[31] Ada Rainey of the *Washington Post* offered a tribute to his success with the method. "Mr. Phillips is doing a great deal to awaken interest in art in Washington," she wrote. "Each time that there is a change of hanging and arrangement … it quickens the understanding of present-day art."[32] She conveyed an example of how he rearranged art for the benefit of interaction. Although it was a simple matter of Phillips displaying two particular Ryders differently, Rainey wrote that "In gallery B, there is a group that includes *Moonlight Cove* and *Macbeth and the Witches* by Ryder. These are the consummation of the romantic spirit which appeals so strongly to the imagination of the spectator."[33] The *Post* published Rainey's piece in the Sunday paper of February 8, 1931. On February 2, Phillips had premiered ten new exhibits, a staggering number for the same opening day even if several of them contained less than a dozen works each. Many of the exhibits were exactly as Rainey described – works from the permanent collection shown anew. The largest of Duncan's exhibits to open that Monday spoke to his and Marjorie's desire to share with the public the connections which form art history; he titled the seventeen-work show "Modern Art and Its Sources." Among the others were "Twentieth Century Lyricism" and "Foreign and American Contemporaries." Most of the February 1931 debuts were designed to close within a few months, making way for further Phillips ambitions. As 1931 continued to unspool, he opened nearly twenty more exhibits. Two of the most on-point regarding his methods of supporting many ways of seeing and painting were "Where Classic and Romantic Meet in Painting" with nine works of art, and "Un-Selfconscious America" with fourteen offerings.

Ambition was not an attribute Phillips tried to stifle in himself. On the contrary, he could function as a veritable public relations machine. In January and February 1927, he wrote a spate of letters to two of the biggest influencers in modern art – Alfred H. Barr Jr. and Alfred Stieglitz. For good measure, he added John Graham, an artist, collector, and curator. The year Phillips contacted him, the Russian-born Graham was living in Baltimore and had become quite renowned in the Charm City's art circles. Phillips's message was forthright to all three men: come to Washington, D.C. to see the Tri-Unit Exhibition he had assembled. In a letter to Graham, he asked no less than three times in two paragraphs to learn details of "the more progressive painters and art lovers of Baltimore."[34] He requested that Graham encourage them to visit the Phillips as soon as possible, and he pressed hard for their contact information. In his pitch to Graham, he used the phrases: "But that is not all;" "Don't fail to come over to see it;" and then to close, "When may we expect you?"[35] Barr, who would become MoMA's first director in 1929, was teaching at Wellesley College in Wellesley, Massachusetts at the time he received his invitation from Phillips. In his second letter to Barr about the three installations, Phillips described "a whole wall of John Marin and another wall of French Modernists, including Matisse and Bonnard at their best ... and a wall containing seven Daumiers, each a masterpiece no matter how small the actual measurements."[36] In that letter, dated February 8, 1927, Phillips entreated Barr: "I can hardly wait to have you know all about this show and I am writing to urge you . . . to see the Phillips Memorial Gallery functioning according to its avowed principles. ... Really it would repay you to come down and to bring some of your pupils."[37] His first letter to Barr about the Tri-Unit Exhibition had been sent a few weeks earlier. In the initial correspondence, as he led up to the topic, Phillips thanked Barr for a soon-to-be-published book review. "I cannot help telling you that I am delighted you are to cover my book for *The Saturday Review of Literature*,"[38] Phillips wrote. He was referring to his 1926 book *A Collection in the Making*. In that letter, dated January 15, 1927, Phillips went into detail about new acquisitions to the collection, such as "superb examples of Winslow Homer and Claude Monet (the latter a Still Life, sumptuous in the quality of its color)."[39] He also shared with Barr that "most important of all, I have found one of my ancient sources of Modern Art in an exquisite, subtle Stone Head from the 18th Dynasty of Egypt."[40] The Stone Head would figure prominently in the Tri-Unit Exhibition that Phillips was so adamant that Graham, Barr, and Stieglitz attend and hopefully, promote. In one of his letters to Stieglitz, Phillips provided the Modernist photographer and gallery operator an account of the arrangement of the Tri-Unit show. The report is packed with the who, what, where, why, and how of Phillips's thinking:

> The three units together, two large and one small, will give a comprehensive picture of what we are doing and the way we want to do it ... The Marins hang on one wall of the Main Gallery where there is daylight and where they can be seen at a proper distance and in comfort, a sofa placed at exactly the right range will enable the serious student who desires to know Marin can look long and intimately at each picture without rising ... In the same Main Gallery modern French paintings will be shown ... And in the midst of all this vitality of the modern mind, expressing itself so diversely in color and form, I will show our Stone Head of the 18th Dynasty in Egypt with its glimpses of a happy moment when the sun came out and the individual was prized, all the spirt of modern artists anticipated.[41]

Hiring Artists to Work for the Museum

Duncan Phillips wrote tirelessly about how he supported many methods of seeing art, beginning with the homelike atmosphere of his and Marjorie's museum. He would reiterate many times the rewards of showing art from the past alongside selections from their collection of modern art. He would assert that displaying American art with European art was the right thing to do, no matter the timeline. He would point out that changing the arrangement of paintings could summon an entirely new viewing experience. There was, however, a Phillips method that went undocumented in his own writings. He hired artists to work various day jobs at The Phillips Collection. Arthur Hall Smith said that most of the employees at the Phillips were painters and that Duncan took pride in providing paychecks to artists. Smith indicated that during his hours on the clock he was more likely to have a hammer in his hand than anything resembling a paintbrush. His own artworks were created on his own time. But Smith said that in Duncan's eyes, his jack-of-all-trades position at the museum did not detract from his identity as an artist. On the contrary, the boss welcomed it. "Mr. Phillips always introduced me to people as a painter who helps us here," Smith said.[42] He added that Phillips respected the other artists on the payroll as well. In addition to Smith, artists who were employed at the Phillips during Duncan or Marjorie's lifetimes included: Jim McLaughlin, John Gernand, Willem de Looper, Bill Koberg, Jane Godfrey, Kevin MacDonald, Michael Green, and Cynthia Griffith. Godfrey was hired as a museum assistant in 1977, "otherwise known as a guard."[43] Although Marjorie had retired from the directorship by then, Godfrey said that when the co-founder visited the museum "she would often remark on particular paintings to the guards and enjoyed knowing that so many of us were working artists."[44] Not long after Marjorie retired, Arthur Hall Smith accepted a teaching position at George Washington University in Washington, D.C. After more than two decades at the school, he fulfilled his dream of living in Paris year-round when he himself retired. It was from his studio on the rue Visconti, where he was known as "le Professeur," that he reflected on the significance of artist-employees at the Phillips. Smith talked about how many of them spent much of their time working in the museum's galleries, which allowed them to converse with visitors who wished to hear the stories behind some of the acquisitions. In addition to the direct impact the artist-employees made when they engaged with visitors, there was the indirect effect of "imbuing the place with artistic sensibilities."[45]

In-depth Collecting, Turnabout on Modernism, and Champion for Individual Thought

One other method which Duncan Phillips felt helped visitors gain insight at his and Marjorie's museum was the in-depth collection of certain artists. With the development of single-artist units, he could demonstrate his commitment to the artists, as well as to the viewing public. In so doing, he was known to reveal something of his personality. Half-way into his twenty years of collecting works by Dove, Phillips wrote to the artist: "I am always citing your case as one of the splendid triumphs of the individual in art, of the fundamental need of artists for standing apart and possessing their own soul."[46] Phillips would stay true to that point of view, even when challenged. Jacob Kainen, a painter and printmaker, used to come to The Phillips Collection and talk with Duncan Phillips in the galleries. Kainen recalled how a conversation about Dove's work could have caused hard feelings between himself and Phillips. "He'd walk around and ask my opinion of this artist, that artist, and we'd have discussions,"[47] Kainen said. During one visit, Phillips asked Kainen what he thought of Dove, and Kainen replied that he did not particularly like him. According to Kainen, Phillips paced up and down and said, "Dove is very much of the earth. He is fruity, nutty. He gets eternal changes in nature, growing things, the sky. It's all part of his outlook."[48] Kainen admitted to being undiplomatic with Phillips about Dove, but years later, remained impressed that "the fact you could talk with him on that level and he wouldn't hold it against you is quite remarkable."[49]

Phillips, however, was not always so open-minded. Just a few years out of Yale, he lashed out at what he then considered the horrors of modern art. His tirade appeared in a review of 1913's International Exhibition of Modern Art, known as the Armory Show because of where it was held. He referred to the New York City exhibition in its totality as "stupefying in its vulgarity,"[50] and to Paul Cézanne and van Gogh as "unbalanced fanatics."[51] Phillips would come to praise and purchase works by some of the artists featured at the Armory Show – Cézanne and van Gogh among them. Indeed, he would come to seek forgiveness for the harsh remarks. He wrote in 1927, by way of apology, "I have in due time graduated to a sharpened consciousness of the need for understanding the artist's methods, and the even greater need for an open door of the mind to many different kinds of aesthetic expression."[52]

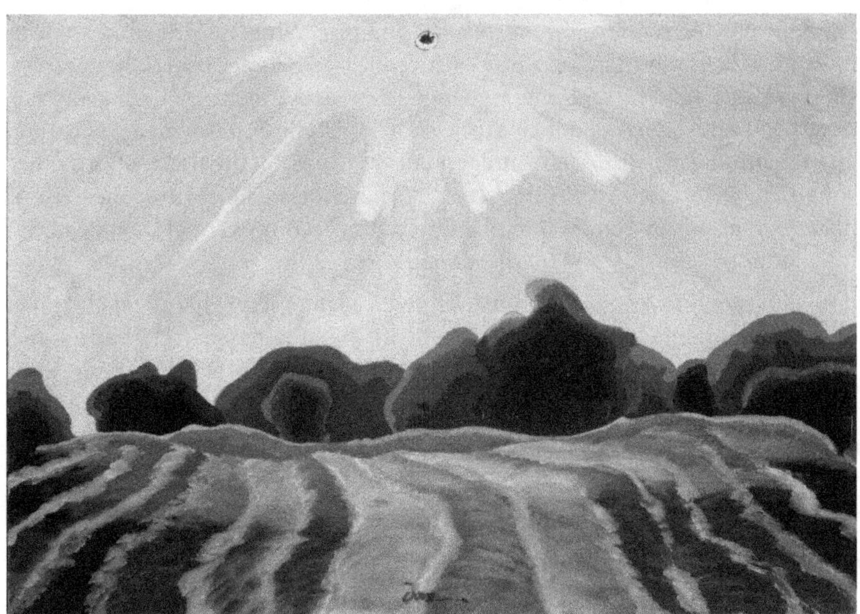

Image 2. 4. Arthur G. Dove, *Morning Sun*, 1935, Oil on canvas 20 x 28 in.; 50.8 x 71.12 cm.; Framed: 22 9/16 in x 30 3/8 in x 1 1/2 in.; 57.31 cm. x 77.15 cm. x 3.81 cm. The Phillips Collection: Acquired 1935. Paintings, 0560, American.

Even while ridiculing Modernists in his 1913 critique, he included the passage "Time winnows the wheat from the chaff, for individuals are greater than schools and their systems and revolutions."[53] His stance on modern art would change dramatically, but his devotion to individualism remained steadfast and in fact, he promoted individual thought beyond art creation and appreciation. One might even say he fretted about what he perceived to be a lack of individualism in civilization at large. "Ours is not an age which prizes individualism," he wrote in 1931. "We can see for ourselves how the disregard of the individual works out in business and social life."[54] Thinking for oneself was what Duncan Phillips meant when he wrote and talked about individualism. He believed it was crucial for artists and for viewers. Mechanization and alienation in the modern world were two of Phillips's concerns, and for the most part, he made his points through his knowledge of art. In 1947, he told an audience at Ohio's Kenyon College: "Art is the last stand and the eternal stronghold of the individual."[55] The "I" which began the word "individual" was capitalized on his prepared remarks, which had been typewritten on hotel stationery. His commitment to individualism, inside and outside the world of art, did not dwindle. A dozen more years would pass before Phillips spoke at the Philadelphia Museum School of Art and discussed what was most dear to him. The 1959 speech was to be about the significance of having collected many different styles of painting. While his prepared remarks indicate he did mention the variety of art at The Phillips Collection, they also show he told his Philadelphia audience that what was more important was "sincerity and the individual expression."[56] Phillips so valued individual expression that he wrote "encouragement for the lone individualist is the hot spot of my endeavors."[57] He also stated: "I stand for the lonely artist in quest of beauty, backed by no political influence and professional organization, independent of all cliques and movements."[58]

Phillips stood for independent viewers as well, and made his stand clear to a different audience, one at Yale University. It must have been bittersweet for Duncan when he returned to campus in March 1931, twenty-three years after he and his big brother James began attending the Ivy League school together, and twelve years after James's death. Duncan arrived at his alma mater to deliver a Trowbridge Memorial Lecture just as he was putting the finishing touches on his book *The Artist Sees Differently: Essays Based upon the Philosophy of a Collection in the Making*. When announcing the lecture, the *Yale Daily News* stated that the museum director from the Class of 1908 had "written a great deal on contemporary art."[59] While Phillips's writing burnished his reputation as an art scholar, the detailed work required in arranging special art exhibitions increased his respect for viewers. By the time of the Yale lecture, he had organized scores of temporary exhibits, either at The Phillips Memorial Gallery or on loan to other museums, including shows featuring paintings by Pierre Bonnard, Arthur Dove, John Marin, Childe Hassam, Berthe Morisot, and Maurice Prendergast. Phillips titled his Yale lecture "The Artist Sees Differently," but he included comments about how he wanted viewers to see differently too – from each other and potentially, as John Dewey agreed in *Art as Experience*, from within themselves. Phillips said that his museum "is based on the conviction that there is no absolute beauty, that what is good for one is not, and could not be good for all."[60] While Phillips was confident in the content of his message to students, faculty, and fellow alumni at the Yale event, he had been hesitant about the formal mode of public speaking. When accepting the invitation to deliver the Trowbridge Lecture, he inquired if it would be permissible to read from a manuscript. "I am not accustomed to lecturing and need a paper to steady me at the start," he wrote. "Of course, I can talk in a gallery any time and almost anywhere, but a lecture platform is very different."[61]

In a slide presentation to a Washington, D.C. audience circa 1935, Phillips continued to encourage viewer autonomy, emphasizing that people who look at art need to trust their personal interpretations. "Art reviewers for the press, art critics generally, and lecturers with their slides are only signposts,"[62] he said.

Duncan and Marjorie Phillips posted some of those signposts. Bonnard's oddness of beauty, Dove's primer on abstraction, O'Keeffe's undiluted courage, Marin's unforgettable rhythms, Lawrence's pure power, and Rothko's ultimate challenge to return inward. Assuredly, The *Phillips Collection is based on a definite policy of supporting many methods of seeing and painting.*

Notes

[1] Duncan Phillips, "The Palette Knife: A Collection Still in the Making." *Creative Art* 4 (May 1929),
[2] Ibid.
[3] D. Phillips, "Modern Art and the Museum," *The American* Magazine *of Art*, October 1931, 275.
[4] D. Phillips, "The Palette Knife," xiii.
[5] Ibid.
[6] Ibid.
[7] D. Phillips, "Art and Understanding," *Art and Understanding* 1 (November 1929): 15.
[8] John Galsworthy, "Vague Thoughts on Art," *Art and Understanding* 1 (November 1929): 17.
[9] D. Phillips, "Art and Understanding," 7.
[10] D. Phillips, *A Collection in the Making: A Survey of the Problems Involved in Collecting Pictures Together with Brief Estimates of the Painters in the Phillips Memorial Gallery* (New York: E. Weyhe, 1926), 6.
[11] Ibid.
[12] D. Phillips, "The Palette Knife," 21.
[13] D. Phillips, "Catholicity Does Not Mean Eclecticism: A Radio Talk by Duncan Phillips," 1954 pamphlet, 5. (Originally presented as "The Pleasures of an Intimate Art Gallery," WCFM Radio, Washington, D.C., February 24, 1954), The Phillips Collection Archives, Washington, D.C.
[14] D. Phillips, *A Collection in the Making*, 6.
[15] D. Phillips, transcript of 1961 lecture, audience and location unknown, audio recording and transcript provided by Federal News Service, Washington, D.C. to The Phillips Collection Archives.
[16] D. Phillips, *The Artist Sees Differently* (New York: E. Weyhe, 1931), 125.
[17] D. Phillips, "The Many Mindedness of Modern Painting," *Art and Understanding* 1 (November 1929), 58.
[18] D. Phillips to Mrs. Marie Sterner, 21 December 1936, The Phillips Collection Archives, Washington, D.C.
[19] D. Phillips, "Expression of Personality in Design," script for slide presentation, 1938, The Phillips Collection Archives, Washington, D.C., 30.
[20] Ibid., 31.
[21] "Are These Men the Best Painters in America Today?" *Look*, February 3, 1948, 44.
[22] John Marin to Duncan and Marjorie Phillips, 18 February 1937, The Phillips Collection Archives, Washington, D.C.
[23] D. Phillips, "Albert Ryder," *American Magazine of Art* 7, no. 10 (August 1916): 388.

[24] Ibid., 391.
[25] D. Phillips, *A Bulletin of The Phillips Collection Relating to a Tri-Unit Exhibition of Paintings and Sculpture*, Phillips Memorial Gallery, Washington, D.C., 1927.
[26] D. Phillips, "Trowbridge Memorial Lecture: The Artist Sees Differently," (Yale University, March 20, 1931), The Phillips Collection Archives, Washington, D.C., 33.
[27] Guy Pene du Bois, "Art By the Way," *International Studio* 77 (1923).
[28] Alice Graeme, "Paintings of Arthur G. Dove in Various Media At Gallery Here Show Artist's Mature Style," *Washington Post*, April 11, 1937.
[29] "A Critic and His Pictures," *Arts*, December 1955.
[30] Arthur Hall Smith, interview with the author, Paris, November 2007.
[31] D. Phillips, *A Collection in the Making*, 6.
[32] Ada Rainey, "Phillips Gallery Exhibition So Arranged As to Throw Light on Art's Meaning," *Washington Post*, February 8, 1931.
[33] Ibid.
[34] D. Phillips to John Graham, 9 February 1927, The Phillips Collection Archives, Washington, D.C.
[35] Ibid.
[36] D. Phillips to Alfred H. Barr Jr., 8 February 1927, The Phillips Collection Archives, Washington, D.C.
[37] Ibid.
[38] D. Phillips to Alfred H. Barr Jr., 15 January 1927, The Phillips Collection Archives, Washington, D.C.
[39] Ibid.
[40] Ibid.
[41] D. Phillips to Alfred Stieglitz, 27 January 1927, The Phillips Collection Archives, Washington, D.C.
[42]A. Hall Smith, oral history interview by Donita M. Moorhus for The Phillips Collection Oral History Project, 2005, The Phillips Collection Archives, Washington, D.C., 9.
[43] Jane Godfrey, email to the author, 9 June 2020.
[44] Ibid.
[45]A. Hall Smith, interview with the author.
[46] D. Phillips to Arthur Dove, 28 February 1935, Arthur and Helen Torr Dove Papers, Archives of American Art, Washington, D.C.
[47] Jacob Kainen, interview by Avis Berman, 10 August-22 September 1982, Mark Rothko and His Times Oral History Project, Archives of American Art, Washington, D.C., 10.
[48] Ibid.
[49] Ibid.
[50] D. Phillips, "Revolutions and Reactions in Painting," *The International Studio*, 51 (December 1913): 123.
[51] Ibid., 126.
[52] D. Phillips, *As Part of the Enchantment of Experience Fifteen Years Later* (Washington, D.C.: Phillips Publications, 1927), 9.
[53] D. Phillips, "Revolutions and Reactions in Painting," 126.
[54] D. Phillips, *The Artist Sees Differently*, 3-4.
[55] D. Phillips, Acceptance Speech for Doctor of Humane Letters from Kenyon College (Gambler, OH, 1947), The Phillips Collection Archives, Washington, D.C.

[56] D. Phillips, Acceptance Speech for Award of Merit from Philadelphia Museum School of Art (Philadelphia, 1959), The Phillips Collection Archives, Washington, D.C.
[57] D. Phillips, *The Phillips Collection Catalogue: A Museum of Modern Art and Its Sources* (New York: Thames and Hudson, 1952), ix.
[58] D. Phillips, *The Palette Knife*, 16.
[59] "Four Lectures Will Take Place in University Today," *Yale Daily News*, March 20, 1931.
[60] D. Phillips, Trowbridge Memorial Lecture, 7.
[61] D. Phillips to Theodore Sizer, 24 October 1930, Trowbridge Lecture, box 13, folder 109, School of Art and Architecture Records, Yale University.
[62] D. Phillips, "Freshness of Vision," slide lecture circa 1935, The Phillips Collection Archives, Washington, D.C.

Chapter 3

World War II Years: Broadening Endeavors

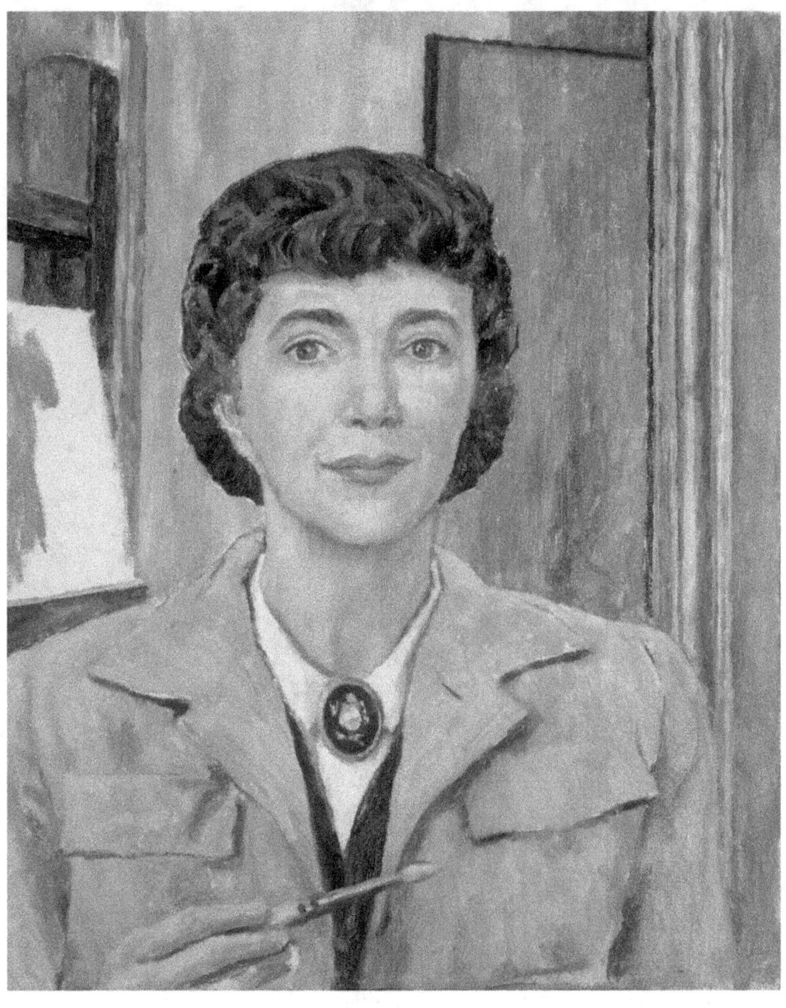

Image 3. 1. Marjorie Phillips, *Self-Portrait*, ca. 1940,
Oil on canvas 20 1/2 x 16 1/2 in.; 52.07 x 41.91 cm. The Phillips Collection:
Gift of the artist, 1985. Paintings, 1538, American.

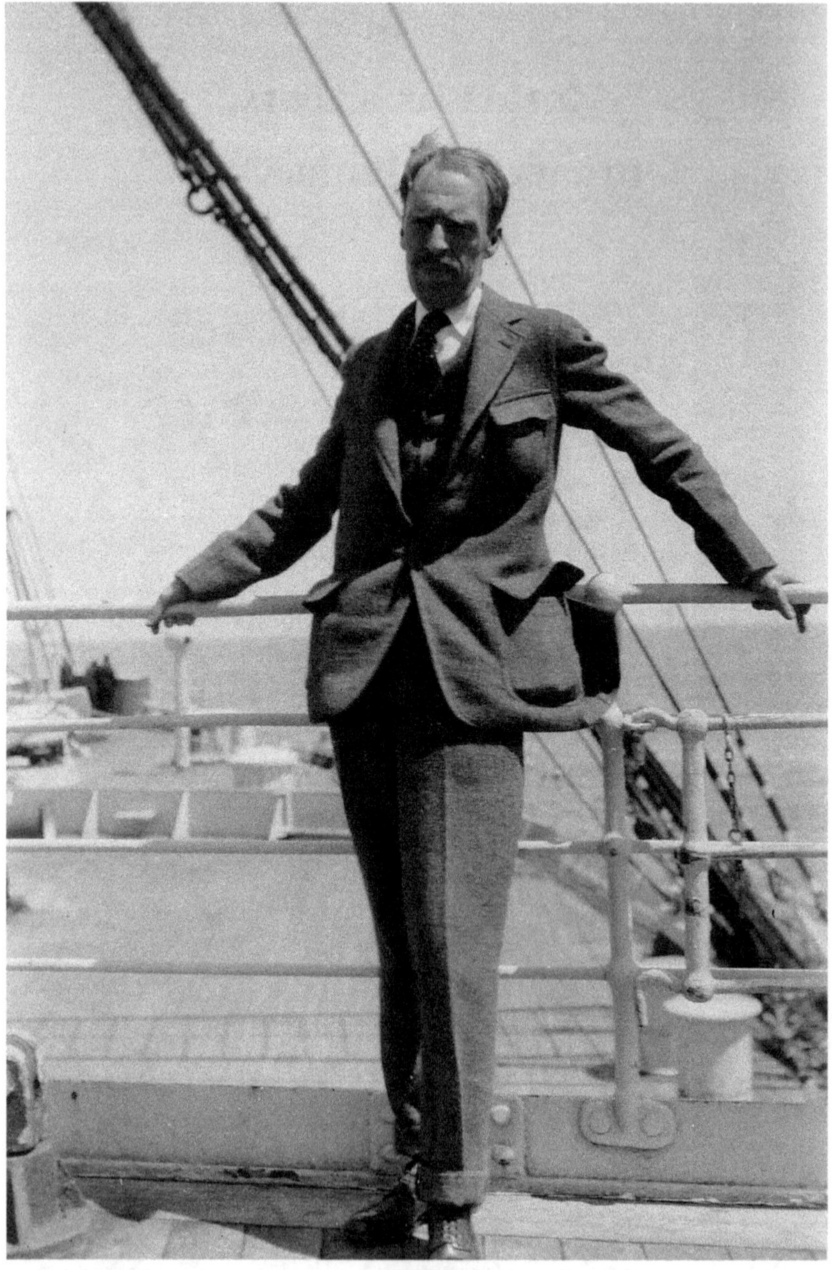

Image 3. 2. Duncan Phillips on a transatlantic voyage prior to World War II. The Phillips Collection Archives.

The reputation of Duncan Phillips as an important figure in art collecting and art scholarship was well-established by the 1940s. He and Marjorie Phillips had made solid decisions in the first twenty years of operating their museum of modern art, which allowed him to pursue art endeavors apart from The Phillips Collection. At least part of the couple's success came from the good sense to rely on two particular employees – Miss Elmira Bier and Miss Minnie Byers. Minnie concentrated on the financial end of things and is credited with keeping the Phillipses solvent throughout the Great Depression. Elmira, who began as a secretary, played an especially significant role as a result of World War II. Minnie worked for Duncan and Marjorie for approximately forty years, and Elmira for fifty.

One of the most important cultural milestones in United States history is the birth of the National Gallery of Art. It began with funds from Andrew Mellon, founder of Alcoa, Gulf Oil, and Union Steel. Designed by the architect John Russell Pope and located on the Mall in Washington D.C., it opened in 1941, but in 1938 Duncan Phillips was already a member of its first board of trustees. In announcing his selection to the National Gallery's board, the *Washington Post* identified him beyond co-founding The Phillips Memorial Gallery with Marjorie Phillips. The *Post* referred to him as a director of the American Federation of Arts, an organization with the mission of enriching the public understanding of visual arts.[1]

Duncan Phillips's special talent for the presentation of art was not lost on National Gallery leadership. John Walker, the original chief curator at the National Gallery of Art and its second director, wrote that in planning for the National Gallery, he and his associates "had to think in terms of millions of visitors. Nevertheless, we always kept in mind the delight afforded by the Phillips Gallery."[2] Walker saw the Phillips Memorial Gallery as the "perfect museum" with its "comfortable chairs, ashtrays on tables, soft carpets, absences of guards."[3] In his memoir, Walker wrote that to wander at the Phillips "is to enjoy what can only be described as spiritual refreshment" adding that "in no other museum have I so enjoyed the contemplation of paintings."[4]

To Duncan Phillips, a personal experience with a work of art was paramount in appreciating it. He was fully aware that his own museum's intimacy could not be duplicated in larger institutions, yet he strove for excellence in all of his art-related activities, whether in Washington, New York, elsewhere in the United States, or abroad. A trustee for the National Gallery until 1960, Phillips wielded influence there by applying his skills as an executive and his knowledge as an art scholar. John Walker cited what he considered Phillips's unparalleled background when he wrote of the inaugural group of high-ranking staff at the National Gallery: "Our ignorance was matched by that of all our trustees except one, Duncan Phillips."[5]

A member of the board's acquisition committee, Phillips did not hesitate to employ his art savvy in shaping the National Gallery of Art. A week before the doors to the institution opened, he sent a letter to the gallery's first director, David Finley, pushing him to try to acquire a particular work by the nineteenth-century French painter Jean-Baptiste-Camille Corot, which was owned at the time by an Italian count. "I cannot urge you too strongly to act promptly if it can possibly be arranged to purchase, out of the Gallery's funds, the beautiful landscape of *Ville d'Avary* by Corot," adding that "the master's mature art, when it was most spontaneous and lyrical, can be seen in its very essence in this delicious canvas."[6] When he sent his missive to Finley, Phillips was already arranging to donate to the nation a painting by another nineteenth-century Frenchman, Honoré Daumier. That spring, Finley formally accepted Phillips's contribution of the Daumier work *Les Conseils a un Jeune Artiste (Advice to a Young Artist)* and thanked him "not only for your great generosity in making such an important gift to the Gallery, but for the discrimination shown by you in the selection of this particular painting."[7]

When the dedication ceremony for the National Gallery was held on March 17, 1941, Duncan Phillips was among the VIPs as President Franklin D. Roosevelt spoke to the assembled crowd. The *Washington Post* wrote of the approaching fanfare: "Leaving his desk burdened with the transient reports of war, the President tonight will enter the marble National Gallery of Art and dedicate its ageless treasures to the American people."[8] The previous evening, Duncan and Marjorie hosted a reception at the Phillips Memorial Gallery prior to a round-table discussion at the Willard Hotel on Pennsylvania Avenue, two blocks from the White House. The *Washington Sunday Star* reported that the round-table event was part of that week's American Federation of Arts convention and that its members were in town to "examine the position of art in light of present world conditions."[9]

While the United States would not enter World War II until after the Japanese bombing of Pearl Harbor on December 7, 1941, Washington, D.C. had already increased in volume of both people and federal offices, partly due to relatively new government jobs created by the New Deal. The population of the nation's capital boomed again after Roosevelt's "a date that will live in infamy" speech. It is difficult to measure the exact number of newcomers to the District during America's involvement in the war because the four years of 1941-45 fall between census counts; however, the U.S. Census shows that Washington's population nearly doubled from 1930 to 1950, with the 1950 tally at 800,000 people. In World War II Washington, there simply were not enough houses, apartments, or even rooms available. Materials that private developers might have otherwise used to build new housing were required for military purposes. As the living conditions grew ever more crowded, the U.S. government itself –

under the umbrella of the Federal Works Agency – began erecting temporary housing for wartime employees. The *Washington Post* reported on relief for at least some civil service women and WAVES – the U.S. Navy's acronym for Women Accepted for Voluntary Service – who would be moving into new quarters in Arlington, Virginia. Describing Kansas Hall, one of ten dormitories which were quickly built in an area known as Arlington Farms, each of them named for a U.S. state, the *Post* article said that "six hundred and ten additional feminine Government workers earning under $1800 a year will reach the end of their housing problems this week." Reporting that "most of the residents are employed at either the Pentagon Building or the Navy Department annex nearby," the *Post* specified that "rooms cost $24.50 a month, whether you live alone or have a roommate, except corner rooms with two exposures, which are $28.50 and probably will be worth the difference when July comes to Arlington."[10]

The heat and humidity of Washington summers and its effect on government workers was also noted in a newspaper article the previous July. With the United States only seven months into the war, the National Gallery of Art proved a popular destination for civil servants, as well as military personnel stationed in D.C. or on leave. "Soldiers and sailors visit this citadel of beauty in such numbers that you get the impression the place must be strictly G.I.," wrote Alan David in the *Washington Post*. "Government employees ... have practically adopted the gallery as their own." Allowing that part of the lure might be the cafeteria and the air conditioning, David continued: "A lunch hour poll probably would reveal two-thirds of the visitors to be Uncle Sam's nephews and nieces engaged in topping off a meal with a stroll through the restful avenues of Gainsborough and Bellini."[11]

The National Gallery was not the only art destination attracting those serving their country. John Walker sent Duncan Phillips a letter about a 1944 exhibit of American painting at the Phillips Memorial Gallery and the most recent sojourn he and his wife had made there. "The gallery yesterday was filled with people, many of them in uniform. I received the impression once more of how much your gallery means to this city," Walker wrote. "Margaret and I were both very moved by the deep enjoyment of the people we watched looking at your pictures."[12]

One of the service members who frequented the Phillips Memorial Gallery in 1944 was Richard Diebenkorn, who would go on to become an internationally acclaimed artist and tell of how much the gallery meant to him. As Walker continued his letter, he again acknowledged Phillips's art expertise, writing: "The pictures you have assembled stand as a wonderful tribute to your judgment."[13] Mr. and Mrs. Walker – and the young Diebenkorn – would have encountered more than a dozen works by Stieglitz Circle artists in *The American*

Paintings of The Phillips Collection show. Two paintings by Georgia O'Keeffe were featured, two by Marsden Hartley, four by Arthur Dove, and six by John Marin.

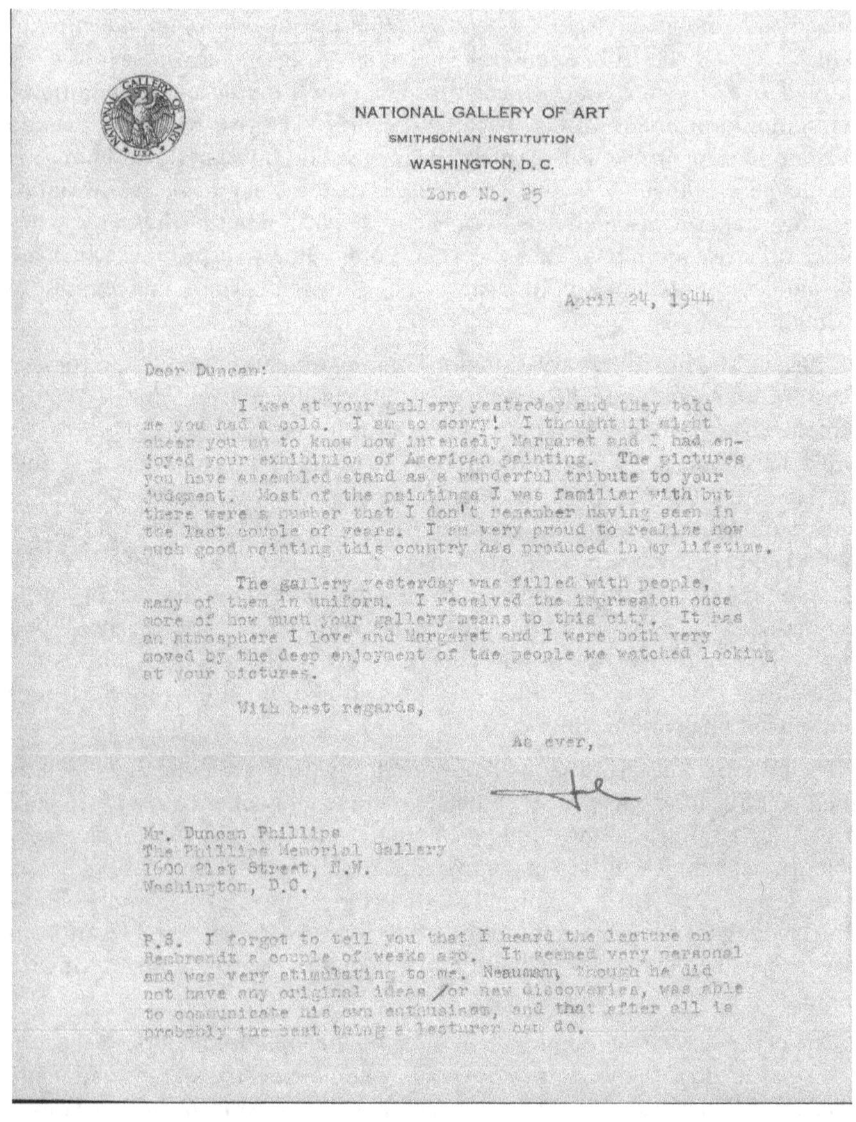

NATIONAL GALLERY OF ART
SMITHSONIAN INSTITUTION
WASHINGTON, D. C.
Zone No. 25

April 24, 1944

Dear Duncan:

I was at your gallery yesterday and they told me you had a cold. I am so sorry! I thought it might cheer you up to know how intensely Margaret and I had enjoyed your exhibition of American painting. The pictures you have assembled stand as a wonderful tribute to your judgment. Most of the paintings I was familiar with but there were a number that I don't remember having seen in the last couple of years. I am very proud to realize how much good painting this country has produced in my lifetime.

The gallery yesterday was filled with people, many of them in uniform. I received the impression once more of how much your gallery means to this city. It has an atmosphere I love and Margaret and I were both very moved by the deep enjoyment of the people we watched looking at your pictures.

With best regards,

As ever,

Mr. Duncan Phillips
The Phillips Memorial Gallery
1600 21st Street, N.W.
Washington, D.C.

P.S. I forgot to tell you that I heard the lecture on Rembrandt a couple of weeks ago. It seemed very personal and was very stimulating to me. Neumann, though he did not have any original ideas /or new discoveries, was able to communicate his own enthusiasm, and that after all is probably the best thing a lecturer can do.

Image 3. 3. The National Gallery of Art's John Walker wrote to Duncan Phillips about a 1944 visit to the Phillips Memorial Gallery. The Phillip Collection Archives.

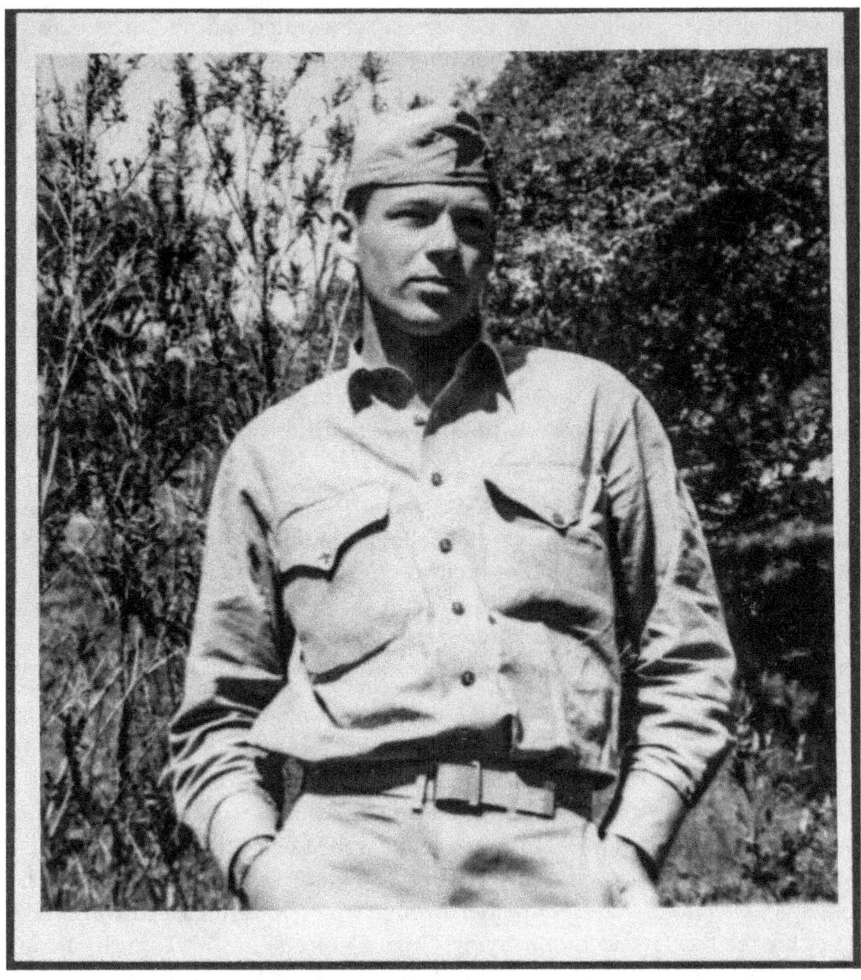

Image 3. 4. *Richard Diebenkorn in the United States Marine Corps, Camp Pendleton, California, 1945* © Richard Diebenkorn Foundation. Courtesy of Richard Diebenkorn Foundation.

Indeed, Duncan and Marjorie welcomed many men and women in uniform to the Phillips Memorial Galley during World War II, as well as civil servants and contract personnel. The Phillipses hoped the young out-of-towners would enjoy its homelike atmosphere. Yet they wanted to do more. Elmira Bier, who had long before proven herself as Duncan's secretary, was put in charge of arranging a weekly public concert at the museum. Miss Bier's responsibilities had already evolved into a combined executive assistant and chief of staff position, but she embraced the additional work with gusto. Newspaper critics lauded her concert programs, noting her openness to include local musicians as well as new music. Meanwhile, she corresponded with a who's who of modern art, including Alfred Stieglitz, Arthur Dove, and Georgia O'Keeffe. While her letters were sent for business purposes on behalf of the museum, Elmira nearly always took the time to include something personal. Often, it would be her own comments about a work of art. In 1943, however, she wrote Stieglitz of her "dream for a small house and large garden where I have put cabbages among my roses and tomatoes with my violets."[14] Stieglitz replied that he hoped her flowers and vegetables would flourish, adding that "The Place [An American Place, his gallery and studio at the time] is my garden."[15] Many years later, O'Keeffe wrote that her late husband, Stieglitz, often spoke of Elmira Bier, who had visited him in New York.[16]

At Elmira's retirement ceremony in 1972, artist John Gernand spoke on behalf of his fellow Phillips Collection employees. His written remarks indicate he told Elmira:

"Your versatility is amazing. You may greet Henry Moore or Kenneth Clark and a few moments later take care of calling a plumber, talking to a musician about his program you have not received or dictating a letter to a publisher about an unsatisfactory color proof, and doing all this with various and frequent interruptions by telephone, intercom or one of us in person with a question."[17]

Like Elmira, Minnie Byers would prove her value time and time again. Minnie's first position for the museum was as assistant to treasurer Dwight Clark, and she became treasurer herself in 1927. Hailing from modest means in Ellenboro, North Carolina, Minnie attended business school in Richmond, Virginia, learning about the stock market as well as acquiring secretarial skills. She also attended American University and St. John's College. According to The Phillips Collection's Karen Schneider, Minnie was a powerful executive. One of Minnie's relatives recalled her saying: "I have a problem with Duncan. I can't tell him how much money we have. He'll go and spend it on works of art."[18] Schneider wrote that Minnie was protective of Phillips and his money. "She began to educate herself about art. She'd say, 'I don't think it's worth that, Duncan,' and he listened to her."[19]

In The Phillips Collection Archives, where Schneider serves as head librarian and archivist, there is a photograph of the inscription of a gift to Minnie from Duncan and Marjorie. It was 1943 when they presented her with a tray to commemorate twenty-five years of "loyal devotion to ourselves and to our creative undertakings." The inscription continued: "As our treasurer in difficult times, in a stormy period of recurring and perplexing crises due to wars and economic depressions … you accepted the challenges of your responsibilities and met them with fortitude, courage and skill."[20]

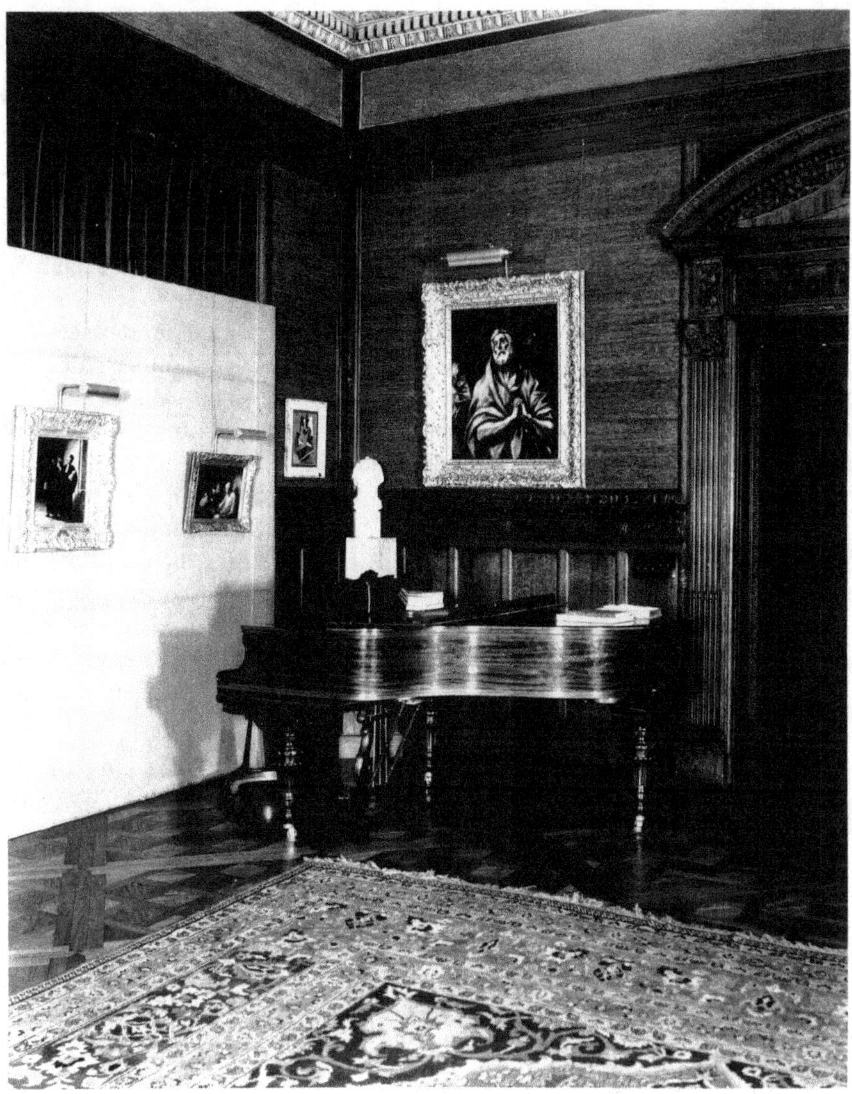

Image 3. 5. The Music Room at the Phillips looks much the same today as it did to visitors during the early and mid-twentieth century. The Phillips Collection Archives.

Were it not for Elmira Bier and Minnie Byers, it is entirely possible that the National Gallery of Art would not have remained such a significant beneficiary of Duncan Phillips's time and energy. He applied his knowledge of art to wide-ranging decisions there for thirty-two years. One of the highlights came as an additional duty to his work on the board. Phillips played an international role in preparation for an event that followed World War II, and his participation was not without a covert caveat.

Two committees appointed by the National Gallery and sponsored by the Department of State selected more than 200 paintings by American artists for an exhibition held in London in the summer of 1946. David Finley wrote to Phillips in October 1944 that the Tate Gallery trustees "would like to hold a retrospective exhibition of American painting as soon as circumstances permit after the war and the bomb damage to the Tate Gallery building has been fully repaired."[21] Finley wrote that he hoped Phillips would be able to serve on the advisory committee responsible for contemporary art. One committee selected art from the eighteenth and nineteenth centuries and the other from the nineteenth and twentieth centuries. For the latter, two of the committee members were Juliana Force, the first director of the Whitney Museum of American Art, established in 1930 by Gertrude Vanderbilt Whitney; and Alfred H. Barr Jr. of MoMA. Force and Barr were two of the most formidable executives in modern art, yet Duncan Phillips was selected to chair the committee. Finley wrote to Phillips in October 1944 that the Tate trustees wanted to hold the exhibit after the war ended in Europe without waiting for the conclusion of the war with Japan. He added that "Our Ambassador at London, Governor Winant, strongly supports this point of view."[22] Finley closed his correspondence to Phillips with an entreaty to keep the idea of the exhibition "confidential for the present, until an announcement can be made in London."[23]

Ultimately, the exhibit opened at the Tate Gallery ten months after Japan's surrender to the Allies. Phillips loaned twenty-three works from the Phillips Memorial Gallery to the June-July 1946 show, which was titled *American Painting: From the Eighteenth Century to the Present Day.*

Notes

[1] "Five Trustees of National Gallery of Art Named: Mellon, Duncan Phillips Head Group Chosen by Regents of Smithsonian," *Washington Post*, June 25, 1937.

[2] Ibid.

[3] John Walker, *Self-Portrait with Donors: Confessions of an Art Collector* (Boston: Little, Brown, 1974), 35.

[4] Ibid.

[5] Walker, *Self-Portrait with Donors*, 35.

[6] Duncan Phillips to David Finley, 10 March 1941, Record Group 7, Series A, Item 2, Gallery Archives, National Gallery of Art, Washington, D.C.

[7] David Finley to Duncan Phillips, 29 May 1941, The Phillips Collection Archives, Washington, D.C.

[8] "Shrine of Permanence: Roosevelt to Put War Aside; Dedicate Art Gallery Tonight," *Washington Post,* March 17. 1941.

[9] "Annual Convention of Arts Federal Opens Here Tuesday: Program Will Include Reception at Phillips Memorial Gallery," *Washington Sunday Star,* March 16, 1941.

[10] "Home for 610: Government Girls Occupy New Dorm," *Washington Post,* April 2, 1943.

[11] Alan David, "National Art Gallery Challenges Museum and Zoo in Popularity," *Washington Post,* July 12, 1942.

[12] John Walker to Duncan Phillips, 24 April 1944, The Phillips Collection Archives, Washington, D.C.

[13] Ibid.

[14] Elmira Bier to Alfred Stieglitz, 28 May 1943, The Phillips Collection Archives, Washington, D.C.

[15] Alfred Stieglitz to Elmira Bier, 31 May 1943, The Phillips Collection Archives, Washington, D.C.

[16] Georgia O'Keeffe to Elmira Bier, 7 March 1967, The Phillips Collection Archives, Washington, D.C.

[17] John Gernand, Remarks at Retirement Ceremony for Elmira Bier (Washington, D.C., 1972), The Phillips Collection Archives, Washington, D.C.

[18] Karen Schneider, "Women's History at The Phillips: Minnie Byers," *Experiment Station* (blog) March 22, 2013, http://blog.phillipscollection.org/2013/03/22/womens-history-phillips-minnie-byers/.

[19] Ibid.

[20] Inscription on a gift to Minnie Byers from Duncan and Marjorie Phillips, January 15, 1943, The Phillips Collection Archives, Washington, D.C.

[21] Finley to Duncan Phillips, 25 October 1944, The Phillips Collection Archives, Washington, D.C.

[22] Ibid.

[23] Ibid.

Chapter 4

Marjorie Phillips: Artist and Executive

The Gilded Age had waned when Marjorie Acker attended the Art Students League of New York. She took the train into the city from Ossining, New York, where she lived with her parents and six siblings. Her routine was to disembark at Grand Central Station on 42nd Street then walk up Fifth Avenue to reach the renowned art school on 57th Street. The Indiana-born painter loved New York City. She would pop into art galleries to see the latest works on display whenever time allowed.

Miss Acker took her art courses seriously, but she missed out on socializing with classmates after hours. She regretted being a "day student" and having to return to Ossining each evening. Her mother, Alice Beal Acker, relied on Marjorie and another daughter to help with the younger children. Her father, chemical engineer and inventor Charles Acker, had suffered a severe financial setback and while Marjorie stopped short of calling it melancholy, she did say that neither he nor Alice was ever quite the same. Fortunately for their children, the Ackers lived only forty miles from Newburgh, New York, where Alice's parents, William "W.R." and Eleanor Beal, owned a hillside manor overlooking the Hudson River. Before the turn of the century, Grandfather W.R. founded a gas company; then in 1900, he established an "electric light" company. He combined the utilities into the Central Hudson Gas and Electric Corporation, and it stayed a family business for several years.

Privilege or Merit?

When Marjorie visited her grandparents at the Beal estate, she also spent time with her uncles, established artists Reynolds and Gifford Beal. Both of them encouraged her to paint without attempting to mold her. In an interview with journalist Susan Drysdale, Marjorie said that she did not actually study with either Reynolds or Gifford, "but probably absorbed a good deal through a sort of osmosis and hearing them talk."[1] Gifford Beal, an award-winning painter who had studied with William Merritt Chase, was president of the Art Students League during Marjorie's enrollment there. The notion that Marjorie was provided certain privileges that her talent did not merit followed her long after she married Duncan. The label of wife-of-a-collector dabbler was sometimes bestowed in haste or by innuendo. There were critics who did not see more than pretty pictures when they looked at Marjorie's works. An example was Florence Berryman of the *Washington Star*, who reviewed Marjorie's one-woman show at the Corcoran Gallery of Art in Washington, D.C. in 1955. Berryman wrote about the views the paintings offered, notable in her opinion simply for their "green of countryside, lofty trees and well-tended gardens."[2]

Although Marjorie would never achieve the level of renown of so many artists shown at The Phillips Collection, she did enjoy noteworthy success at the New York, San Francisco, and London galleries that exhibited and sold her paintings. In addition to the gallery shows, her work has appeared at some of America's most prominent art museums, among them: the Whitney Museum of American Art, MoMA, the Art Institute of Chicago, the Cleveland Museum of Art, and the Carnegie Institute. Moreover, two leaders of the art world, David Finley, the first director of the National Gallery of Art, and Alfred Stieglitz, fine arts photographer and promoter of Modernism, documented their respect for her paintings. Finley sent a letter to Marjorie about visiting her 1952 one-woman show at Durlacher Brothers in New York City. "I was greatly impressed and send you my warmest congratulations," the fellow Washington resident wrote. "I think you should be very proud of your exhibition."[3] The tribute from Stieglitz is even more remarkable because it was unusual for him to laud an artist not considered a Modernist. The Bignou Gallery in New York City held two one-woman shows of Marjorie's works in the 1940s; Stieglitz penned a letter to Duncan after accompanying the Phillipses to her 1941 exhibit there. "I would not have given up this experience this morning for anything. Seeing you and your wife standing amongst her pictures, seeing the landscapes, the still lifes, the portrait of you, the city outside, made me feel as if I had visited and seen an exceptionally fine world,"[4] the aging photographer and gallery owner wrote. From his own New York City gallery and studio, The Place, Stieglitz continued to reflect on his morning with the Phillipses, stating that Marjorie's pictures remained "alive very vividly before me."[5] He added his thanks for "calling for me and taking me to Bignou's to see the paintings of Marjorie Phillips. And I am glad we saw them together, and undisturbed by anyone."[6]

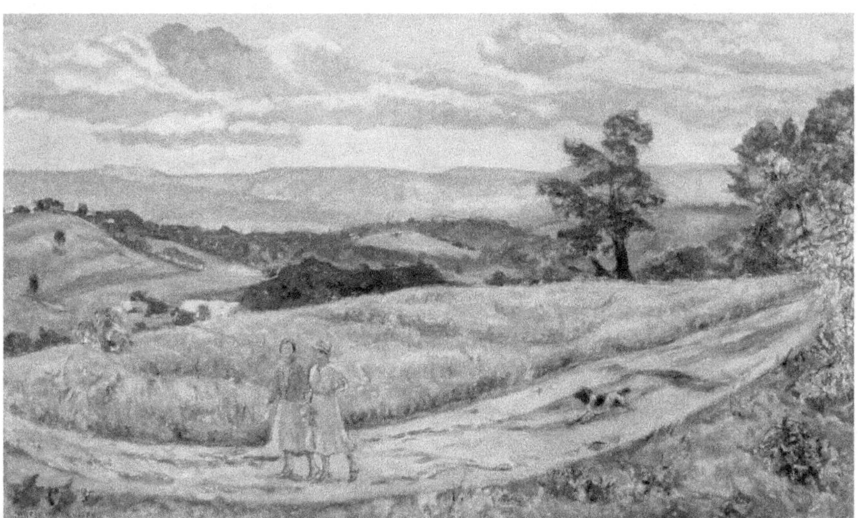

Image 4. 1. Marjorie Phillips, *Morning Walk*, 1939, Oil on canvas 22 x 36 1/4 in.; 55.88 x 92.075 cm. The Phillips Collection: Acquired 1940s. Paintings, 1516, American.

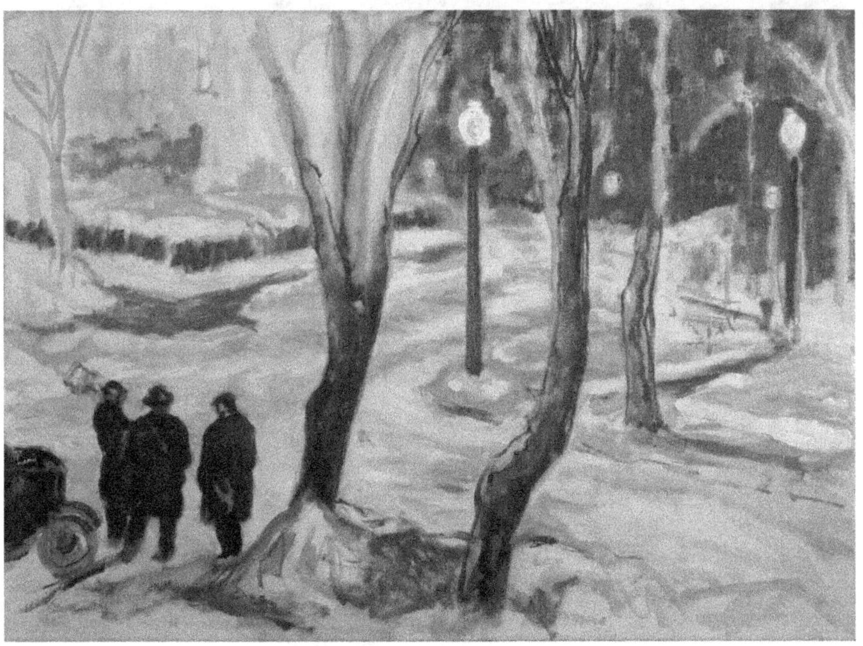

Image 4. 2. Marjorie Phillips, *After the Snowfall*, 1922,
Oil on canvas board 17 7/8 x 24 in.; 45.4025 x 60.96 cm. The Phillips Collection: Gift of the artist, 1984. Paintings, 1490, American.

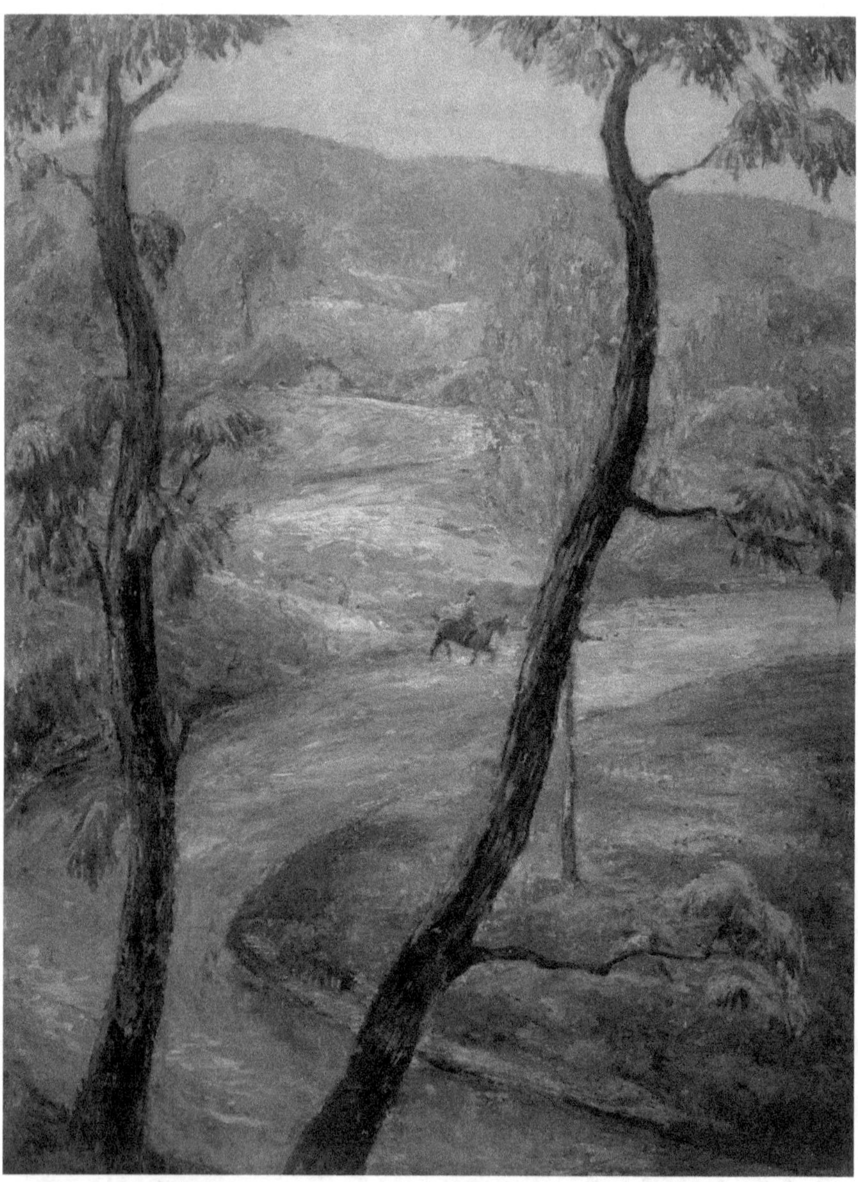

Image 4. 3. Marjorie Phillips, *Rock Creek Park*, early 1920s,
Oil on canvas 24 x 17 3/4 in.; 60.96 x 45.085 cm. The Phillips Collection: Gift of the artist, 1984. Paintings, 1534, American.

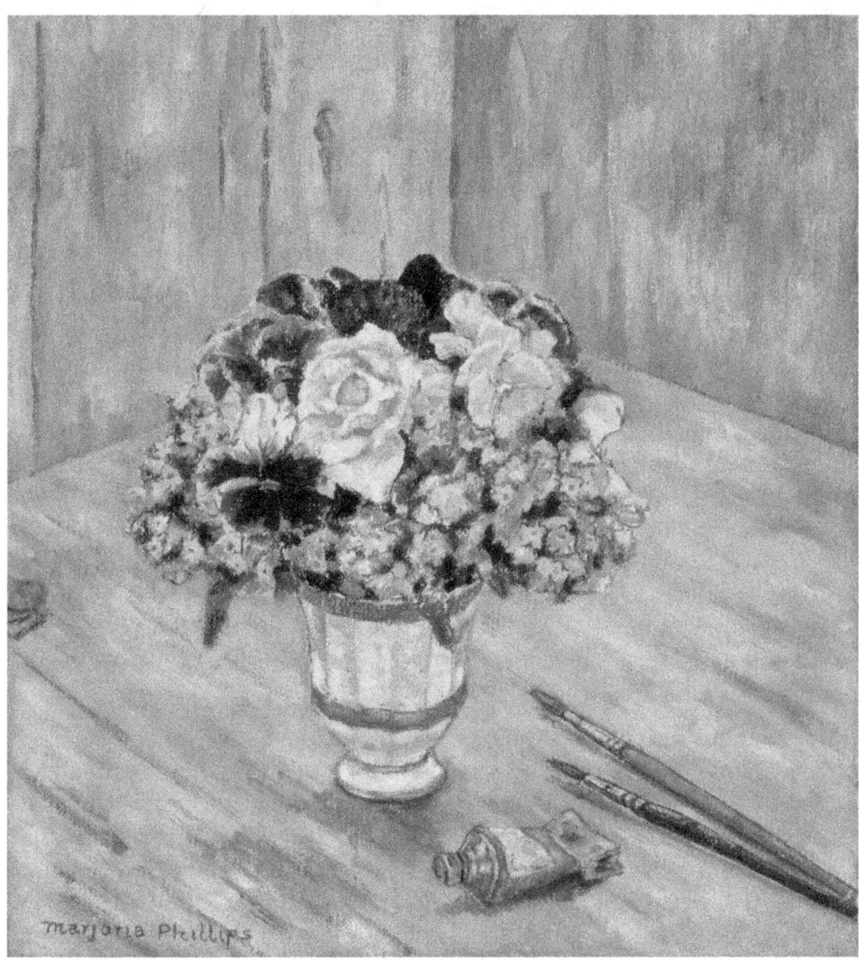

Image 4. 4. Marjorie Phillips, Little Bouquet, 1934,
Oil on canvas 15 1/2 x 14 1/8 in.; 39.37 x 35.8775 cm. The Phillips Collection: Acquired by 1941 (?). Paintings, 1512, American.

Determined to Paint

Please don't disturb read the sign Marjorie put on the door to her studio, a dedicated space first located within the Phillipses' Dupont Circle property and later at their Foxhall Road home. She had always been a disciplined creator, even painting on her honeymoon. The newlyweds' get-away would not be the only time she packed palette and easel. During her years with Duncan, she made the most of their summers in the Alleghenies. "It was a wonderful place for painting," she said of rural Ebensburg, Pennsylvania. "Social life didn't follow you there. You could walk, paint. I'd work in my studio, from the car or in a field on the spot."[7] Back in Washington, Marjorie set aside mornings for painting. On those afternoons when she was tempted to return to a work-in-progress, the duties of being a museum executive usually prevented her from opening the studio door again until the next day. While Marjorie did not become director of The Phillips Collection until after Duncan's death in 1966, she served as its associate director for forty-one years and bore responsibility for the minutiae of organizing temporary exhibitions in the museum's Prints and Drawings Room.

There were other commitments stemming from her expected roles as a married woman during the early to mid-twentieth century. While she benefited from the luxury of hiring domestic help, Marjorie ran the household. In addition to motherhood, she took on a plethora of social obligations, sometimes directly related to the museum, but often as a function of the couple's place among the wealthy families in Washington. Marjorie attended countless luncheons and charity events throughout her adult life, and she hosted them as well. A lead item on the society page of the *Washington Evening Star* from 1940 told of a buffet dinner she and Duncan provided to aid the British war effort. The Phillipses' "large gathering" that evening followed a lecture at the National Theatre on "Shakespeare in Peace and War."[8] Her participation in fund-raising events continued throughout World War II, principally for the American Red Cross.

More tranquil times found Marjorie welcoming friends, artists, and members of the Phillips Gallery staff to meals both simple and grand. John Gernand was a long-time employee at the museum and a painter who recalled meeting fellow artist John Marin and the poet Dylan Thomas at separate Phillips soirees. In an oral history commissioned by the Archives of American Art, Gernand said that he was "often asked" to the Phillips's house for dinner because he was one of the only employees "to have dinner clothes."[9] Whether the Phillipses were entertaining at home or accepting an invitation from a senator or an ambassador, it was Marjorie who made sure that their son had his supper and that Duncan had all the requisite accouterments for his formal attire.

Her Greatest Cheerleader

No matter the task at hand, Marjorie saw the world as an artist. Duncan admired her for it, and throughout her career, he cheered her on. In 1948, Duncan composed the foreword for an exhibition brochure about works by Marjorie. The exhibit was first mounted at the Bignou Gallery and then shown at the Phillips Gallery. In his description of her art, Duncan wrote: "What we need today is not just another group movement but a few individuals who love that real light, which is the life of everything it touches. Such an artist is Marjorie Phillips who, in spite of keen understanding and appreciation of many [artistic] techniques is never distracted from her course. She is a luminist with a truly classic feeling for composition of pictorial space."[10] In the context of art history, Luminism was a term coined a half-dozen years *after* Duncan wrote the foreword. It referred to a group of artists who could use light to turn the sky or sea ethereal. With pervading light came a feeling for the universality of nature. As an art movement, Luminism encompassed painters in the nineteenth century's Hudson River School, among them Frederic Edwin Church and Albert Bierstadt. Marjorie would have been familiar with Church's interpretation of Niagara Falls and Bierstadt's of the Rocky Mountains, among other sweeping renditions. When Duncan called Marjorie a luminist, he was not comparing her to the great American landscape artists. Rather, he was referring to how she used light to enhance what he saw as her individualism.

One of Marjorie's artistic heroes was Pierre Bonnard. References to his use of color can be found in some of her oil paintings, most notably those of flowers. His deep coral is in her poppies. Brush strokes of his purples appear in her African violets. However, she was too schooled of an artist to take her homages to Bonnard too far. She was influenced by Impressionism and Post-Impressionism, but Marjorie Acker Phillips did not stop there. Some of her works employ Realism without straying into the dark grittiness of America's Ashcan School, although she did admire its members which included Robert Henri and John Sloan.

In her most popular painting at The Phillips Collection, *Night Baseball*, Marjorie mixed elements of the artistic movements she had studied – and in the process displayed her skill in guiding the viewer's eye. The year is 1951. The New York Yankees are in D.C. to play the Washington Senators. Joltin' Joe DiMaggio is at bat. The artist's vantage point is behind the home-team dugout. Prior to that night, she had attended many games with Duncan, an avowed baseball fanatic. It was the visual spectacle more than the actual sport that appealed to Marjorie, who regularly sketched the activity on the field from her seat in the stands. "I would make innumerable small pencil drawings while observing aspects that I thought were characterful for a painting," she wrote.[11] For *Night Baseball*, she purposefully emphasized the tension of the moment through the game's natural geometry. Marjorie wrote that she "always loved that group of three: the squatting catcher just behind the man at bat and, standing behind him, the eagerly watching umpire leaning forward."[12] She chose the experience of that particular night to move beyond sketching and commit to oil-on-canvas because of the Yankee Clipper's presence. Although she joined other Washingtonians in rooting for the Senators, she fully acknowledged that "Joe DiMaggio topped them all in style and special character!"[13] Marjorie was proud that "the final version of all my studies must have seemed authentic" because years later a man wanted to buy her painting for the Baseball Hall of Fame. "I said I could not sell it as I had given it to my husband."[14]

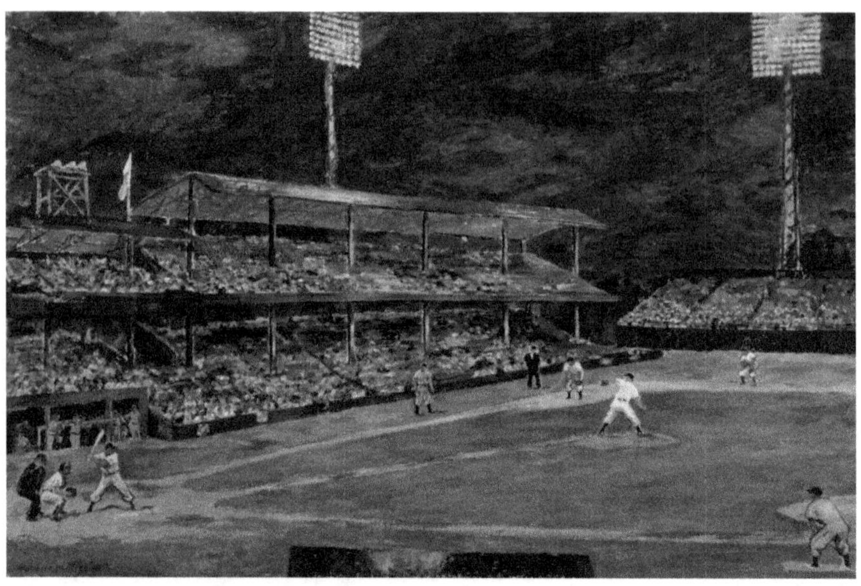

Image 4. 5. Marjorie Phillips, *Night Baseball*, 1951, Oil on canvas 24 1/4 x 36 in.; 61.595 x 91.44 cm. The Phillips Collection: Gift of the artist, 1951 or 1952. Paintings, 1521, American.

Up from the Basement Rooms

Like most of Marjorie's works in their turn, *Night Baseball* rested on her easel after morning studio sessions. The mornings-only painting became routine when she was made associate director of the museum. Most of her museum work during her tenure as an associate director "was done with Duncan"[15] and included selecting art, discussing plans, and traveling to meet artists and art dealers. "I concentrated on the basement rooms," she wrote. "They were called the print rooms but there were paintings shown there too. My responsibility was to get up exhibitions for these rooms."[16] Like exhibitions anywhere, works were sought on loan from other institutions as well as private collectors. When Marjorie organized the 1940 exhibition "Great Modern Drawings in April," for instance, she borrowed Pierre-Auguste Renoir's *The Bathers* from the Wadsworth Atheneum in Hartford, Connecticut and Paul Cézanne's *L'amour de Puget* from the Brooklyn Museum. For the same show, she received correspondence from Mrs. John D. Rockefeller Jr.'s secretary affirming that "Mrs. Rockefeller has asked me to tell you that she would be glad to let you have the Van Gogh drawing of a landscape any time that you wish it."[17]

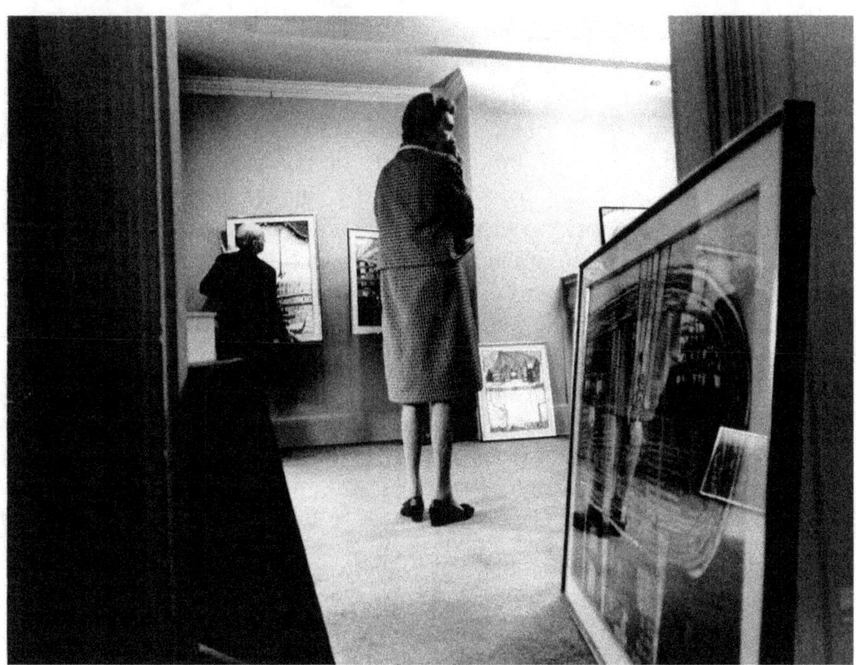

Image 4. 6. Marjorie Phillips installing a traveling art exhibition at The Phillips Collection, 1969. The Phillips Collection Archives.

While Marjorie succeeded with the majority of exhibitions she worked to organize, not all of them came to fruition. In 1964, as her duties were expanding due partly to Duncan's ill health, she wrote to artist Edward Hopper informing him that The Phillips Collection was planning to hold an exhibition of his work only months from the date of her letter. "We have both always been great admirers of your work and have some unusually fine examples, as you know. We are wondering if you have any suggestions to make about the show, particularly as to some favorite canvasses of your own or in private collections that you would like to have included?"[18] She continued the letter by inviting him to the opening of the show. Hopper replied that his "pictures are not available at the present time" because the Whitney Museum of Art had arranged for a retrospective of his works through the fall, after which it would be traveling to Chicago, Detroit, and St. Louis. "This is all planned and underway," Hopper wrote in longhand, adding how much he appreciated "your wishing to have a show of my works in Washington, but it seems not possible just now."[19]

By contrast, one of Marjorie's major achievements came two years later, in the spring of 1966, when she presented the multi-artist show "Birds in Contemporary Art." She borrowed sculpture, paintings, and drawings from owners of works by Bonnard, Morris Graves, Arthur Dove, Georges Braque, Pablo Picasso, Joan Miro, and Constantin Brancusi. Other artists were also represented, including Marjorie herself by way of a 1965 oil she called *Mr. Snowman.* Her purpose in selecting birds as a theme for the exhibit was two-fold: it would show the public how important form is to an artist, and it would reveal something of each artist's singularity. In the introduction to the exhibition catalogue, Marjorie wrote: "So here we have creations, from wit and humor, from pathos to the sinister, depending on how the artist's personality endows the bird, along with his appreciation of its essential character and the life-giving all-time basic and experimental art forms."[20] One of her many thank you letters to the show's lenders was sent to Katharine Graham, who by that time had succeeded her late husband, Philip Graham, to become president and publisher of the *Washington Post.* Marjorie told "Dear Kay" that her Brancusi sculpture *Oiseau d'Or (Golden Bird)* was "greatly admired and appreciated (especially by Duncan). It played a very important part in what proved to be an unusually lively, varied and fascinating group of sculpture and painting."[21]

Correspondence had been a big part of Duncan's decades as a director, and so it was for Marjorie during her time at the helm. Some of the day-to-day considerations could be as simple as a request from a journalist, a publisher, or another art museum for a photograph to use in an article, book, or promotional materials. For the collaboration of a book series between MoMA and the Book-of-the-Month Club, the New York museum asked for a color transparency of The Phillips Collection's Braque painting *Le Gueridon.* Duncan Phillips had strongly preferred Georges Braque's Cubism to Pablo Picasso's, and *The Guitar* was one of several Braque oils the Phillipses had purchased over the years. Marjorie deeply respected the author of the book series, art critic John Russell. He had been to dinner at the Phillips home and had once been given a special tour of The Phillips Collection with his wife. Russell sent a thank you note to Marjorie in which he reflected on the couple's impressions from the tour. He shared that both he and Mrs. Russell "said with one voice" that the Phillips museum was unrivaled for its "depth and delicate sureness of judgment which it displays at every point." Russell added that he hoped to "say something of this sort" in his pending piece for the *London Times.*[22] In response to MoMA's request for the then-preferred format for reproduction of images, Marjorie wrote instructions to administrative supervisor Elmira Bier: "Please say that we will be glad to send transparency for John Russell series."[23]

In reply to a request from the director of the Art Institute of Chicago to borrow the actual *Le Gueridon* painting, Marjorie emphatically said yes. "How wonderful the masterpieces you are including will look in those beautifully lighted galleries," she wrote Charles Cunningham about Chicago's planned Braque show. "Such an exhibition is thrilling to think about; we will all look forward to seeing it!" Marjorie closed her director-to-director letter with insight into the challenges of bringing together works of art. "Best wishes for good luck in getting the things you want most."[24]

Another full-hearted approval was sent to Antoine Terrasse, a great-nephew of Pierre Bonnard. Terrasse was helping the French government organize a Bonnard exhibit for Japan, to be shown at venues in Tokyo and Kyoto. In reply to Monsieur Terrasse's request for Madame Phillips to loan one painting of her choice, Marjorie wrote: "I have thought it over a great deal and would like to send a particularly fine one. I have therefore decided on *Woman and Dog* [*Woman with Dog*], knowing you like it, and it is illustrated in the fascinating new book on Bonnard which you brought to me."[25]

Marjorie said yes whenever she could, but she was protective of The Phillips Collection's reputation for quality. In a letter to the Dissemination of Culture Section of the United Nations Educational, Scientific, and Cultural Organization, she wrote that she would be glad to have a reproduction of Cézanne's *Pomegranate and Pears* included in a forthcoming UNESCO publication, but she attached a condition. "I should very much like to see a proof ahead of time," Marjorie stipulated. "There have been so many poor reproductions of paintings in The Phillips Collection of late."[26]

When Marjorie turned down any type of request, she did it as diplomatically as possible. She told France's cultural affairs office that "The Phillips Collection appreciates the honour [she used the British spelling] you pay our beautiful painting by Manet, *The Ballet Espagnol*" by asking to include it in an exhibition at the Louvre on poet and art critic Charles Baudelaire. She bowed out by explaining that the Phillips could "not spare" the painting "because it is the only Manet in the collection." Marjorie closed her letter with kudos to the Louvre curators. "The idea back of your exhibition is so good that I am doubly sorry that we cannot grant your request."[27] She said no to another petition from Paris the following year. The same French cultural affairs office that wrote on behalf of the Louvre asked to borrow a Phillips Collection work by Paul Klee for the Musee National d'Art Moderne. Marjorie replied: "We have loaned important Klees to exhibitions for the last two years including *Arab Song* and cannot lend it so soon again. We must keep the 'unit' or small gallery of his work intact this year as one of our most important features." Whether she responded to a request in a positive or negative way, Marjorie always wanted to end on an upbeat note. Above her signature in the Klee denial letter, she added that she was certain the exhibition "will be very fine."[28]

Another institution to be disappointed was the Museum of Fine Arts in St. Petersburg, Florida. They were planning an exhibition titled "Color in Control" and asked to borrow one of the Rothkos in The Phillips Collection's Rothko Room. Marjorie explained that she could not grant their request for *Ochre and*

Red on Red for two reasons. “First of all, the artist does not approve of their traveling and in the past has been much upset when he heard we had sent any on loan,” she wrote. “The other reason is that we cannot spare any in our present hanging as their installation in the gallery you wrote you liked so much is a very important feature of this museum.”[29]

Sometimes Marjorie would say a concurrent yes and no to a would-be borrower. In 1969, the centennial of Henri Matisse’s birth, a representative for a celebratory retrospective asked for a loan of the two Matisse oil paintings owned by the Phillips. They remain among the most formidable works in the collection. A view of the French master’s studio, titled *Atelier, Quai Saint*-Michel was painted in 1916, when he was forty-six years old, and his *Interior with Egyptian Curtain* was completed in 1948, his seventy-eighth year. Marjorie wrote that she would be “glad to send one of the paintings which you invited for the Henri Matisse Exposition du Centenaire, but that we could not possibly spare them both for so long a time. The one I have chosen to send is *Atelier, Quai Saint-Michel*, which I believe is probably the finest of the two.”[30] In another split decision regarding the loaning of Phillips Collection art, Marjorie informed the American Federation of Arts that she would be happy to lend the painting *Offices* by Charles Sheeler “even though we may miss it sorely.” However, she turned down their request for a second work for their exhibition “From Synchronism Forward: A View of Abstract Art in America.” She wrote: “I am sorry I cannot grant your request to borrow *Golden Storm* by Dove for the same circulating exhibition. It is far too fragile as well as an important feature of The Collection.”[31]

The condition of a work of art was often a determining factor in Marjorie’s decisions on loans for special exhibitions. Peter Selz was the founding director of the University Art Museum at the University of California, Berkeley, which opened in 1970. When the California museum was in its infancy, he asked Marjorie to borrow the painting *Resurrection* by Albert Pinkham Ryder. The occasion was a show titled “The Hand and the Spirit: Religious Art in America 1770-1900.” Marjorie replied that while the concept “sounds very interesting indeed … I cannot possibly lend the painting … It is not only constantly on display here in a group of American old masters but is in fragile condition and it would be exceedingly hazardous for it to be sent on such a long tour as you outline.”[32] She underlined the words “fragile” and “exceedingly hazardous.”

“She Turns Tiger”

Marjorie Phillips herself was far from fragile. Jane Morse, author of a May 1970 *Look* magazine profile titled “The Marjorie Phillips Story,” wrote that she found the museum director to be shy, but stated that “shyness is not to be confused with softness in backbone.” Morse explained: “For art or her husband’s reputation, she turns tiger."[33] There is no more perfect example than the March 1970 letter Marjorie wrote to a man in the upper echelons of the art world hierarchy. She formalized communication to J. Carter Brown, the director of the National Gallery of Art, after talking with him on the telephone. "I am sure you will understand how excited we are about plans for celebrating The Phillips Collection's fiftieth anniversary with a small but distinguished Cézanne exhibition in early 1971," she wrote as part of her rebuttal to Brown's idea to hold a Cézanne show at the same time. "Unfortunately, a simultaneous showing at the National Gallery of Cézanne's paintings owned by Washingtonians would inevitably create confusion and divert attention from the commemoration."[34]

J. Carter Brown acquiesced to the widow's wishes, and her presentation of eighty-three works by Paul Cézanne proved a resounding triumph. She considered it the accomplishment that gave her the greatest satisfaction of her directorship.[35] Marjorie had been orchestrating the exhibition for quite some time. In 1969, she sent a letter to Charles Cunningham in Chicago seeking his input and asking for a face-to-face discussion. "It was good to hear that you are coming to the meeting of The International Exhibitions Foundation, and after the meeting and lunch hope you will give some suggestions as to paintings by Cézanne you would especially want included in the 1971 Exhibition of his work."[36] Marjorie knew the value of bringing other museum professionals on board. She persuaded not only the Art Institute of Chicago but also the Museum of Fine Arts, Boston to partner with The Phillips Collection on assembling the exhibition, and it traveled to both cities after the Washington debut. During the duration of organizing the show, Marjorie relied on Cézanne authority John Rewald. A world-renowned expert on Impressionism and Post-Impressionism, Rewald was on the faculty of the University of Chicago in their Department of Art. In the catalogue that accompanied the Cézanne exhibition, Marjorie wrote that Rewald's "extensive writings are the source of much of our knowledge of the artist" and that she deeply appreciated the professor "who constantly advised."[37]

Phillips Collection employee Arthur Hall Smith was privy to many of the behind-the- scenes details that brought the Cézanne show together. "Every institution Mrs. Phillips asked came through," Smith said.[38] Marjorie confessed it was no easy feat. "The organization of a Cézanne exhibition presents many difficulties," she wrote, "not the least of which is that the artist's works are so prized by museums and private collectors that there is a general reluctance to lend them."[39] The paintings and drawings came from locations across the United States and Europe, from Baltimore to Berlin. Marjorie felt that the willingness to lend was a tribute to her late husband. Smith allowed that Duncan's reputation as an arts connoisseur provided a foundation but believed the real success of obtaining Cézanne works from other museums was more a matter of reciprocation. Smith said it was "like calling in the chits," explaining that over the years when others asked to borrow, "Mr. Phillips had lent, lent, lent, lent."[40]

The *New York Times* covered the black-tie gala opening of "Cézanne: An Exhibition in Honor of the Fiftieth Anniversary of The Phillips Collection." In addition to national recognition in the press, Marjorie was rewarded with record-breaking attendance during the show's run. "People lined the street waiting to see it," she recounted.[41] Indeed, "the crowds were not to be believed by Phillips standards," said Smith, who estimated 300 to 400 visitors per day.[42]

Well before the Cézanne show, Marjorie cultivated amicable relationships with members of the media who covered the arts. For instance, she sent a letter to Frank Getlein of the *Washington Evening Star* in late August 1965 to inform him of two autumn events which would be sponsored by The Phillips Collection. One item detailed her museum's recognition of the bicentennial of the Smithsonian Institution; the other announced an exhibit of photographs of sculpture. Most notable in the letter, however, is her compliment to Getlein for a piece that had appeared in the *Star*: "I liked your recent review of my Retrospective at the Phillips Collection, especially the part about understanding figures in motion, etc."[43] When British journalist Susan Drysdale was working for the *Christian Science Monitor*, Marjorie wrote her a letter filled with praise and gratitude for a 1971 newspaper story. "This is to tell you I thought your article about The Phillips Collection was splendid," Marjorie began. She shared how it made her "really very happy" that so many friends and acquaintances "read it with enjoyment." Drysdale's article highlighted Marjorie's book *Duncan Phillips and His Collection* which had been published the previous year. In the continuation of her letter to the arts reporter, Marjorie wrote: "Your personal response to the book - that meant a lot to me!" Mrs. Duncan Phillips signed the letter "with thanks and admiration."[44]

In 1973, when London's Marlborough Gallery sought someone to craft the introductory essay for a catalogue of their show of Marjorie's works, Drysdale was selected. In her introduction to the exhibit on Old Bond Street, Drysdale sounded like Duncan Phillips with regard to Marjorie Phillips's individualism. "Despite constant exposure to innumerable styles of painting both as artist and collector, she has quietly and steadily pursued her own way," Drysdale wrote.[45]

By the time of the London opening, Marjorie had retired as director of The Phillips Collection. She no longer had to balance the life of an executive with that of a working artist. "I had more time for painting," was how Marjorie Acker Phillips put it.

Notes

[1] Susan Drysdale, "Introduction," *Marjorie Phillips,* Marlborough Fine Art, London, 1973, 6.

[2] Florence Berryman, "News of Artists and Exhibitions: Inspired by Nature," *Washington Sunday Star,* April 3, 1955.

[3] David Finley to Marjorie Phillips, 16 October 1952, The Phillips Collection Archives, Washington, D.C.

[4] Alfred Stieglitz to Duncan Phillips, 2 April 1941, The Phillips Collection Archives, Washington, D.C.

[5] Ibid.

[6] Ibid.

[7] Drysdale, "Introduction," *Marjorie Phillips,* 5.

[8] "Large Gathering Hears Mr. Evans' Lecutre for British War Relief: Mr. and Mrs. Duncan Phillips Give Buffet Supper After Performance at National," *Washington Evening Star,* November 11, 1940.

[9] John Gernand, oral history interview by Julia Haifley for the Archives of American Art, 18 January-14 February 1979, Archives of American Art, Washington, D.C., 6.

[10] "Centennial Art: Marjorie Phillips," *Cosmos Club Bulletin,* January 1978, 9.

[11] Marjorie Phillips to Susan Drysdale, 29 September 1971, The Phillips Collection Archives, Washington, D.C.

[12] M. Phillips, *Marjorie Phillips and Her Paintings* (New York: W.W. Norton, 1985), 68.

[13] M. Phillips to Susan Drysdale, 29 September 1971.

[14] M. Phillips, *Marjorie Phillips and Her Paintings,* 68.

[15] Ibid., 20

[16] Ibid.

[17] E. B. Robinson to Marjorie Phillips, 14 March 1940, The Phillips Collection Archives, Washington, D.C.

[18] M. Phillips to Edward Hopper, 30 June 1964, The Phillips Collection Archives, Washington, D.C.

[19] Edward Hopper to Marjorie Phillips, 8 July 1964, The Phillips Collection Archives, Washington, D.C.

[20] M. Phillips, *Birds in Contemporary Art, A Loan Exhibition,* (Washington, D.C.: The Phillips Collection, 1966).

[21] M. Phillips to Katharine Graham, 18 April 1966, The Phillips Collection Archives, Washington, D.C.

[22] John Russell to Marjorie Phillips, 6 April 1960, The Phillips Collection Archives, Washington, D.C.

[23] Patricia White to Marjorie Phillips, 3 December 1971, The Phillips Collection Archives, Washington, D.C.

[24] M. Phillips to Charles Cunningham, 11 January 1972, The Phillips Collection Archives, Washington, D.C.

[25] M. Phillips to Antoine Terrasse, 11 December 1967, The Phillips Collection Archives, Washington, D.C.

[26] M. Phillips to J. Cuzelin, 21 January 1969, The Phillips Collection Archives, Washington, D.C.
[27] M. Phillips to the Ministere des Affaires Culturelles, 22 March 1968, The Phillips Collection Archives, Washington, D.C.
[28] M. Phillips to the Ministere des Affaires Culturelles, 8 August 1969, The Phillips Collection Archives, Washington, D.C.
[29] M. Phillips to Lee Malone, 8 August 1969, The Phillips Collection Archives, Washington, D.C.
[30] M. Phillips to Pierre Schneider, 16 October 1969, The Phillips Collection Archives, Washington, D.C.
[31] M. Phillips to Konrad G. Kuchel, 1 August 1967, The Phillips Collection Archives, Washington, D.C.
[32] M. Phillips to Peter Selz, 5 August 1971, The Phillips Collection Archives, Washington, D.C.
[33] Jane Morse, "The Marjorie Phillips Story," *Look,* May 5, 1970, T10-12.
[34] M. Phillips to J. Carter-Brown, 18 March 1970, The Phillips Collection Archives, Washington, D.C.
[35] M. Phillips, *Marjorie Phillips and Her Paintings*, 21.
[36] M. Phillips to Charles Cunningham, 30 October 1969, The Phillips Collection Archives, Washington, D.C.
[37] M. Phillips, "Foreword," *Cézanne : An Exhibition in Honor of the Fiftieth Anniversary of The Phillips Collection,* (Washington, D.C.: The Phillips Collection, 1971), 7.
[38] Arthur Hall Smith, oral history interview by Donita M. Moorhus for The Phillips Collection Oral History Project, 2005, The Phillips Collection Archives, Washington, D.C., 42.
[39] M. Phillips, "Foreword," *Cézanne,* 7.
[40] A. Hall Smith, oral history interview, 42.
[41] M. Phillips, *Marjorie Phillips and Her Paintings*, 21.
[42] A. Hall Smith, oral history interview, 42.
[43] M. Phillips to Frank Getlein, 31 August 1965, The Phillips Collection Archives, Washington, D.C.
[44] M. Phillips to Susan Drysdale, 7 September 1971, The Phillips Collection Archives, Washington, D.C.
[45] Drysdale, "Introduction," *Marjorie Phillips,* 5.

Part Two: Six Artists Through a Phillips Collection Lens

"In painting, let there be surprise, mystery, indefiniteness."

— Marjorie Phillips

Chapter 5

Pierre Bonnard: Unsettling Calmness

The paintings of Pierre Bonnard welcome viewers who are mindful of opposites in art. Duncan Phillips saw the yin and yang in Bonnard's pictures, contrasts which foster the type of independent encounters with art that Phillips and *Art as Experience* author John Dewey advocated for individuals. Marjorie Phillips saw it too, but for her, it was from the perspective of a fellow artist. "I love the strength and subtlety of his painting," she wrote. "The combination is striking."[1] Another striking aspect of Bonnard's work – and one which encourages viewer imagination – is its phantomlike quality. While he brings the familiar such as a dog enveloped in its owner's arms or simply a chair placed to the side of an open window, the situations Bonnard provides are not straightforward. His art can unsettle. It can also soothe. Duncan and Marjorie Phillips believed in the dual capacities of art to both enchant and challenge viewers. They acquired so many of Bonnard's paintings not just for their ethereal beauty, but because of the artist's enticements to ponder them.

Young Pierre Eugene Frederic Bonnard studied law in Paris, where he also took art classes at the École des Beaux-Arts and the Académie Julian. Although he earned a law degree and briefly held a position in the legal profession, he disappointed his civil service father by deciding to paint full-time. In the 1890s, along with one of his art teachers, Édouard Vuillard, he became known as a member of Les Nabis, translated as the prophets. In fact, Duncan Phillips referred to Bonnard as a "prophet of much that we call modern."[2] As the Nabis were direct descendants of Paul Gaugin, a noted Post-Impressionist, it may seem out of place to even consider Bonnard as an Impressionist. Yet, Bonnard described himself as "the last of the Impressionists"[3] and admired the work of Claude Monet, his elder by nearly thirty years. Stanley Meisler, who spent much of his career as a foreign correspondent for the *Los Angeles Times*, supplied an apt distillation of Bonnard and Vuillard's place in the unfolding of modern art: "Instead of trying to capture the effect of light and color in nature like the Impressionists, the Nabis would try to manipulate color and composition to evoke a feeling or mood."[4] For Princeton art history professor William Seitz,

Bonnard's strongest connection to Impressionism was to give an extended life to its themes "with his sun-filled paintings of kitchens, windows and gardens."[5]

In Bonnard's *The Terrace*, painted in 1918 and purchased by the Phillipses in 1935, both Nabis colors and Impressionist themes appear. The abnormal shape of the trees and Lucy-in-the-sky-with-diamonds colors above the horizon line assuredly pay tribute to Gaugin contemporary Vincent van Gogh. Prominent flora and a smaller representation of human figures, in this case, a woman and a man, bring to mind many a Monet garden painting. Paul Cézanne's presence is felt too, through Bonnard's altering of realistic planes on a tray of food behind the terrace's table. As occurs in a Cézanne still life of apples or pears, the prepared outdoor meal in the Bonnard painting would be sliding to the ground in real life. Thankfully, Bonnard is not content with real life. His great-nephew Antoine Terrasse, an art historian, wrote that Bonnard had "the gift of the fairies that can metamorphose a yellow pumpkin into a golden carriage."[6] In *The Terrace* it is not the Cinderella tale which comes to mind so much as an epilogue to a Jane Austen novel. Those relatively small human figures are an elderly woman and man believably living happily ever after. Spectacular swatches of orange cross the painting and treats of pink dance through the garden, landing in stripes on a white tablecloth with one last *jeté* into the fabric of the woman's dress.

Duncan Phillips praised Bonnard for his "freedom from formula,"[7] admiring how his art could not be pigeonholed. An examination of how Phillips described the characteristics of Impressionist and Expressionist painters leads one to believe that if forced to categorize Bonnard's art in such a manner, he would have called him an Expressionist. "The Expressionist aims to do for the mind what the Impressionist is content to do for the eye," Phillips wrote. "[The Expressionist's] response is not to light and air as an end in itself but … as thought-compelling or mood producing agencies for emotional self-expression."[8] Phillips offered the comparison in "The Many Mindedness of Modern Painting," an article in the first issue of *Art and Understanding*, a magazine Phillips published. In one of the other articles he wrote for that issue, Phillips explained why he felt the need to create *Art and Understanding*. He was worried that the public saw artists becoming "more and more mysterious alchemists working for a few fascinated patrons" and he hoped "to show that the world is in sore need of reconciliation" between artists and the general public. He wrote that he believed art "is synonymous with the proper functioning of human life" and is therefore a "universal human concern."[9]

In much of art, the intimacy of pictures – a woman with a dog, for instance – can elicit universal human concerns. Yet, while there may well be shared thoughts within individual responses, each viewer's experience with a painting will differ. For Phillips, and art reviewers from the past hundred-plus years, it is Bonnard's use of color that contributes to generations of viewers appreciating his art. In the brochure accompanying a small 1958 exhibition at his and Marjorie's museum, Phillips wrote of Bonnard as an innovator with his "seemingly casual and surprising color combinations" who created "intimate states of being."[10] Colors feature prominently in works by an abundance of the artists Phillips collected, but none more so than Bonnard and later, Mark Rothko. Bonnard imbued his paintings with strange blues and greens, unpredictable pinks and oranges, and memorable purples. As if composing a perfect little poem, he made notes about certain colors and the nuances he saw in them:

> Violet in the grays.
> Vermillion in the orange-tinted
> Shadows, on a cold day of fine weather.[11]

The cold day of fine weather is in February 1927, the exact month Duncan Phillips wrote "nature is never too sacred for Bonnard to rearrange, but ever a source-book."[12] In that 1927 essay, composed for attendees of an exhibition that featured some of Bonnard's paintings, Phillips made clear he found something otherworldly in Bonnard's work. "He leaves glimpses of Fairyland where the commonplace had been before,"[13] Phillips wrote. More than thirty years later, Phillips maintained that the artist "created a vivid sense of reality in landscapes, still life, and interiors far more fantasy than like realism."[14] Bonnard's *Open Window* makes the collector's point. He painted the oil on canvas in 1921, and the Phillipses purchased it in 1930. Lush with light against turquoise windowpanes, the room in the picture welcomes onlookers. A woman appears curled in a rocking chair. The viewer is allowed to see only part of her body. She is poised to pet a cat, which adds to the overall contentment of the indoor scene. Yet something is not right with the view outside the window. The outdoor portion of the picture seems untrue in the distance and height of the trees as well as with the unusual blue-green of the sky. No doubt, Bonnard purposefully composed more fantasy than reality with *Open Window*, and one can conjecture that he did so to affect viewers. He once wrote "In art, it is only reactions that count."[15]

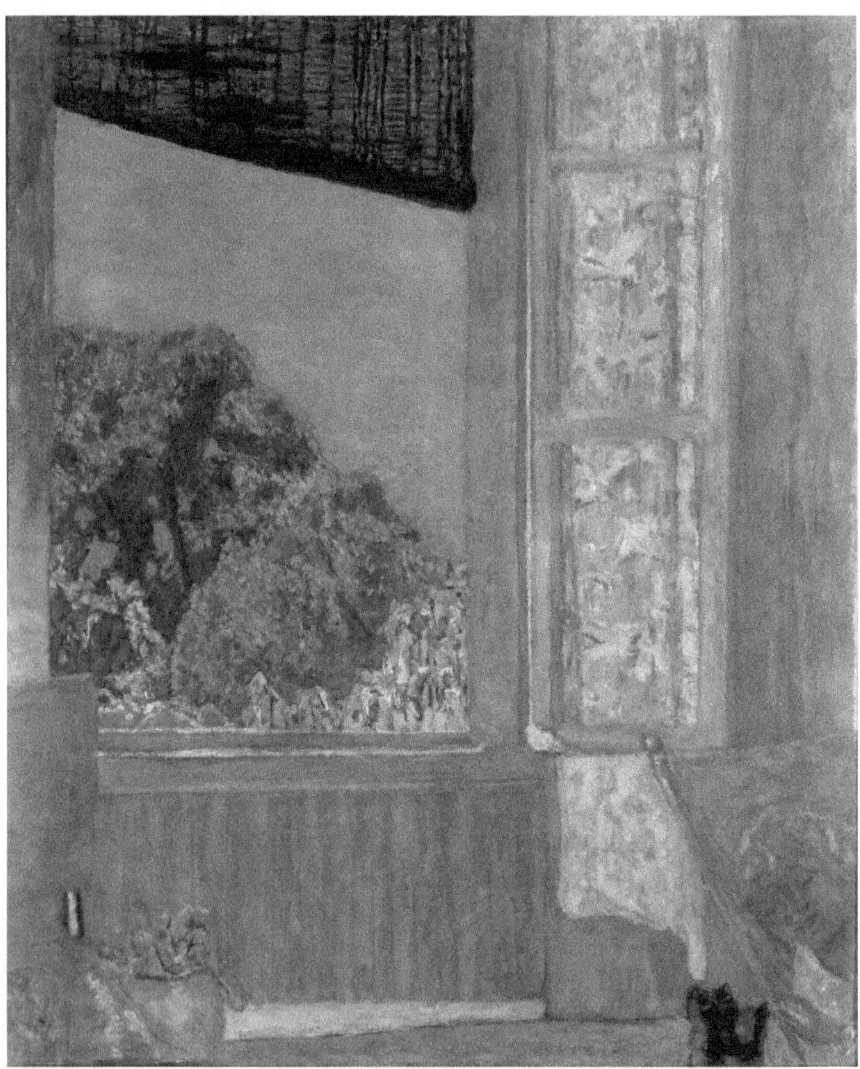

Image 5. 1. Pierre Bonnard, *The Open Window,* 1921, Oil on canvas 46 1/2 x 37 3/4 in.; 118.11 x 95.885 cm. The Phillips Collection: Acquired 1930; © 2015 Artists Rights Society (ARS), New York / ADAGP, Paris. Paintings, 0172, French.

Traditional Comparison of Bonnard to Matisse

Bonnard's work has been compared to that of his more famous contemporary, Henri Matisse. One commonality between Bonnard and Matisse in their pictures is the frequent presence of large windows that offer indoor and outdoor perspectives. Another is that both artists painted with unexpected and sometimes unprecedented colors. Duncan Phillips wrote that in Bonnard's subtlety of touch he seemed to "invent a new art of melted color,"[16] and much of Matisse's reputation as a creator would come from his novel palette. A founding member of the Fauvists or wild beasts, Matisse said he constructed his art "by means of color" and used color to "convey his response to his subject."[17] A fine example of Matisse's revolution of color is the Baltimore Museum of Art's *Large Reclining Nude*, also known as *The Pink Nude*, in which he tints the flesh of its reclining woman a curious hue. *The Pink Nude* also shows how Matisse, who has at times been measured against Pablo Picasso, incorporates some Cubism into his works. While the eyes, nose, and mouth appear in realistic proximity to one another, the Cubist feel comes from the diminutive size of the head in relationship to the woman's torso, and also from the overly long arms, one dangling and the other behind her neck. The Phillipses owned two works by Matisse, but they had collected numerous Bonnards by 1930, when Matisse visited The Phillips Collection. Duncan Phillips enjoyed telling the story of serving as a docent to one of the early twentieth century's most renowned artists. According to an article in the *Washington Post*, Matisse said he was "so happy to see so many Bonnards" in the collection and added, "He is a much better painter than I am."[18] Marjorie Phillips recalled Matisse's words as all-encompassing rather than a one-to-one comparison. Per Marjorie, Matisse said of Bonnard: "He is the best of us all."[19]

Matisse once refused to commit to sending any paintings to a particular exhibition in Nice until he knew if his friend Bonnard would be showing work there. When Bonnard made his decision of not showing known, Matisse stated he would not participate either. In their letters to each other from the 1920s, 30s, and 40s, they discuss: the progress of paintings they are working on; specific tubes of paints they are procuring; the logistics of obtaining a preferred type of canvas; and most emphatically, their enjoyment and admiration of one another's work. Then, in their old age, the two artists dwell on their health and the effects of the weather upon it. Their late correspondence features back-and-forth advice on how not to catch a chill.

Connections to Earlier Eras in Art

Others may link Bonnard to Matisse, but Duncan Phillips took a more comprehensive approach, writing of Bonnard's connections to Edgar Degas, Henri de Toulouse-Lautrec, Vincent van Gogh, Pierre-Auguste Renoir, and Claude Monet. He wrote that "Bonnard is the heir of Degas, Lautrec and Van Gogh in his Japanesque caprice of composition, of Renoir in his subtle color reflections, of Monet and again of Van Gogh in his sparkling luminosities of landscape."[20] While those connections are certainly meant as compliments, Phillips revealed his most ardent comparison to Bonnard when he spoke of a kinship to Renaissance painter Giorgio Barbarelli da Castelfranco (1477-1510), better known as Giorgione. The author of numerous books and articles, Duncan broadened his platform for making connections among different art eras when he participated in a television special about his and Marjorie's museum. The Greater Washington Education Television Association produced the 1959 TV show, which was called "A Gallery of Modern Art and Its Sources." While the Channel 5 camera followed him at predetermined stops in The Phillips Collection, Duncan Phillips explained for his expanded audience how various paintings reach across time. A script for the production indicates that while pointing out Bonnard's painting *The Palm*, Phillips said that "Bonnard's feeling for time passing and for the abundance of nature, carries us back to Giorgione."[21] In the book Phillips wrote about Giorgione for the American Federation of Arts, he placed the Venetian between his teacher Giovanni Bellini and his pupil Titian. Despite the outsized talents of Bellini and Titian, Phillips stated that Giorgione remained independent of both, adding that through his art, Giorgione demonstrated he "knew the rhythms of nature and the rhythms of life itself."[22] While a celebration of nature was apparent to Phillips when he looked at works by Bonnard and Giorgione, their shared theme of remembrance resonated even more powerfully with him. Phillips wrote that Giorgione "will always be a favorite of the few who, in every age and not merely his own, cherish in life the memoried pause which is the music of fine moments."[23] The notion that Giorgione could stir a memoried pause was similar to how Phillips felt about Bonnard. Both artists heightened Phillips's ability to encounter art and experience it for himself, just as he and Dewey encouraged others to do. Not only did Phillips indicate that Bonnard was an artist who capably provides visitors opportunities to draw on their pasts, but Bonnard himself wrote of the significance of creating environments to stimulate viewer participation. He would awaken their senses when they stood before his paintings. In personal notes, he wrote: "Identity of the individual: character, sensations of hearing and smelling. Consciousness, the shock of feeling and memory."[24]

Romanticism without Forsaking Classicism

Nature and its primacy to life was another topic Bonnard addressed head-on. In his notes, the artist wrote: "That an inner feeling of beauty coincides with nature, that's the point."[25] Bonnard also displayed a keen understanding of how the romantic combines with the classic in nature and carries over into art. "Everything has its moment of beauty," Bonnard wrote. "Beauty is the fulfillment of seeing. Seeing is fulfilled by simplicity and order."[26] Duncan Phillips agreed with the idea of order in painting and wrote in prepared remarks for a 1934 gallery talk that "the greatest romantic art has structural unity and classic order."[27] Generally, the hallmarks of classicism are: serenity, restraint, reason, and society over self. In contrast, romanticism is marked by: excitement, passion, spirituality, and the individual as more important than the group. Phillips indicated in the remarks for his gallery talk, which he titled "Classic or Romantic in Modern Landscape," that "we associate the word classic with unalterable perfection in formal relations."[28] But perfection did not mean optimum to Phillips; he made his partiality for romantic over classic art clear. The clarity stems from his emphasis on individual thought: "The closed and compact symmetry of classicism will not correspond to many of our most personal states of mind and the romantic must ever be one of the fundamental artistic points of view."[29] In the prepared remarks for his gallery talk, however, Phillips did not hesitate to elaborate on the value of classicism, explaining that the "restraint upon romanticism accounts for the greatness of Michel Angelo [*sic*], Rembrandt, Daumier, and our own American Ryder."[30]

Serenity engulfs Bonnard's painting *Nude in an Interior* and restraint resounds throughout the picture. Painted circa 1935, and acquired by the Phillipses in 1952, it is an ode to symmetry. The subject of the painting, a woman in the process of sponging herself, offers the viewer a banquet of angles. Her left elbow bends sharply back. Her knees are spread apart as she washes an inner thigh. The right knee bends to achieve balance – for the picture and the woman. Bonnard keeps the woman's face featureless, but he allows sunlight to reach her head. Rays of the sun are also reflected on the radiator in the room, but strong shadows are painted among pieces of furniture. The picture brings to mind a description of Bonnard's work written twenty years prior to the creation of *Nude in an Interior*. In a 1915 book titled *Modern Painting: Its Tendency and Meaning*, author Willard Huntington Wright found that within Bonnard's paintings "are hot sunlight and cold shadow in scintillating succession."[31]

Spurring Independence in Viewers

Bonnard's push and pull of sunlight and shadow – or the familiar measured against the otherworldly – builds up the kind of tension that can spur viewers to approach art independently, something that visitors to New York City's Museum of Modern Art would get to experience courtesy of Duncan Phillips. In October 1929, A. Conger Goodyear, the first president of MoMA and the chairman of its original organizing committee, notified Phillips that "subject to your acceptance you were elected a Trustee."[32] The Washington, D.C. collector and co-founder of America's first museum of modern art did accept the position on MoMA's first board, thus expanding his sphere of influence over visitors to art museums as well as exhibition curators and museum administrators. Very quickly, Phillips made an important loan to MoMA for what would be their third exhibition. "I am sending our very finest Bonnards at great personal sacrifice," Phillips cabled Alfred H. Barr Jr. regarding the 1930 show *Paintings in Paris.*[33] Phillips then dispatched a letter to Barr confirming that he would loan five Bonnards for the exhibit of French paintings, adding that he could also loan works by Georges Braque; André Derain; Jean Fautrier; and if desired, by the Spaniard Pablo Picasso, who had relocated to France. The bulk of the letter was about the Bonnards and how Phillips had painstakingly selected: *The Palm, Woman with Dog, Le Midi* (also known as *The Riviera*), *Interior with Boy,* and *Early Spring.* Phillips seemed to refer primarily to his Bonnards when he closed the letter: "This is a very precious shipment and I can only trust that all will go well and my treasures will come back unharmed."[34] The Bonnards that Phillips selected for MoMA illustrate points that he made about the relationship between romantic and classic art in his 1934 gallery talk. However, Phillips is not the only art expert to comment on how romantic painters often used classic elements in composing their pictures, nor the only one to reference Bonnard as successful in using classicism to enhance romanticism. In a review of MoMA's 1948 Bonnard exhibition, art critic and painter Guy Pene du Bois wrote that "a checkered tablecloth, a bowl of flowers, a brilliant wallpaper could carry as satisfying a message as a Greek god upon an Olympian pedestal."[35] Additionally, when *New York Times* critic John Canaday reviewed MoMA's 1964 Bonnard show, he wrote that the artist "not only transforms [his] wildly varied palette from chaos into harmony, from confusion into structure, but retains enough of the feeling of water on flesh, of towels and tile floors."[36]

The floors in *Nude in an Interior* are dappled a cool blue-green, in contrast to the leopard-skin rug appearing in the picture. Tile floors would have been a more expected choice for the intimate slice-of-life painting, but the odd combination of ocean color and animal print lends credence to another art critic's summation of Bonnard's many works. "Underneath the lushness of his color is a shiver of the strange,"[37] wrote Paul Richard in his review of a Bonnard exhibit at The Phillips Collection in 2002. Richard's turn-of-the twenty-first-century prose is also apropos for the 1922 painting *Woman with Dog,* the first Bonnard acquired by Duncan and Marjorie. A woman sits at a table with a dog in her lap. All seems correct, at the outset. Somehow, Bonnard depicts a potential disturbance within the picture's tranquility. The woman appears contemplative as she looks down at the dog, who stares forward – at the viewer or more likely, the food on the table. The strong vertical shape of the painting emphasizes the long face of the reddish-brown dog and the part in the red-headed woman's hair. The dog seems the model of domestication with its paws resting over the woman's arm, as if posing for a photograph. The assortment of food is painted assorted shades of red, most of them subdued. But the woman's dress contains vertical white stripes on material the color of the inside of a blood orange.

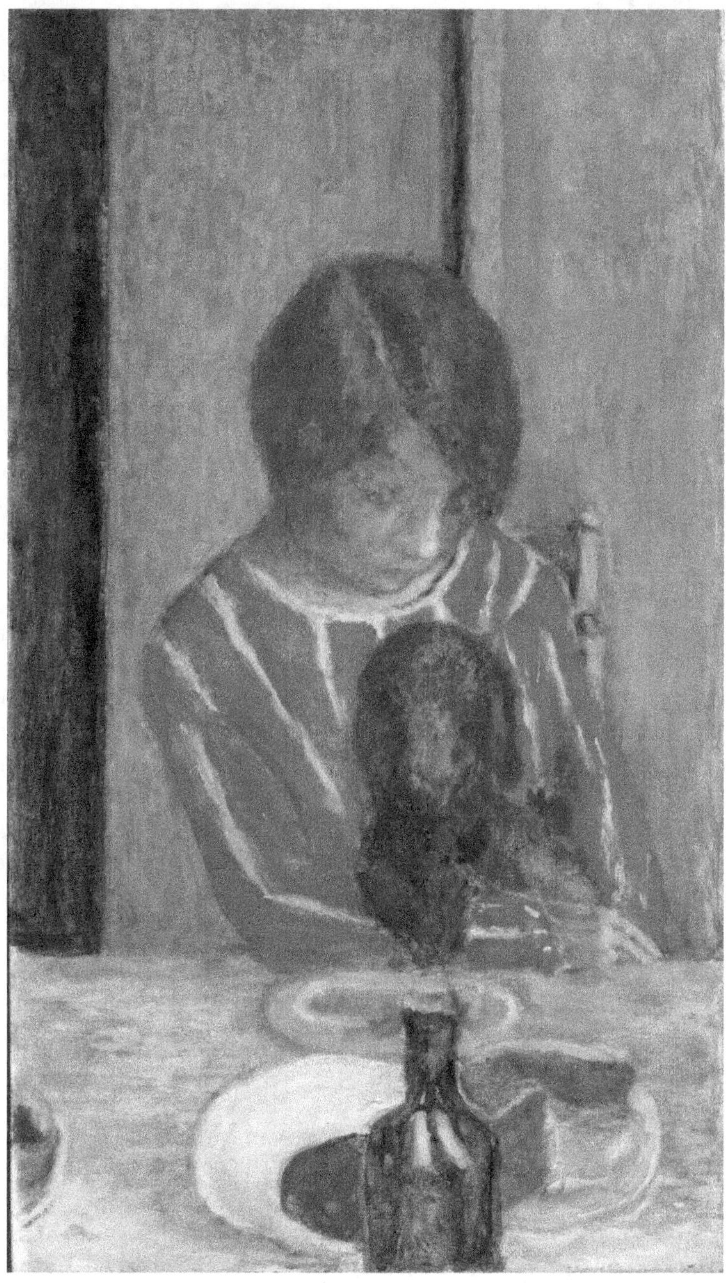

Image 5. 2. Pierre Bonnard, *Woman with Dog*, 1922, Oil on canvas 27 1/4 x 15 3/8 in.; 69.215 x 39.0525 cm.; Framed: 33 in x 21 1/2 in x 2 3/4 in; 83.82 cm. x 54.61 cm. x 6.99 cm. The Phillips Collection: Acquired 1925; © 2015 Artists Rights Society (ARS), New York / ADAGP, Paris. Paintings, 0179, French.

A Prophet of the Modern

Duncan Phillips called Bonnard a prophet of the modern and two modern artists come to mind courtesy of *Woman with Dog*: Rothko, so famed for his reds that a play about him was named for the color, and Milton Avery, Rothko's friend and mentor. The Avery painting at The Phillips Collection which correlates with *Woman with Dog* is the 1941 oil *Girl Writing*. Using his daughter March as the model, Avery painted abstractly but with enough realism to communicate actual objects. In the vertical picture, the girl's red socks rekindle Bonnard's reds and anticipate Rothko's. Like Bonnard's painting, Avery's offers an everyday situation that does not feel everyday. It, too, has the dreamlike quality of some of Duncan and Marjorie's Bonnards. One of those Phillips-owned Bonnards caused some momentary consternation when the artist came to their museum in 1926. Bonnard journeyed to the United States that year to serve as a juror for the Carnegie International at the Carnegie Institute in Pittsburgh. During Bonnard's trip to the U.S., he also stopped in Washington, D.C., where he was accompanied by Homer Saint-Gaudens, director of the Carnegie Institute's Department of Fine Arts. Saint-Gaudens, son of sculptor Augustus Saint-Gaudens, brought Bonnard to the Phillips Memorial Gallery. Duncan and Marjorie were giving him a tour when suddenly, Bonnard announced that he wanted to alter his 1908 picture *Early Spring*, which Duncan and Marjorie acquired in 1925, a year before the visit. Aware that Marjorie was an artist, Bonnard asked for a brush and some paints. "We had come from our country place in Pennsylvania to meet him, so I had a good alibi," Marjorie wrote. "All my paints were either locked up or in the country!"[38] Believing his work to be imperfect was not confined to that one incident. In 1931, Bonnard wrote to Duncan: "I am touched by the interest you take in my painting despite its great flaws."[39]

During Bonnard's lifetime and beyond, reviewers have been inclined to agree with the Phillipses in admiring the work of the Frenchman. Not only have some of the twentieth century's most esteemed art critics not pointed out any great flaws in the paintings of Pierre Bonnard, but portions of their written praise may well be considered over-the-top. Thomas B. Hess, long-time editor of *ARTNews*, wrote that "Pierre Bonnard seems able to enchant and narcotize the critical eye," adding that "there is nothing one can say against Bonnard except that there is nothing to be said against him."[40] John Russell, the *Sunday Times of London* and *New York Times* contributor who was charmed by Duncan Phillips wearing gloves to dinner, wrote that in Bonnard's late paintings "a daring that knew no limits took over. It was as if God the father had allowed himself an eighth day in which to reinvent the world."[41]

The reinvention comes one viewer at a time. With Bonnard, a "mood both of celebration and loss permeates his art."[42] Poignancy becomes beauty, and vice versa. His works are "at once immediately accessible and permanently elusive."[43] Pierre Bonnard brings an unsettling calmness.

Notes

[1] Marjorie Phillips, *Marjorie Phillips and Her Paintings* (New York: W.W. Norton, 1985), 103.
[2] Duncan Phillips "Pierre Bonnard," *A Loan Exhibition: Six Paintings by Bonnard* (Washington, D.C., The Phillips Gallery, 1958), 1.
[3] Andrew Hudson, "Phillips Is the Place to Study Bonnard," *Washington Post*, June 26, 1966.
[4] Stanley Meisler, "Pierre Bonnard," *Smithsonian*, July 1998, 34.
[5] William Seitz, "The Relevance of Impressionism," *ARTNews*, January 1969, 56.
[6] Antoine Terrasse, *Bonnard: Shimmering Color* (New York: Harry N. Abrams, 1999), 121.
[7] D. Phillips, "Pierre Bonnard," *A Loan Exhibition*, 1.
[8] D. Phillips, "The Many Mindedness of Modern Painting," *Art and Understanding* 1 (November 1929): 64.
[9] D. Phillips, "Art and Understanding," *Art and Understanding* 1 (November 1929): 9.
[10] D. Phillips, "Pierre Bonnard," *A Loan Exhibition*, 1.
[11] Terrasse, 130.
[12] D. Phillips, "Pierre Bonnard," *A Bulletin of The Phillips Collection Relating to a Tri-Unit Exhibition of Paintings and Sculpture*, Phillips Memorial Gallery, February and March 1927, 14.
[13] Ibid., 16.
[14] D. Phillips, "Pierre Bonnard," *A Loan Exhibition*, 3.
[15] Elizabeth Hutton Turner, *Pierre Bonnard: Early and Late* (London: Philip Wilson, 2002), 253.
[16] D. Phillips, "Pierre Bonnard," *A Bulletin of The Phillips Collection*, 16.
[17] John Elderfield, *Henri Matisse; A Retrospective* (New York: Museum of Modern Art, 1992), 133.
[18] Jean White, "Duncan Phillips Policy: Art Is for All the People," *Washington Post*, May 12, 1966.
[19] M. Phillips, *Duncan Phillips and His Collection* (New York: W.W. Norton, 1982), 178.
[20] D. Phillips, *The Artist Sees Differently* (New York: E. Weyhe, 1931), 53.
[21] "A Gallery of Modern Art and Its Sources," Greater Washington Education Television Association, aired October 6, 1959, on Channel 5, Washington, D.C.
[22] D. Phillips, *The Leadership of Giorgione* (Washington, D.C.: American Federation of Arts, 1937), 4.
[23] Ibid., 12.
[24] Terrasse, 70.
[25] Turner, 252.
[26] Ibid., 249.
[27] "A Gallery of Modern Art and Its Sources," Channel 5.
[28] Ibid.
[29] Ibid.

[30] Ibid.

[31] Willard Huntington Wright, *Modern Painting: Its Tendency and Meaning* (New York, John Lane, 1915), 317.

[32] A. Conger Goodyear to Duncan Phillips, October 5, 1929, The Phillips Collection Archives, Washington, D.C.

[33] D. Phillips to Alfred H. Barr Jr., 2 January 1930, The Phillips Collection Archives, Washington, D.C. The telegram is dated 2 January *1929*, but given the context of the message, the use of the previous year is an error.

[34] D. Phillips to Alfred H. Barr Jr., 4 January 1930, The Phillips Collection Archives, Washington, D.C.

[35] Guy Pene du Bois, "Bonnard as Artist and Democrat," *New York Times*, June 13, 1948.

[36] John Canaday, "Bonnard and His World of Sensuous Delight," *New York Times*, October 11, 1964.

[37] Paul Richard, "Moving in Place: Steadfast Pierre Bonnard's Fidgety Feast," *Washington Post*, September 25, 2002.

[38] M. Phillips, *Duncan Phillips and His Collection*, 74.

[39] Turner, 72.

[40] Thomas B. Hess, "Bonnard: Or How to Be Modern and Charming," *ARTNews*, February 1954, 29.

[41] John Russell, *Bonnard: The Late Paintings*, ed. Sasha M. Newman (Washington, D.C.: The Phillips Collection, 1984), 10.

[42] Nicholas Watkins, *Bonnard: Colour and Light* (London: Tate Gallery Publishing, 1998), 7.

[43] Terry Teachout, "Bonnard in the Home of His Champion," *Wall Street Journal*, October 9, 2002.

Chapter 6

Arthur Dove: Close to the Soil and the Stars

Most elements of Arthur Dove's abstractions are easily recognizable to onlookers, offering an entryway into modern art. The sun or the moon appear often in his works, sometimes accompanied by a pending change in the weather. In one particular work, Dove painted the sun deeply orange. Strong spiral lines within emphasize its circular nature. Grey clouds partially cover the heat-giving orb as rippled ground yields to its presence. The painting, which he titled *Red Sun*, is not unlike Native American art in its boldness of tribute to earth and sky. Dove created the oil on canvas in 1935, in the middle of the Great Depression. Duncan and Marjorie Phillips bought *Red Sun* the same year, and in a letter that summer, Duncan told Dove it had become his favorite picture.[1]

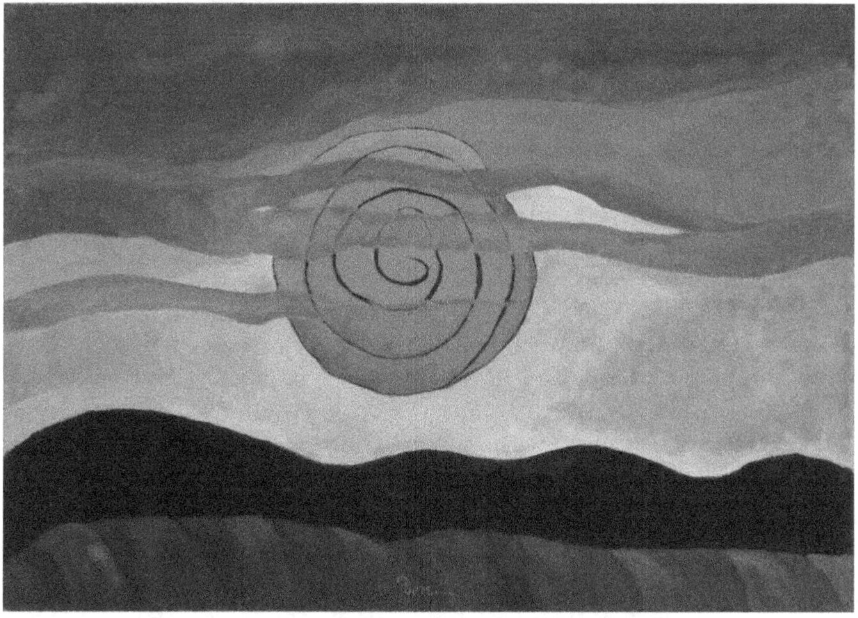

Image 6. 1. Arthur G. Dove, *Red Sun*, 1935, Oil on canvas 20 1/4 x 28 in.; 51.435 x 71.12 cm.; Framed: 22 1/2 in x 30 3/8 in x 1 3/4 in.; 57.15 cm. x 77.15 cm. x 4.45 cm. The Phillips Collection: Acquired 1935. Paintings, 0569, American.

The two years prior to the purchase of *Red Sun* were especially hectic for Duncan Phillips because of his duties for the Public Works of Art Project. Part of the New Deal's Works Progress Administration, it was created in 1933 to provide government employment for artists. Phillips had been appointed chairman of the PWAP regional committee which covered Maryland, Virginia, and the District of Columbia. The position, Phillips wrote to Dove in December 1933, is "now taking practically all of my time," adding that "we have already put twenty painters to work on decorating walls of public schools, etc."[2] In June 1934, Phillips stood on stage at Yale University with the architect of the New Deal, Franklin Delano Roosevelt, and was awarded an honorary master of arts degree. In its report of the New Haven, Connecticut event, the *Washington Post* referred to Phillips as "a patron of the arts."[3]

As the Depression continued, Duncan Phillips presented a retrospective exhibition of Dove's works in the nation's capital. Phillips wrote that some of the paintings in the 1937 show "have been compared to the great Venetian Masters because of their luminous and sumptuous chromatic surfaces. And yet they come to us from the orchards and the ploughed fields."[4] He had once written to Dove: "There is an elemental something in your abstractions. They start from nature and personal experience."[5] Later, Phillips would write that Dove's artistic inspiration sprang from a life "close to the soil and the stars."[6]

Dove grew up in Geneva, New York and attended Hobart College there. He transferred to Cornell University, where he enrolled in a pre-law curriculum, but also took art classes. Upon graduation in 1903, Dove moved to New York City where, as Phillips wrote, he "won immediate success"[7] as an illustrator for top periodicals such as *Harper's Weekly, Collier's,* and *The Saturday Evening Post.* Dove had "joined the best-paid illustrators – much to his father's satisfaction – and was accounted one of the most distinguished among them,"[8] wrote Jerome Mellquist in his book *The Emergence of an American Art.* Early in his illustrating career, however, Dove was encouraged by artists John Sloan, Robert Henri and William Glackens to focus instead on painting. As Dove considered the advice from the members of the Ashcan School – named for their gritty urban realism, a trip abroad seemed in order. Dove had married his childhood sweetheart, Florence Dorsey, in 1904, and in 1908, they traveled to Europe and remained in France for more than a year. Back in the United States, he no longer sought work as an illustrator. As Mellquist put it, Dove gave up "his certain income for the troubled way of an independent painter."[9]

Reflections of Inner Consciousness

Arthur Dove knew what he wanted from his life and his art. Ten years before the Phillipses began collecting Dove's work, the artist stated that his wish was "not to revolutionize nor to reform, but to enjoy life out loud." In that 1916 declaration, Dove put into words the essence of the art he was making: "Sensations of light from within and without have reflected from my inner consciousness. Theories have been outgrown ... the reality of the sensation alone remains."[10] Duncan Phillips understood. He often communicated about Dove in the context of the senses, encouraging viewers to internalize their encounters with the paintings. "His abstractions of color and form are based on a profoundly felt and intimately personal acceptance of life both as tactile substance and immaterial illusion,"[11] Phillips wrote of Dove. Referred to as a "pioneer abstractionist artist,"[12] Dove has often been discussed alongside Russian painter Wassily Kandinsky because of their similarly early callings to abstraction. Art critic Vivien Raynor wrote that while "Kandinsky got most of the credit for inventing abstraction ... it was the accomplishment not of one, but several painters working in the years immediately preceding World War I. One of these was Arthur Dove."[13] In 1912, Kandinsky authored *Concerning the Spiritual in Art,* considered by many art historians to be the seminal treatise of modern art. Kandinsky put forth that an artist who does not simply replicate nature is more spiritual than one who does because he must rely on himself to create. Duncan Phillips would also come to write about "the spiritual" in nonrepresentational art, as well as corporeal reactions to it. For example, Phillips wrote to Dove that in the hands of the right artist "abstract art ceases to be an amusement for the aesthete and becomes a divine activity."[14]

The artist Georgia O'Keeffe spoke freely about her friend Dove in an interview for *The New Yorker,* directly addressing the issue of whether he was influenced by Kandinsky. "I think Dove came to abstraction quite naturally. It was his way of thinking," O'Keeffe said. "Kandinsky was very showy about it, but Dove had an earthy, simple quality that led directly to abstraction. His things are very special. I always wish I'd bought more of them."[15]

Collecting and Supporting an Interpreter of America

The Phillipses did buy more of them. Over a twenty-year period, they acquired forty-seven of Dove's works, the greatest number of any artist in their collection. The couple first purchased Dove's work in 1926 when they visited the Intimate Gallery, one of a succession of Manhattan galleries operated by Alfred Stieglitz, photographer, art impresario, and husband to O'Keeffe. It was Stieglitz who introduced the United States to *Concerning the Spiritual in Art* by publishing excerpts in an issue of his journal *Camera Work* in 1912. A fierce proponent of Modernism, especially the American Modernists, Stieglitz served as an art dealer for Dove, exhibiting the artist's work first at his gallery 291, which closed in 1917; then at his Intimate Gallery, open from 1925-1929; and finally, at his gallery An American Place, which he ran from 1929 to 1946. Marjorie Phillips spoke about the trips she and Duncan would make to New York and the freedom they were given to browse the works of art at a Stieglitz gallery. "He didn't try to influence you at all,"[16] she said of Stieglitz. The first time they bought art through Stieglitz, Duncan and Marjorie chose two paintings by Dove, *Golden Storm* and *Waterfall*, as well as one by O'Keeffe. Four years later, in 1930, Phillips started providing Dove a stipend of fifty dollars a month, with modest increases until the artist's death in 1946. The arrangement afforded Phillips first pick of the works from Dove's annual exhibitions. Through his commitment to Dove in the form of a stipend, Phillips did more than help the artist with financial stability. It was a way Phillips could demonstrate to the public his belief in the artist's significance to modern art.

When Duncan Phillips wrote articles or essays about Dove, he often wove in references to the American Modernist's hardscrabble life as a farmer and that for a period of time, he lived on a boat. The Long Island dockside years began in 1921 when Dove left Florence and their son to live with Helen "Reds" Torr, who would become his second wife. Phillips wrote of Dove in connection with "weathered wood and rusty iron," elaborating on his "sensitivity to damp soil and ore from the mines."[17] In the brochure for the 1937 retrospective he organized of Dove's works, Phillips emphasized the artist's affinity to capture the spirit of his nation: "Strange to say the new pleasure stirs a vague old nostalgia. And this art is American to the core."[18] Publicly and privately, Phillips linked Dove to another interpreter of America, the painter Albert Pinkham Ryder. In a piece for the *Magazine of Art*, Phillips wrote that he recognized in Dove "the heir of our romantic Ryder"[19] and in an early correspondence to Dove he referred to "your spiritual ancestor Albert P. Ryder."[20] Waldo Frank, a contributor to *The New Republic* also made a connection between Dove and Ryder when he anticipated how Dove would be remembered. Frank wrote in a 1926 essay that Dove "will long since be sleeping with his fathers, among whom are Ryder, Thoreau, Melville."[21] Henry McBride in the *New York Sun* shared the sentiment that Dove was among America's great creative minds. "There are still poets, dreamers, and idealists in our midst," McBride wrote in a 1944 review of Dove's paintings, "and when another twenty years roll around, it will be found that we have been neglecting our Walt Whitmans and Emily Dickinsons just as our forbearers did." Long before McBride's piece, art critic Elizabeth McCausland, later an art history professor at Sarah Lawrence College, wrote about Dove in connection to an American author undeniably heralded in his own time. Noting Dove's "color, wit, and superb sense of fun," she wrote that "someone said he has that American tang (and twang) which Mark Twain had."[22]

Golden Storm, Dove's oil and metallic paint on plywood panel from 1925, evokes Whitman more than Twain, most specifically the collection of poems *Leaves of Grass*. The painting and the poetry share an evocativeness of nature and a feeling of place. Undeniably abstract, the painting seems to incorporate land, air, and sea. In the picture, waves look like leaves and the sky might be blades of grass. Much of the painting features the color of wheat in sunshine, but tension and movement predict a storm breaking. A viewer can imagine standing on the porch of a prairie homestead, hearing the first claps of thunder. Phillips likely considered the picture to be more of a seascape than a landscape. Of *Golden Storm*, he wrote that "an opening of the sky gleams with a dust of gold leaf applied directly to a block of unpolished wood"[23] and "cloud forms of copper red threaten black waves which toss in agitation."[24]

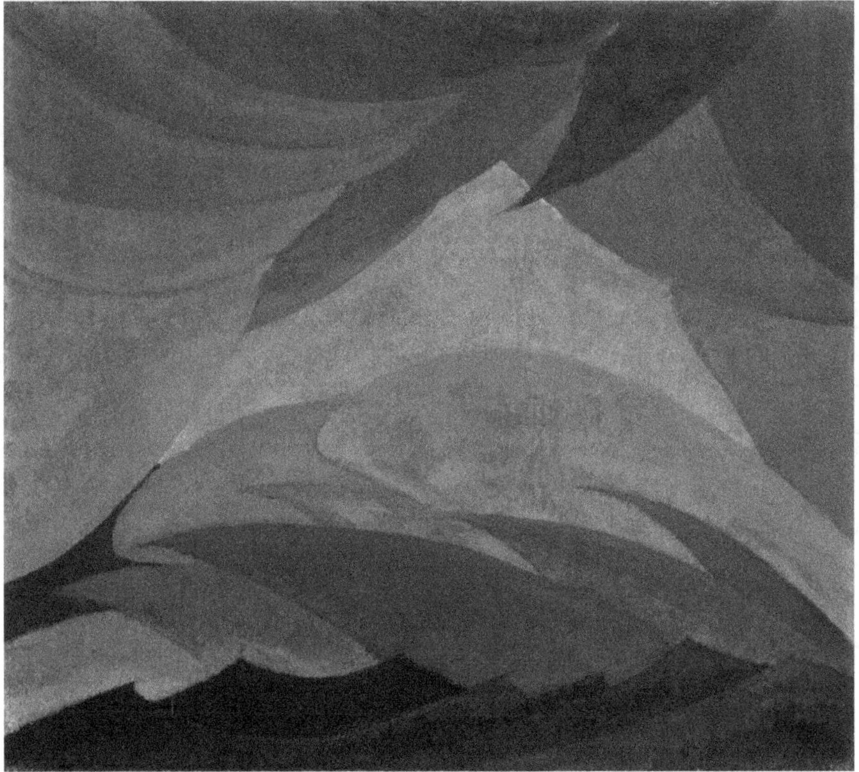

Image 6. 2. Arthur G. Dove, *Golden Storm*, 1925,
Oil and metallic paint on plywood panel 18 9/16 x 20 1/2 in.; 47.14875 x 52.07 cm.;
Framed: 19 1/2 in x 21 1/4 in x 1 3/8 in.; 49.53 cm. x 53.97 cm. x 3.49 cm.
The Phillips Collection: Acquired 1926. Paintings, 0553, American.

Duncan Phillips continuously conveyed the importance of Dove's physical surroundings to his work as an artist. In a 1947 essay, he wrote that Dove "would work on a farm far away from gallery distractions, close to nature and the elements," and that the countryside "would be his research laboratory and his haven of creative independence."[25] Phillips wrote the piece for *New Directions in Prose and Poetry*, a publication reaching an audience devoted to literature, thus expanding the potential for appreciation of Dove's art beyond readers interested in visual art. Paul Rosenfeld, in an article for *The Dial*, told of Dove's ability to paint the nuances of rural America. "The mustard browns, the dull rich greens, the fawns and tans and soft warm whites call to mind the smell of hay, the breath of kine, the taste of warm-squirted milk," Rosenfeld wrote. "One hears perforce the grunting of piglets, the lowing of oxen, the swishing of great slow tails."[26] Dove himself described farm life as difficult, but not without the inclusion of lighthearted quips, particularly notable in his letters to Elizabeth McCausland. When inviting McCausland to visit him and Reds, he wrote that the "old farm house and estate that has been leaning against the wind for support for years is a job. … We have a frying pan and a dog that came with the place. … You will be in time for green corn and lima beans, so come on."[27]

While Dove's personality shines in his letters to McCausland and Stieglitz, his letters to his patron Phillips are understandably less whimsical and more earnest. Even with their serious tone, Marjorie Phillips said in her oral history interview for the Archives of American Art that her husband had "a delightful correspondence with Dove."[28] Responding to what Duncan Phillips penned for an upcoming Dove exhibition at the Phillips Memorial Gallery, the artist wrote: "Your notice was beautiful. It and a letter from Sherwood Anderson I consider to be the finest things that have been said of the paintings."[29] Duncan had invited Dove to Washington, D.C. on a number of occasions. In one letter, he wrote instead of a retreat to the Phillipses' country home, suggesting "come and visit us in the mountains of Pennsylvania. You would find some good subjects," he coaxed, "with splendid skies over checkerboard landscapes."[30]

Duncan Phillips did not limit his prodding of Dove to accepting extensions of hospitality. For a two-month period in December 1933 to January 1934, Phillips wrote to Dove about the PWAP, encouraging, then badgering him, to apply for the temporary government work. In his December 16, 1933 letter to Dove, Phillips wrote that "the rate is forty-two fifty a week" and because Dove is living in New York state, suggests he contact the regional chair there, specifying Juliana Force of the Whitney Museum of Art.[31] On January 8, 1934, Phillips wrote to Dove: "Your letter left me uncertain whether you had applied with Mrs. Force or with Gordon Washburn at Buffalo, but since you expressed interest in doing a mural project, I wrote to Mrs. Force about you. She wires me in reply that she has not heard from you and hopes that you will do so promptly."[32] Two weeks later, on January 22, 1934, Phillips began his letter to Dove: "I am anxious to hear whether you have applied to the New York Regional Committee of the Public Works of Art Project. Unless and until you do apply it is obvious that you could not be put on the payroll. I went beyond discretion and also beyond my local jurisdiction."[33] Phillips ended the letter with a reference to his personal patronage of Dove. "I only wish our subsidy could be a little larger ... I am going to New York tomorrow for a few days and I will go to see Stieglitz and talk with him about you. It would be great if you just happened to be in town at that time as I am so anxious to meet you."[34] Phillips did not get to meet Dove in the winter of 1934. Dove did not apply for a PWAP job, nor did he ever journey to visit the Phillipses in the Keystone State or the District of Columbia. Marjorie talked about the one time they met him in person, which was in 1936. "He was always going to come to Washington, but his health, you know he had heart trouble and so we met him in New York and liked him tremendously."[35] Dove also suffered from Bright's disease, a debilitating kidney condition. In Duncan's letters to Dove, which almost always featured admiration for one or more paintings, he would often include hope for Dove's well-being. In one such letter, Duncan wrote about "the very real world of pure art which you inhabit," and sent "best wishes for your health and your creations."[36]

In a letter written in April 1940, Duncan Phillips shared with Dove some of his thoughts and his daily life as a collector: "Now I have some work to do at my desk and then on Wednesday I hope to go to New York especially to see your paintings. Each year this is an event to which I look forward with the most intimate delight for you know how strongly I react to your creative ardor and genius." Phillips continued with a reference to their stipend arrangement: "Never doubt that it is a privilege to help you in any way and I hope with all my heart that you have recovered your health, for your art is one of the best things in America today."[37] Shortly before Dove died, he wrote to Phillips: "You have no idea what sending on those checks means to me ... after fighting for an idea all your life, I realize that your backing has saved it for me, and I want to thank you with all my heart and soul for what you have done."[38]

The Moon, the Sun, and America Singing

In one of his letters to Dove, Duncan Phillips wrote: "Your pictures give constant and growing pleasure and there are no pictures in the Collection in the modern idioms to which I am more closely attuned." Phillips specifically mentioned the work *Me and the Moon*, a wax emulsion on canvas that Dove created in 1937 and the Phillipses would purchase in 1938. Astounding shades of blue are stacked layer upon layer between black and pale yellow. Unlike most renderings of the moon, it appears near the bottom of the picture, showing not as a sliver or a perfect circle but as an egg freshly cracked into a skillet, the yoke forming a slightly odd shape as it cooks. Rings of olive green and charcoal grey surround Dove's moon. A jiggled line crosses it, perhaps an electric wire. Elsewhere, a similar wire dangles with devices that look like Christmas lights, two of them glowing yellow and a third one a bluish green. Because the moon itself is placed so close to the ground, it seems to be nestling in – or hovering just above – the blacks and browns of the soil. *Me and the Moon* was painted the year acclaimed writer Sherwood Anderson sent the letter that meant so much to Dove. The author of *Winesburg, Ohio* wrote that he was "deeply stirred" by Dove's latest paintings. "It seems to me, Arthur, that your work of the last year has got something in it that is mighty fine to see ... there is in this new work of yours a sureness of touch."[39]

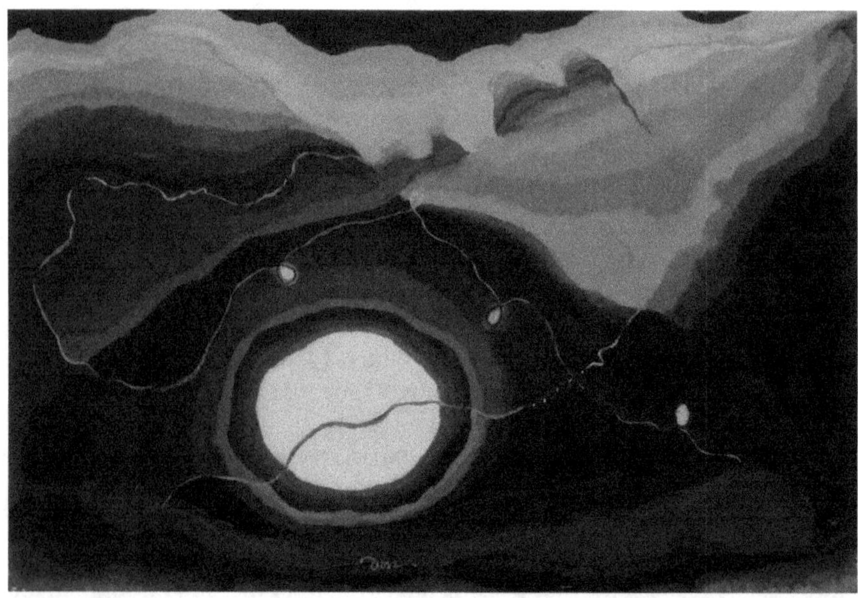

Image 6. 3. Arthur G. Dove, *Me and the Moon*, 1937, Wax emulsion on canvas 18 x 26 in.; 45.72 x 66.04 cm. The Phillips Collection: Acquired 1939. Paintings, 0559, American.

Leslie Judd Portner served as an art critic at the *Washington Post* in the 1950s and into the 1960s, often covering exhibitions at The Phillips Collection. In one of her "Art in Washington" columns, Portner pointed out that Dove painted "not only sights but sounds and moods." In her viewing of Dove's works, she imagined "the deep velvet boom of a foghorn" and saw "the pulsating brilliance of a rising moon."[40] Portner seemed a kindred spirit with Duncan Phillips in her review of Dove's art. Phillips described Dove as "expressing unashamed worship of sun and moon. He looked right into the glow of the morning sun or into the face of the full moon as it rose above the haunted hills."[41] Phillips also referred to Dove's "radiations of sunshine in vast expanses of sky, over glistening, thawing snow."[42]

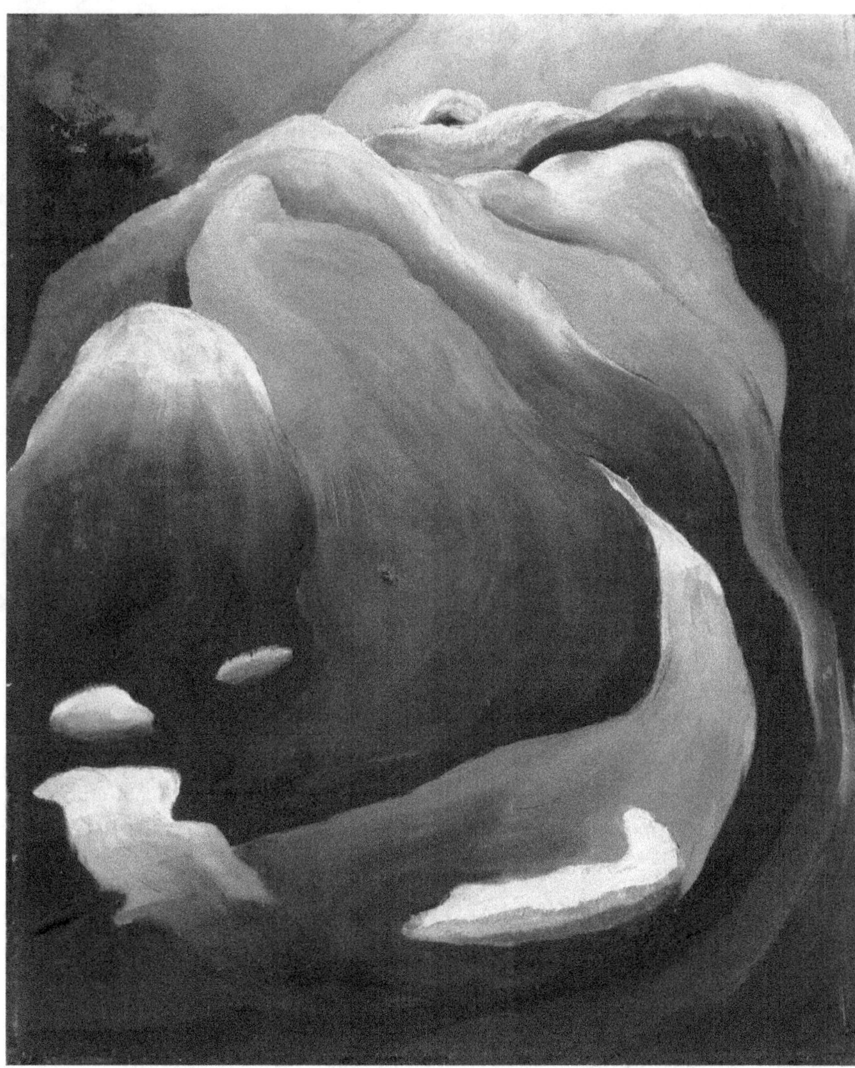

Image 6. 4. Arthur G. Dove, *Waterfall*, 1925, Oil on hardboard 10 x 8 in.; 25.4 x 20.32 cm. The Phillips Collection: Acquired 1926. Paintings, 0586, American.

Thawing snow appears in *Waterfall,* an oil on hardboard Dove painted in 1925 and the Phillipses acquired in 1926, at the same time they bought *Golden Storm.* Art critic Hilton Kramer wrote that Dove's paintings are "small, intimate, moody and lyrical," adding that they "require a certain concentration and inwardness – precisely the qualities of mind that went into their making."[43] Measuring only ten-by-eight inches, *Waterfall* nonetheless inspires with a near-magical placement of greys and blacks and browns. Curves in the fall's wet stones cascade as if water themselves. Immersed in this corner of America, water could be running up instead of down, especially since Dove draws the onlooker's eye up with white foam pointing north. James Thrall Soby might have been thinking of *Waterfall* when he wrote in his monthly art column for the *Saturday Review of Literature* about Dove's relationship with the viewer: "He does not seize our attention but woos it slowly."[44]

In the wooing, senses beyond vision blossom. Stones may be cold to the touch. Falling water may emit a gentle sound or a loud rush. Visitors standing before any of the many Arthur Dove abstractions that Duncan and Marjorie Phillips collected might well imagine they can hear America singing.

Notes

[1] Duncan Phillips to Arthur Dove, 6 June 1935, Arthur and Helen Torr Dove Papers, Archives of American Art, Washington, D.C.
[2] D. Phillips to Arthur Dove, 16 December 1933, Arthur and Helen Torr Dove Papers, Archives of American Art, Washington, D.C.
[3] "Patron of the Arts Here Honored With President: Duncan Phillips Presented Degree at Yale: Other Leaders There," *Washington Post*, June 21, 1934.
[4] D. Phillips, "Retrospective Exhibition of Works in Various Media by Arthur G. Dove, March 23d to April 18th 1937," *Phillips Memorial Gallery Bulletin*, Washington, D.C.
[5] D. Phillips to Arthur Dove, 3 May 1933, Arthur and Helen Torr Dove Papers, Archives of American Art, Washington, D.C.
[6] D. Phillips, "Art of Arthur G. Dove," *New Directions in Prose and Poetry*, no. 11 (1947): 509.
[7] Ibid.
[8] Jerome Mellquist, *The Emergence of an American Art* (New York: Charles Scribner's Sons, 1942), 363.
[9] Ibid., 177.
[10] Arthur Dove, *The Forum Exhibition of Modern American Painters* (New York: Anderson Galleries, 1916).
[11] D. Phillips, *A Collection in the Making: A Survey of the Problems Involved in Collecting Pictures Together with Brief Estimates of the Painters in the Phillips Memorial Gallery* (New York: E. Weyhe, 1926), 63.
[12] "Arthur Dove Dies; Abstractionist, 66," *New York Times*, November 24, 1946.
[13] Vivien Raynor, "Out of History's Mists Comes Arthur Dove," *New York Times*, October 16, 1983.
[14] D. Phillips to Arthur Dove, 13 March 1928, Arthur and Helen Torr Dove Papers, Archives of American Art, Washington, D.C.
[15] Calvin Tomkins, "The Rose in the Eye Looked Pretty Fine," *New Yorker*, March 4, 1974, 62.
[16] Marjorie Phillips, oral history interview by Paul Cummings for the Archives of American Art, 27 June 1974, Archives of American Art, Washington, D.C., 31.
[17] D. Phillips, "Original American Painting of Today," *Formes*, January 1932, 198.
[18] D. Phillips, "Retrospective Exhibition."

[19] D. Phillips, "The Critic – Partisan or Referee?" *Magazine of Art,* 1953, 88.
[20] D. Phillips to Arthur Dove, 13 March 1928, Arthur and Helen Torr Dove Papers, Archives of American Art, Washington, D.C.
[21] Waldo Frank, essay for *The New Republic,* 1926, Arthur and Helen Torr Dove Papers, Archives of American Art, Washington, D.C., 4.
[22] Elizabeth McCausland, "Dove's Oils, Water Colors Now at an American Place," *Springfield Sunday Union and Republican,* April 22, 1934.
[23] D. Phillips, "Art of Arthur G. Dove," 511.
[24] D. Phillips, *A Collection in the Making,* 63.
[25] D. Phillips, "Art of Arthur G. Dove," 509.
[26] Paul Rosenfeld, "American Painting," *The Dial,* December 1921, 665.
[27] Dove to Elizabeth McCausland, 11 August 1933, Elizabeth McCausland Papers, Archives of American Art, Washington, D.C.
[28] M. Phillips, oral history interview, 25.
[29] Dove to Duncan Phillips, 28 May 1937, Arthur and Helen Torr Dove Papers, Archives of American Art, Washington, D.C.
[30] D. Phillips to Arthur Dove, 6 June 1935, Arthur and Helen Torr Dove Papers, Archives of American Art, Washington, D.C.
[31] D. Phillips to Arthur Dove, 16 December 1933, Arthur and Helen Torr Dove Papers, Archives of American Art, Washington, D.C.
[32] D. Phillips to Arthur Dove, 8 January 1934, Arthur and Helen Torr Dove Papers, Archives of American Art, Washington, D.C.
[33] D. Phillips to Arthur Dove, 22 January 1934, Arthur and Helen Torr Dove Papers, Archives of American Art, Washington, D.C.
[34] Ibid.
[35] M. Phillips, oral history interview, 26.
[36] D. Phillips to Arthur Dove, 9 March 1943, Arthur and Helen Torr Dove Papers, Archives of American Art, Washington, D.C.
[37] D. Phillips to Arthur Dove. 9 April 1940, Arthur and Helen Torr Dove Papers, Archives of American Art, Washington, D.C.
[38] Dove to Duncan Phillips, late October 1946, The Phillips Collection Archives, Washington, D.C.
[39] Sherwood Anderson to Arthur Dove, 12 April 1937, Arthur and Helen Torr Dove Papers, Archives of American Art, Washington, D.C.
[40] Leslie Judd Portner, "Dove Retrospective at the Phillips," *Washington Post,* December 14, 1958.
[41] D. Phillips in Foreword to Frederick S. Wight's *Arthur G. Dove* (Berkeley, University of California Press, 1958), 17.
[42] D. Phillips, "Original American Painting of Today," 198.
[43] Hilton Kramer, "The Intimate Art of Arthur G. Dove," *New York Times,* November 28, 1975.
[44] James Thrall Soby, "Arthur Dove and Morris Graves," *Saturday Review of Literature,* April 17, 1956, 33.

Chapter 7

Georgia O'Keeffe: Courage

Sorry to have missed you.

That was the gist of the note Georgia O'Keeffe left for Duncan Phillips on a day in 1936. She wrote it on a Phillips Memorial Gallery envelope.[1] It read:

> *Dear Mr. Phillips,*
> *I came in this afternoon with my friend Anita Pollitzer and was very sorry not to see you. When I asked this morning if the gallery would be open it did not occur to me to ask if you would be here.*
> *I enjoyed the paintings very much.*
> *My greetings to Mrs. Phillips.*
> *Sincerely,*
> *Georgia O'Keeffe*

By 1936, Duncan and Marjorie Phillips owned four of their eventual six O'Keeffe paintings. In addition to showcasing O'Keeffe's abstractions in their collection, Duncan had written about her work more than once before the missed visit. Rarely had he been more unreserved in praising the integrity of an artist. To *Formes* magazine readers, he stated that her "concentrated study of details in nature, her magnified flower forms, her stylized New Mexico mesa, her very personal patterns of modulated color planes ... may either delight or repel, inspire or estrange, according to what one sees or fails to see in them."[2] His 1932 *Formes* review concluded that "she is undeniably an original genius."[3] Earlier still, in 1926, he had gone into depth about O'Keeffe in his book *A Collection in the Making.* "A young painter of vivid personality and extraordinary skill," is how he began his profile of the Modernist. He described her as "amazing," then spelled out what to him was most central about her work. "It is courage which commands our attention – the courage of her challenging philosophy and especially her courage in so often prolonging the intensity of a theme based on one color, or on the intricate elaboration and enlargement of one linear motif."[4] Jack Cowart of the National Gallery of Art saw the boldness in O'Keeffe's color and form in a likeminded way to Phillips. When Cowart boiled down O'Keeffe's painting to its essence, he wrote of "the direct hard punch of the form, the astonishing key of her color."[5] O'Keeffe herself addressed form. "A hill or a tree cannot make a good painting just because it is a hill or a tree," she wrote. "It is lines and colors put together so that they say something. For me, that is the very basis of painting. The abstraction is often the most definite form for the intangible thing in myself that I can only clarify in paint."[6]

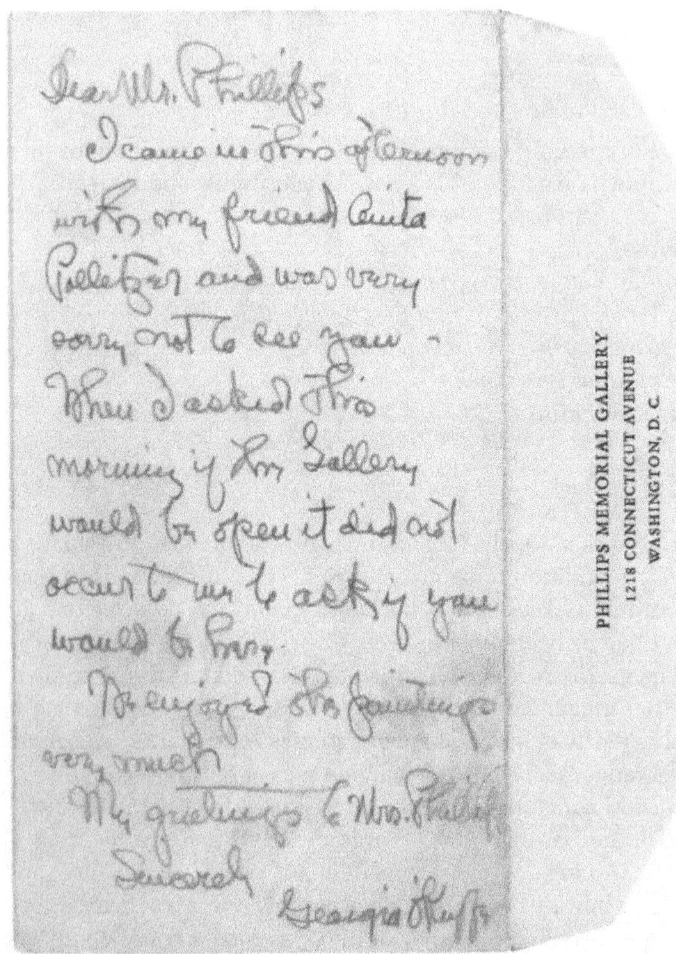

Dear Mr. Phillips
I came in this afternoon
with my friend Anita
Pollitzer and was very
sorry not to see you –
When I asked this
morning if the Gallery
would be open it did not
occur to me to ask if you
would be there.
We enjoyed the paintings
very much
My greetings to Mrs. Phillips
Sincerely
Georgia O'Keeffe

PHILLIPS MEMORIAL GALLERY
1218 CONNECTICUT AVENUE
WASHINGTON, D. C.

Image 7. 1. Georgia O'Keeffe wrote an impromptu note for Duncan Phillips on a Phillips Memorial Gallery envelope during a visit to the museum in 1936. The Phillips Collection Archives.

Georgia O'Keeffe's courage was not limited to her art. Throughout her long life – she lived to be ninety-eight – internal fortitude got her to the places she felt she needed to be. The daughter of Wisconsin dairy farmers who lived on the outskirts of a town named Sun Prairie, she was quite literally born to open spaces. Although it later developed into a suburb of Madison, Sun Prairie was truly prairie during Georgia's girlhood in the late 1880s and the 1890s.

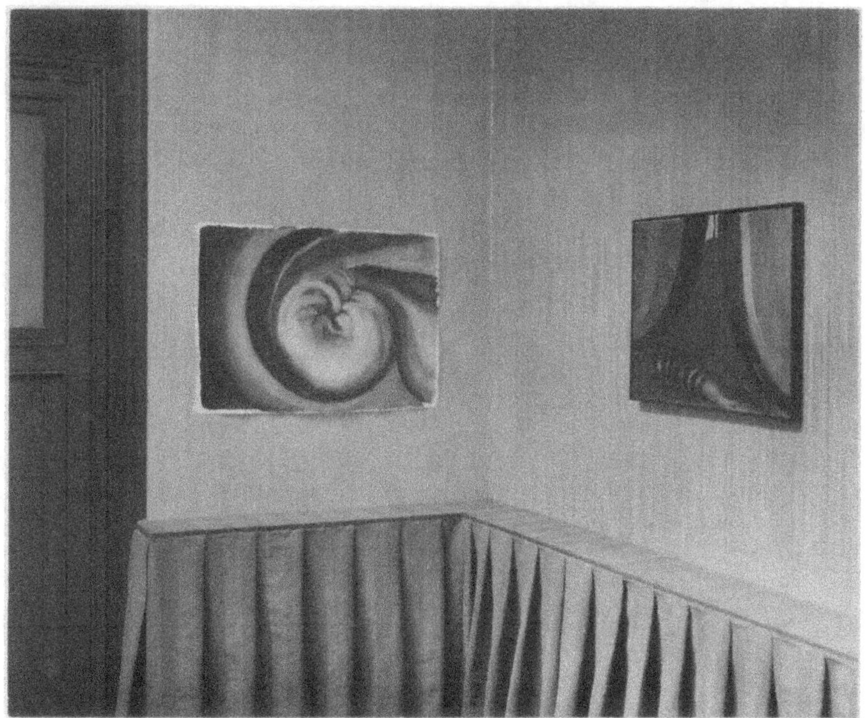

Image 7. 2. Alfred Stieglitz, *Georgia O'Keeffe - Exhibition at '291,'* 1917, Gelatin silver print 6 15/16 × 8 3/8 in.; 17.7 × 21.2 cm. Mount: 8 7/16 × 11 in.; 21.5 × 28 cm. Philadelphia Museum of Art: From the Collection of Dorothy Norman, 1997, 1997-146-73, American.

Talent got her into art school and tenacity led her to study with some of America's most respected art educators, among them Arthur Wesley Dow. Although O'Keeffe had been to New York City for some of her art studies, it must have taken courage to move there in 1918 and live with Alfred Stieglitz, a married man. She was thirty, he was fifty-five, famous for his photography and promotion of modern art. Even before moving to New York, O'Keeffe had become a member of the Stieglitz Circle, her works shown at his gallery 291; and after it closed in 1917, his subsequent galleries. Unlike fellow painters Arthur Dove, John Marin, and Marsden Hartley, she was talked about for more than her art. O'Keeffe posed nude for Stieglitz numerous times and while many art historians consider the resulting photographs among his best works, the quality of the muse's own art was sometimes questioned because of their relationship, even after he became her husband. Duncan and Marjorie Phillips were not among the naysayers. It would be six years after Stieglitz and O'Keeffe began living together before his divorce was granted. Three months after the final decree, the two were wed by a justice of the peace with Marin bearing witness. Undaunted by long-running rumors and innuendo, she continued to pose for Stieglitz, clothed and unclothed.

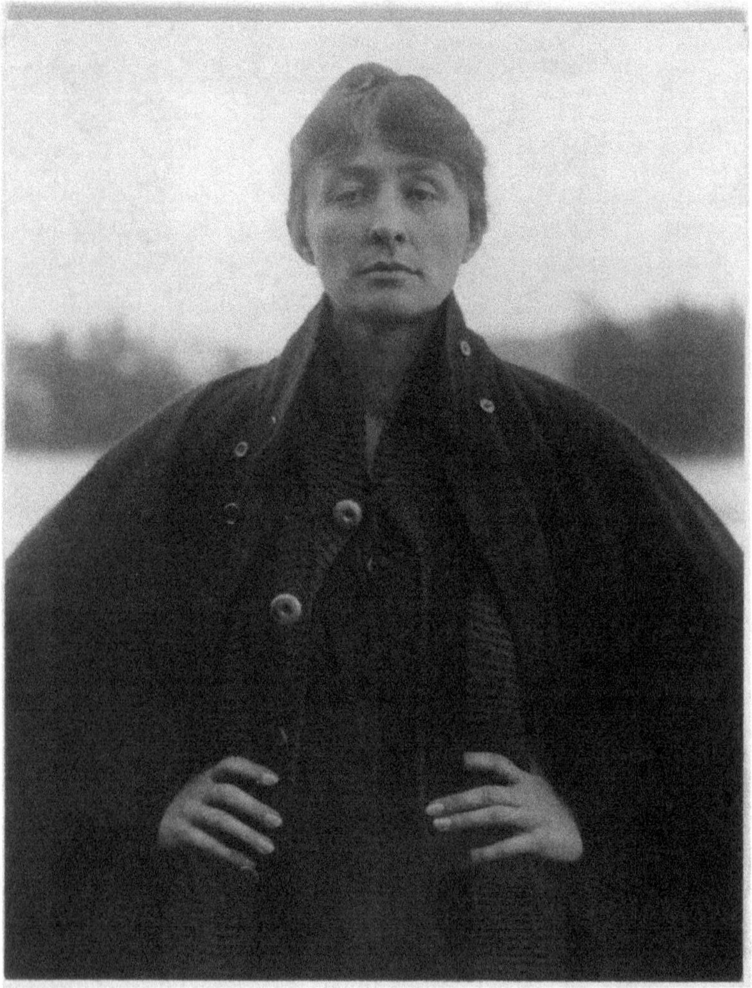

Image 7. 3. Alfred Stieglitz, *Georgia O'Keeffe*, 1918, Gelatin silver print 4 11/16 × 3 5/8 in.; 11.9 × 9.2 cm. Mount (secondary): 12 7/16 × 9 15/16 in.; 31.6 × 25.3 cm. Philadelphia Museum of Art: Purchased with the Lola Downin Peck Fund, 1978, American.

To be with Stieglitz, O'Keeffe had chucked her job as an art instructor at West Texas State Normal College, a teacher's college in Canyon, Texas. The college bulletin from 1917 did a fine job summarizing her education and experience. Sandwiched between H. W. Morelock, Professor of English, and Jessie Eulalia Rambo, Director of Home Economics, Miss O'Keeffe's entry read:

> Chicago Art Institute, 1905-6; New York Art Students' League, 1907-8; University of Virginia Summer School, 1912; Teachers' College New York City, 1914-16; Supervisor Art Amarillo Public Schools, 1912-14; Teacher in University of Virginia Sumer School, 1913-1916. Present position 1916 –

It was a risk to leave her faculty position for love. Teaching art to would-be teachers may not have been the most glamorous job for the woman who would become one of America's foremost Modernists, but she appreciated the natural beauty of Canyon, named for nearby Palo Duro Canyon. Her year and a half in the small Texas town could be read as a prequel to the vastness of New Mexico, the area of the United States most closely associated with O'Keeffe's middle and late years. When Canyon celebrated the one-hundredth anniversary of its 1889 founding, the centennial committee funded a slim publication about their renowned resident. The author, Fred Stoker, a retired professor from West Texas State University, wrote that O'Keeffe "often walked to the west side of town in the evening. ... Even though there were some dusty days, the air, particularly at night, was ... unusually clear and beautiful."[7] O'Keeffe wrote about those frequent walks. "There were no paved roads and no fences – no trees – it was like the ocean but it was a wide, wide land."[8] In his booklet about O'Keeffe's stay there, Professor Stoker wrote that "She gloried in the beautiful sunsets and was particularly impressed by the evening star (Venus)."[9] When organizing the National Gallery's retrospective of her works in 1987, Jack Cowart also wrote about O'Keeffe and the outdoors. He, too, homed in on her penchant for day's end. "Sunset," Cowart wrote in the catalogue that accompanied his O'Keeffe show, "is the time when the world appears least structured, when forms tend to dissolve and are replaced by new colors and sensations."[10] It is the time that inspired one of The Phillips Collection's most sublime works of art.

The Phillips sunset by O'Keeffe is officially titled *Red Hills, Lake George* but Marjorie Phillips had been known to refer to it as "Red Hills and the Sun," arguably a more fitting title since Earth's energy source wins the gaze of any onlooker to the painting. *Red Hills* was painted in 1927 and although the Phillipses had purchased two O'Keeffes the prior year, *My Shanty, Lake George,* painted in 1922, and *Patterns of Leaves,* painted in 1923, they did not acquire the sunset picture until 1945. On its canvas, the hills are painted tomato red. They rise and fall. Rather than provide stability to the landscape, they seem to shift like sand. The sun first catches a viewer's eye as a ring of lemon yellow.

Inside the yellow is a milky white; outside it is a faint gray. Circles more distant from the center of the sun are shown in distinct shades of pink, soon mixed with layers of brown. Eventually, because of the purple-tinged browns, the sky looks more like soil than sky. While the setting sun may be the focal point of the painting, the vivid red hills will not be denied. Their soft curves could be interpreted as a woman's torso. Or, a viewer with a different imagination might feel the sun's heat beginning to ease on what is perhaps Arabia, and Colonel T. E. Lawrence rides through the still-scorched sands on horseback.

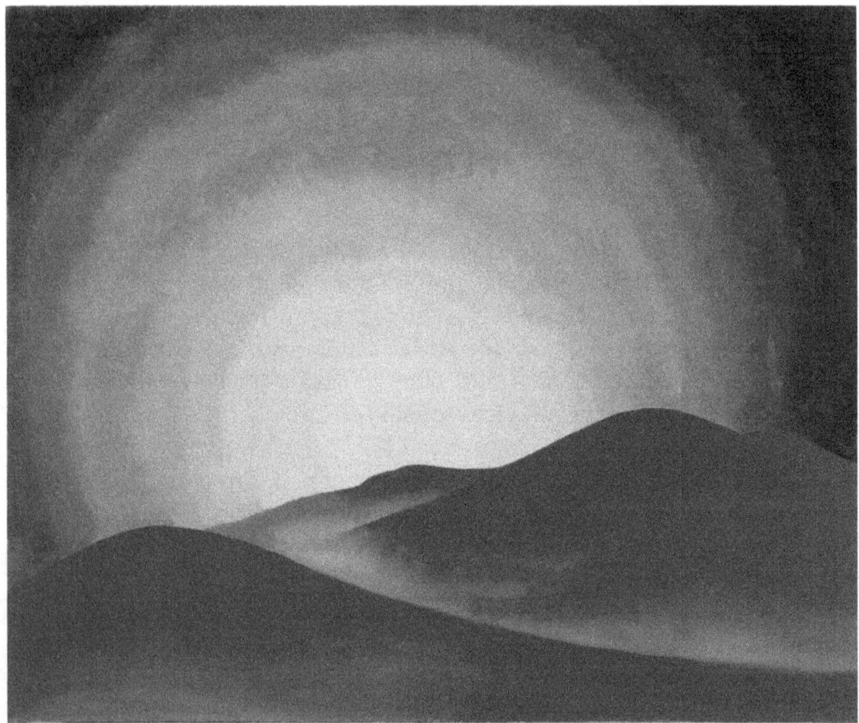

Image 7. 4. Georgia O'Keeffe, *Red Hills, Lake George*, 1927, Oil on canvas overall: 27 in x 32 in.; 68.58 cm. x 81.28 cm.; framed: 28 1/4 in. x 33 3/8 in. x 2 in.; 71.75 cm. x 84.77 cm. x 5.08 cm. The Phillips Collection: Acquired 1945; © 2008 The Georgia O'Keeffe Foundation/Artists Rights Society (ARS), New York. Paintings, 1450, American.

Finding Something of Her Own

Well into her art career, O'Keeffe was asked to name the strongest influence on her work. "Some people say nature, but the way you see nature depends on whatever influenced your way of seeing," she replied. "I think it was Arthur Dow who affected my start, who helped me find something of my own."[11] Dow, a teacher to O'Keeffe as well as to her friend Anita Pollitzer, figured prominently in the letters the two women sent each other; they affectionately referred to him as Papa Dow. He encouraged students to look to nature for ideas in composition. O'Keeffe was intrepid painting nature. A certain notoriety came from her depictions of flowers, said by many to resemble elements of the female body, most notably the vagina. "The critics wrote extensively if somewhat evasively about this aspect of her art," according to art historian Lloyd Goodrich, long associated with the Whitney Museum of American Art. Goodrich stated that when her flower paintings were first exhibited "Freudianism (and pseudo-Freudianism) was very much in the air."[12] O'Keeffe went on record as saying she thought the paintings were improperly analyzed. She felt that some art critics "hung all your associations with flowers on my flower and you write about my flower as if I think and see what you think and see of the flower – and I don't."[13] In spite of her intent coming into question, O'Keeffe succeeded in getting the paintings noticed. In 1961, she spoke with art historian Katharine Kuh about the origin of what she called her "blown-up flowers." During her interview with Kuh, O'Keeffe said that in the 1920s, skyscrapers seemed to be going up overnight in New York. At that time, she saw a still life with flowers by Henri Fantin-Latour that she found very beautiful, but, as she told Kuh, "I realized that if I were to paint the same flowers so small, no one would look at them because I was unknown. So I thought I'll make them big like the huge buildings going up. People will be startled, they'll *have* to look at them – and they did."[14]

Fifteen years after the Kuh interview, Viking Press published an elaborate volume of O'Keeffe's paintings of flowers, bones, and other subjects accompanied by the artist's writing. At the beginning of the 1976 book, O'Keeffe stated that some of her writing was done in the early 1930s and some of it was continued in the first half of the 1970s. It is not made clear exactly when she first documented the following idea, but it correlates to what Duncan Phillips believed about individual encounters with art and is apropos to experiencing her flower paintings. O'Keeffe wrote: "I long ago came to the conclusion that even if I could put down accurately the thing that I saw and enjoyed, it would not give the observer the kind of feeling it gave me."[15]

Always an Individual

Another aspect of O'Keeffe's individualism was expressing that beauty could be found in unpredictable sources and circumstances. Not unlike flowers, which multitudes consider pleasing to the eye, she found animal bones beautiful. She would gather both flowers and bones and would "take them home to use to say what is to me the wideness and the wonder of the world as I live in it."[16] O'Keeffe's passion for the Southwest extended beyond flora and fauna to architecture. She wrote of "one of the most beautiful buildings left in the United

States by the early Spaniards,"[17] the Ranchos Church of Taos. One of Duncan and Marjorie Phillips's prized possessions was a 1929 O'Keeffe of the Ranchos Church. Theirs is the second in a series of eight known paintings of the old church. Duncan thought so highly of it that he placed a stand-alone photograph of the painting in the March 1930 issue of his magazine *Art and Understanding* to illustrate an article titled "The Current American Art Season." The photo of The Phillipses' *Ranchos Church, No. II, N.M.*, appeared across from Ralph Flint's description of O'Keeffe's general treatment of the Taos terrain. Flint wrote: "Suggestive of the strange dark beauty of the place, she chose to paint a series of rude, wayside crosses, now hugely black and bleak against the sun-fired, hummocking New Mexico mountains, now pale and weathered against a cool vault of rain-washed blue."[18]

O'Keeffe was always true to herself. The year she painted Duncan and Marjorie's *Ranchos Church* was the year she stopped spending summers with Stieglitz in Lake George, New York. The artist and her art impresario would remain married until Stieglitz's death, and while she would visit him in New York City, her home had become New Mexico where she bought acres of ranch land.

Duncan and Marjorie acquired their final O'Keeffe in 1945, a year before Stieglitz died. Each of their O'Keeffe's was purchased through him. Duncan would sometimes write to Stieglitz about how he had arranged or rearranged works by Stieglitz Circle artists at the Phillips Memorial Gallery. In one such letter, Duncan explained why they had not been to New York City to see O'Keeffe's latest paintings. Part of the reason was that Phillips was especially busy that season with curator duties. Another reason, he explained to Stieglitz, involved admiring O'Keeffe's art too much. "Of course we wanted to see the O'Keeffe exhibition though I admit we were a little afraid of it, afraid to be tempted to buy any more when our funds are all gone. But we have O'Keeffe represented in three different aspects and must be content to wait for another year to add to the group."[19]

O'Keeffe and Stieglitz are forever linked in art history, and in the history of The Phillips Collection. Although she chose New Mexico over Stieglitz, by all accounts, the two remained in love.[20] A few years after his death, O'Keeffe sent a letter to Duncan and Marjorie concerning their official acceptance of a gift of Stieglitz photographs. "I know I should send them to you because Stieglitz so often spoke of intending to send them himself," O'Keeffe wrote. "I think they will feel very much at home with you."[21]

Georgia O'Keeffe was a young artist when Duncan Phillips wrote that it is her courage which commands our attention. Later in her career, as if conversing with the Washington, D.C. collector of modern art, she wrote: "I believe that to create one's own world in any of the arts takes courage."[22] Certainly, Duncan and Marjorie Phillips would create their own world of art – an art collection they shared with visitors from near and far.

Notes

[1] The envelope with Georgia O'Keeffe's 1936 note to Duncan Phillips was found by Processing Archivist Juli Folk in 2019 during a digitization project at The Phillips Collection Archives, Washington, D.C.
[2] Duncan Phillips, "Original American Painting of Today," *Formes*, January 1932, 198.
[3] Ibid.
[4] D. Phillips, *A Collection in the Making: A Survey of the Problems Involved in Collecting Pictures Together with Brief Estimates of the Painters in the Phillips Memorial Gallery* (New York: E. Weyhe, 1926), 66.
[5] Jack Cowart, "Georgia O'Keeffe: Art and Artist" in *Georgia O'Keeffe: Art and Letters* by Cowart, Juan Hamilton and Sarah Greenough (Washington, D.C.: National Gallery of Art, 1987), 3.
[6] Georgia O'Keeffe, *Georgia O'Keeffe: A Studio Book* (New York: Viking Press, 1976), n.p.
[7] Fred Stoker, *Georgia O'Keeffe in Canyon* (Canyon, TX: Canyon-Randall Centennial Committee, 1990), 26.
[8] O'Keeffe, *Georgia O'Keeffe: A Studio Book.*
[9] Stoker, 26.
[10] Cowart, 2.
[11] Katharine Kuh, *The Artist's Voice: Talks with Seventeen Modern Artists* (1962; reprint New York: DaCapo Press, 2000), 189.
[12] Lloyd Goodrich, "Georgia O'Keeffe," in *Georgia O'Keeffe* by Goodrich and Doris Bry (New York: Whitney Museum of American Art, 1970), 18.
[13] Goodrich, 19.
[14] Kuh, 191.
[15] O'Keeffe, *Georgia O'Keeffe: A Studio Book.*
[16] Ibid.
[17] Ibid.
[18] Ralph Flint, "The Current American Art Season," *Art and Understanding* 2 (March 1930): 214.
[19] D. Phillips to Alfred Stieglitz, 27 January 1927, The Phillips Collection Archives, Washington, D.C.
[20] For a thoughtful examination of the relationship between O'Keeffe and Stieglitz see Sarah Greenough's editing of their correspondence in *My Faraway One: Selected Letters of Georgia O'Keeffe and Alfred Stieglitz* (New Haven, CT: Yale University Press, 2011). Greenough heads the department of photographs at the National Gallery of Art.
[21] O'Keeffe to Duncan and Marjorie Phillips, 11 August 1949, The Phillips Collection Archives, Washington, D.C.
[22] O'Keeffe, *Georgia O'Keeffe: A Studio Book.*

Chapter 8

John Marin: A Strong and Bracing Wind

Duncan and Marjorie Phillips collected works by John Marin long before *Look* magazine named him the best painter in America. They would show Marin's art with works by established European painters, beckoning viewers to the American Modernist. Duncan Phillips regarded the abstract artist from Maine as "one of the most provoking, challenging innovators in the history of painting,"[1] writing that he "blows through the world of modern art like a strong and bracing wind."[2] The pursuit of rhythm and a life-long love of the outdoors guided much of Marin's painting. His own imagination and his ability to engage the imaginations of viewers are key to Marin's place in art history.

Summing up Marin's biography, Duncan Phillips wrote: "Yankee birth and independence – training as an architect – the influence of Whistler – then of the Chinese, then of Cézanne and Stieglitz – that is the story."[3] Marin was almost thirty years old when he became a student at the Pennsylvania Academy of Fine Arts in 1899. After attending New York's Art Students League at the dawn of the twentieth century, he lived in France for four years and studied briefly at the Académie Julian. Approaching forty years of age, he moved back to the United States, where he would divide his time between New York City and the Maine coastline, the two predominant inspirations for his art. Like his kindred painters of the Stieglitz Circle, Marin did not concern himself with purposeful representation, writing that his works "are meant as constructed expressions of the inner senses, responding to things seen and felt."[4] He later added to how he functioned as an artist, writing: "I don't paint rocks, trees, houses, and all things seen. I paint an inner vision."[5]Alfred Stieglitz served as Marin's art dealer, much as he did for other artists of the Circle, including Arthur Dove, Georgia O'Keeffe, and Marsden Hartley. Buying from Stieglitz, the Phillipses would come to own a half-dozen Marin oil paintings, but mostly they bought Marin watercolors. Like Phillips, Hartley admired Marin's originality as well as his skill. "He paces his strokes to a new beat," Hartley wrote of his fellow Modernist. "He is keen as a whip, alert as a razor, and has the grip of steel on his medium. Strength is always a personal thing, and this is the case of the mighty Marin."[6]

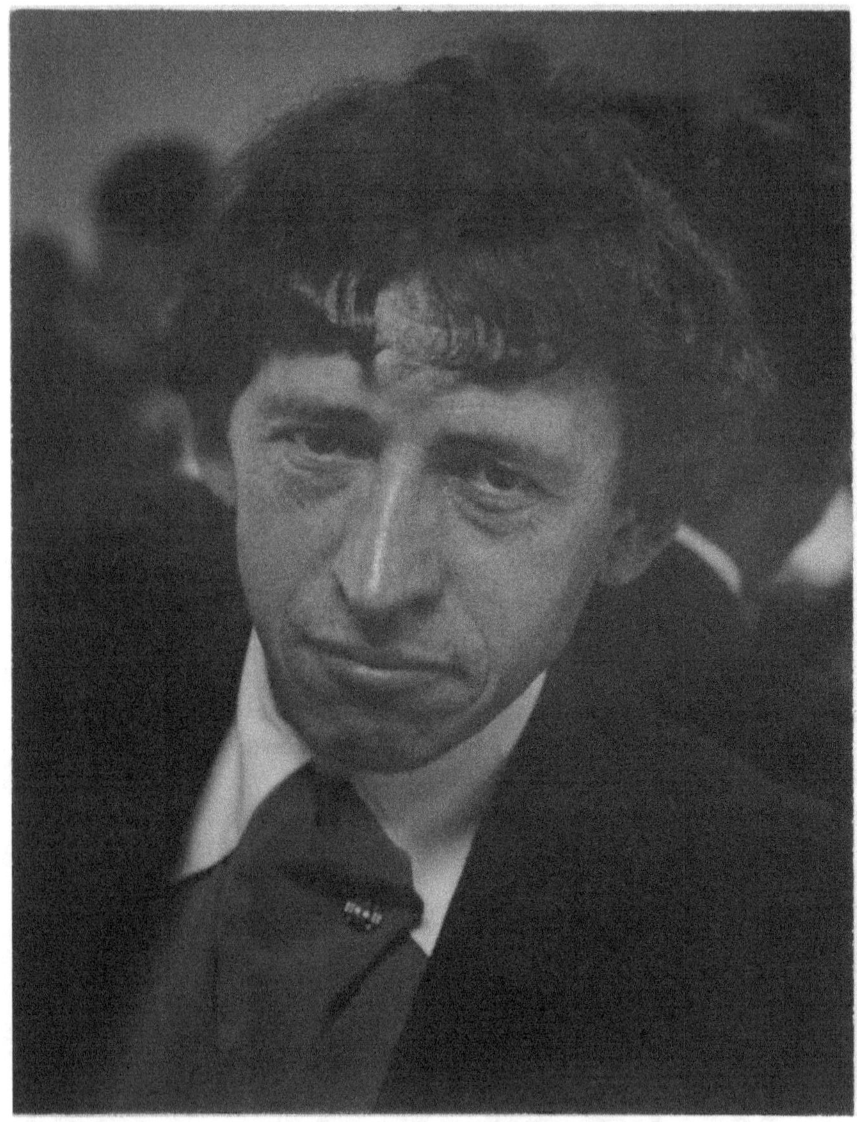

Image 8. 1. Alfred Stieglitz, *John Marin*, 1921,
Gelatin silver print Image/Sheet/Mount: 9 1/4 × 7 in.; 23.5 × 17.8 cm. Mount (secondary): 10 5/8 × 8 1/2 in.; 27 × 21.6 cm. Philadelphia Museum of Art: From the Collection of Dorothy Norman, 1967, 1967-285-40, American.

Proud of his and Marjorie's Marin purchases, Duncan sent a letter to Alfred H. Barr Jr. in January 1927 about a forthcoming display of Marin's works at the Phillips Memorial Gallery. "In February and March I will give Washington a bracing shock in the work of this stimulating creator," Phillips wrote to the future MoMA director, describing Marin "with his incisive brain, his flashing eye, his startling intuition and magic with his medium."[7] In highlighting works by Marin in the winter of 1927, Phillips blazed the trail for New York City's Museum of Modern Art, still two years from its opening. It would take ten years after Phillips's boast for Barr to present a Marin retrospective at MoMA, the first for an American artist there. Phillips, however, did not wait a decade to broaden potential appreciation for Marin. He reached an international readership with an assessment of Marin's importance in his 1932 article about American art for the journal *Formes*, published in French and English. "Never safe and sane," Phillips wrote of Marin's paintings, "with details often askew and out of focus, but with the essential part intensified and magnetic."[8] The following year, 1933, *New York Times* art columnist Edward Alden Jewell called Marin "an American artist of genius."[9] About the same time, art critic Lewis Mumford wrote a remarkable essay for the *New Yorker* which can supply context for the multitudes of accolades Marin amassed. Mumford contrasted the act of viewing works by Marin to those painted by Edward Hopper, famous for restaurant and theater slices of life, sometimes featuring men with fedoras and women in fashionable cloche hats, and almost always conveying a struggle to cope with modernity. Hopper's best-known work is *Night Hawks*, which hangs in a place of pride at the Art Institute of Chicago. The iconic *Night Hawks* was not painted until 1942, but Phillips had purchased another Hopper, an imposing oil-on-canvas titled *Sunday* in 1926, the year the artist created it. In *Sunday*, the scene is barren save for disturbingly hued building fronts and a lone man sitting on the edge of a wood sidewalk, his feet planted in the street. It is a stunning work of art and will compel all but the most jaded visitors to stop and ask the questions who, what, when, where, and why. In the *New Yorker* essay, titled "Two Americans," when Mumford praises Marin at the expense of Hopper it is high praise indeed. "Visually speaking," Mumford wrote, "one may follow Hopper on the pedestrian level; following Marin, one must risk one's neck in an airplane."[10] Mumford offered an additional opinion on the impact works by the two artists might have on viewers: "Both Marin and Hopper have been interpreters of America, but while Hopper has utilized our limitations and made the most of them, Marin has demonstrated our possibilities."[11]

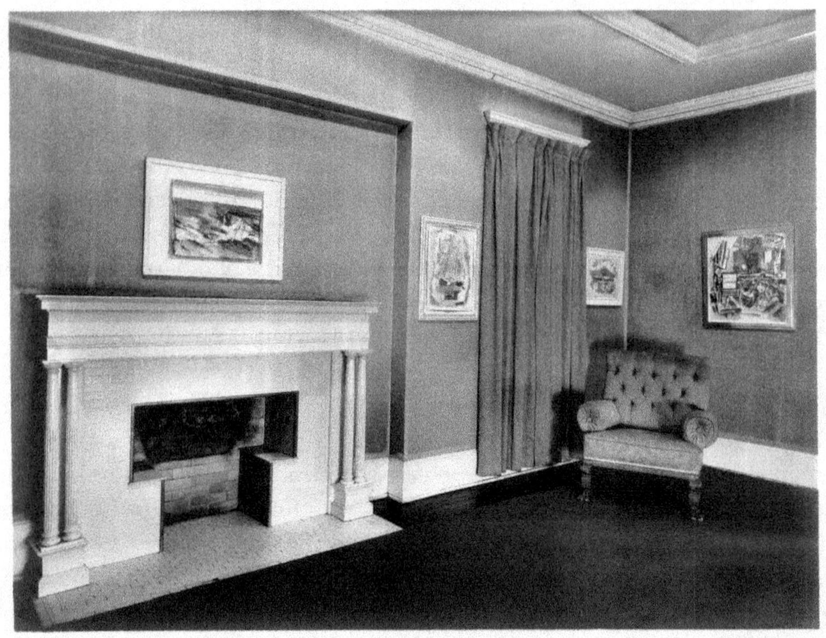

Image 8. 2. Gallery B at the Phillips, ca. 1955, four works by John Marin. Left to right: *Grey Sea,* 1924; *Ship Fantasy,* 1928; *Franconia Range, White Mountains, No. 1,* 1927; and *Street Crossing, New York,* 1928. © 2020 Estate of John Marin / Artists Rights Society (ARS), New York.

"Let the Picture Happen to You"

Part of Marin's strength as an artist comes from his ability to coax the viewer to spend time with his work. Journalist Herbert Seligmann wrote about a visitor to Stieglitz's Intimate Gallery in 1927 who initially remarked that the Marins on exhibit were "hard to see." Following a conversation with Stieglitz, she said "Then you have to let the picture happen to you."[12] It was exactly the attitude Duncan and Marjorie Phillips encouraged in visitors to the rooms of art within the family home that became The Phillips Collection. Playwright and novelist Thornton Wilder thought about Marin in a similar vein when he highlighted the painter's connection to the outdoors in a 1955 essay. Wilder, the author of *Our Town* and *The Bridge of San Luis* Rey, wrote that with Marin "one seems to be learning from him that the visible world is constantly speaking," and that in his art "nature seems to have been caught surprised."[13] Marin's own expressions about his feelings for nature carried over into his writing. "It is raining," he wrote in a letter dated 1920. "Grey skies, grey sea, scurrying clouds, wind this way blowing, that way blowing, weather vane says eastward and eastward it is,

I guess. And the wind whistles that mournful sound and I like it."[14] In a letter to the journalist and art critic Louis Kalonyme, Marin typed: "the other day I picked up Thoreau's Walden and – Well he goes to the woods where he could contemplate. I go to the woods because I love the woods."[15] A few weeks earlier, in June 1945, Marin wrote to Duncan and Marjorie of "brilliant days to come when everything sparkles . . . and it's then I'll play truant and get out and wander to those lovable spots I have discovered not so far away – where the Earth has a sweet smell."[16]

The watercolor and chalk work *Quoddy Head, Maine Coast* speaks to "those lovable spots" and also to Mumford's insight about possibilities. Created in 1933 and purchased by the Phillipses in 1937, it presents the meeting of sky and water. Waves are breaking, and a myriad of blues blacken as stones and shells form a human-like crowd on the beach. White clouds drift in a sky of purest blue, pausing in the shape of a mountain range. What appears to be a buoy settles next to a rounded bit of jagged rock. Fish or fish fossils stud the foreground. It's as if the painting is inviting the viewer into a conversation that is already taking place on the canvas.

Setting the Stage for Conversations among Paintings

Conversations among paintings themselves was an idea Duncan Phillips implemented when hanging and rearranging his and Marjorie's permanent collection. He also used the technique as a way to get visitors to maximize their personal experiences with art in the many temporary exhibits he organized at their museum. One of the most dramatic examples of strategically placing works by more than one artist was when Duncan showcased Marin with Pablo Picasso, the man who was widely considered to be the greatest of modern artists. In 1938, a year after he organized the Dove retrospective at the Phillips Gallery, Duncan held an exhibition titled *Picasso and Marin*. The *Washington Post* announced that the works by Picasso were "personally selected by Duncan Phillips and show the usual distinction of his taste," noting that "Mr. Marin himself will be in town for the occasion of the opening of the exhibition."[17] Most of the Picassos at the show were lent to Phillips for the three-week-long spring event; several of them were owned by Miss Etta Cone of Baltimore. As a collector, Duncan Phillips had not jumped on the Picasso bandwagon; for Cubism, he preferred Georges Braque, for whom he established a unit of works. The Phillipses did, however, own three Picassos at the time of the 1938 exhibit. *Early Morning* (1901) from the Blue Period, and *Bull Fight* (1934) remain two standout works at The Phillips Collection. Certainly, it was bold – some might say brazen – to show Marin with Picasso, but Duncan Phillips went further in his devotion to Marin. In the literature which accompanied the show, Phillips made some strong remarks about both the famous Spaniard and the lesser-known American, speaking harshly of Picasso while promoting Marin. Of *Bull Fight*, Phillips wrote: “Symbolical clashes of color and a swirl of ferocious lines mark this new Baroque with the special significance of an aesthetic dictator's impetuous and ruthless calligraphy.”[18] Phillips crafted separate descriptions for each of the twenty-five Picassos on display. Yet in the Marin portion of the brochure, he wrote only: “Marin needs no annotation as Picasso needs it. His dynamic designs speak for themselves and there is a unity of purpose and plan which pervades them all.”[19]

Friend and Houseguest

In her memoir of Duncan, Marjorie Phillips wrote that her husband was congenial with the artists he liked and that he liked Marin “from the first.”[20] She recalled the protocol for Marin's visits to Washington, D.C.: “For some years he came frequently to see his elderly stepmother, of whom he was very fond, and his stepbrother Commander Bittinger. He would either stay with them or with us: sometimes he came alone, and sometimes with his wife.”[21] The *Washington Evening Star* mentioned a 1948 visit, noting that “John Marin has been a guest of Mr. and Mrs. Duncan Phillips during the past week. Washington's acquaintance with Mr. Marin's paintings is due largely to the Phillips Gallery's several comprehensive exhibits of his work,” adding that during Marin's stay, “Mr. Marin's stepbrother, Charles Bittinger, one of Washington's most distinguished artists, invited a few friends to meet him.”[22] Bittinger, who attended MIT for two years, not only made a life for himself as a painter but was awarded the Legion of Merit from the U.S. Navy for his expertise in ship camouflage.

Marjorie Phillips wrote that she and her husband both enjoyed Marin's visits, no matter where he stayed overnight. One visit stood out for both historical and personal reasons; it coincided with V-J Day (August 14, 1945). It was, she wrote, “a day when Duncan and I were eager to hear every scrap of war news, since our son Laughlin was in the Philippines – and we asked Marin to join us in listening to the radio.”[23] It is unclear if Marin, whose son also served in the Pacific, knew by then that John Jr. was safe. The artist had written to Herbert Seligmann in January 1945: “John Jr. is still from last letter going on now 4 weeks – in the Philippines – we can only hope for the best & try and keep up spirits – I can see it's pulling his mother pretty hard.”[24] Marie Jane Hughes Marin died only a few weeks later, on Valentine's Day. “You may have heard,” Marin wrote to Louis Kalonyme, “that I lost the one who was near and dear to me on Feby 14 – So you see my plan of life is somewhat altered whether I will or not.”[25] John Jr. did make it home from the war, but Marin noted in a postscript on July 2, 1945, that he was “still somewhere out on one of his Pacific islands.”[26]

Between their in-person visits with Marin over the years, Duncan and Marjorie stayed in touch with him by post. In some of their letters, the couple shared with Marin their excitement about his art. Marjorie wrote Marin in 1938 that they were "crazy about" a newly acquired piece and that they could "never tire of it."[27] In New Year's greetings for 1946, Duncan wrote Marin that his "genius as a painter flourishes as never before which is saying a great deal."[28] In March 1947, Duncan wrote to Marin about the painter's latest trip to D.C., conveying that the couple "enjoyed every moment of your visit and hope it did you as much good as it did us." Duncan included in his 1947 letter the tribute that he had been "simply swept off my feet by the power and loveliness" of a recent Marin work.[29] Marin reciprocated the admiration. When he learned, in early 1937, that Duncan and Marjorie had purchased his painting *Pertaining to Fifth Avenue and Forty-Second Street,* the artist wrote to the collectors: "I do hope it will wear well – whether it will hold its own – for you know – and I know – it will be in some mighty good Company. But as I respect your judgment of pictures –I must respect your purchase – and say quite probably you have a good picture."[30] Marin's most heartfelt message to the Phillipses was yet to come. His July 12, 1948 letter to Duncan and Marjorie began: "It seemed I had written you but – I hadn't – Guess I dreamt it – anyway it would have been a good dream – because it would have been based on a real beautiful experience – that of us being with you – our talks – our lookings – our goings."[31]

The letters and the visits were about the business relationship as well as enjoyment of art and each other's company. In the New Year's letter of 1946, Duncan told Marin how he had asked Stieglitz to cooperate with a proposed exhibit of Marin's works at the Phillips Gallery. "He [Stieglitz] did not say no and we think that if you like the idea and tell him so, it would decide him." Before signing off with "our affectionate greetings and sincere homage," Phillips extended an invitation for Marin to stay at the Phillips home on Foxhall Road in Washington, D.C. for the occasion of the intended show. Originally, Phillips had written the words "Marjorie and I hope that you could come down during that time for a short visit" but it is clear he altered the letter, probably because he thought limiting the length of proffered hospitality could be interpreted as impolite. In Duncan's handwriting, a "t" has been added to make the "a" before "short" into the word "at," followed by the insertion of "least a" so the edited letter reads "at least a short visit."[32]

Engaging the Imaginations of Viewers

John Marin was of like mind with Duncan Phillips about not dictating meaning for a work of art. Marin expressed a preference for the avoidance of over-interpretation when he wrote to Elizabeth Navas after she had selected his picture *Region, Trinity Church, New York* for the Murdock Collection of the

Wichita Art Museum. Navas had been hired through a bequest in her friend Louise Caldwell Murdock's will to assemble a collection of American art in honor of Louise's late husband Roland P. Murdock, who had been the publisher of the *Wichita Eagle.* It is obvious in Marin's undated letter to Navas that he was responding to her request for insight into the work. At first, he seems reluctant to say too much. "It should represent nothing but itself," Marin told her, "being itself – being a creation in its own right." However, Marin did share that "this particular picture came into being as the result of my wanderings thereabouts" and that when he painted it, "rhythm throughout was looked for – balance and construction."[33] In an interview in 1949, given long after he had completed *Region, Trinity Church* but a couple of years before Navas purchased it, Marin made it known that he enjoyed rhythm in the making of art and not just the final product. "I like the feel of paint," he said, and spoke of "the drag of the brush across the tooth of the canvas."[34]

Rhythm saturates Marin's 1928 work *Street Crossing, New York,* a watercolor with graphite pencil and black chalk, acquired by the Phillipses in 1931. The picture conjures the magical realism of Marc Chagall heightened by the musicality of Stuart Davis, an American for whom Phillips established a unit in his collection. Motion pervades in the Marin, even in the buildings themselves, squeezed so close to one another that their flags and banners provide a canopy to passersby. The abstraction in *Street Crossing* is to a degree where it is hard not to wonder if the figures in the painting are meant as they appear. Has the flapper with the bobbed hair been shopping, and is she now hailing a cab? Is the man slightly behind her a policeman or a street vendor? Nearby, partial objects such as the wheel of a motorcycle add to the scene's frenzy and uncertainty.

Alfred Barr Jr. wrote of another Marin cityscape in his 1943 book *What is Modern Painting?* Referring to *Lower Manhattan,* a 1920 turquoise-dominated work owned by MoMA, Barr offered words about the art and the artist: "The fifty-story buildings scraping the sky – John Marin felt the excitement of the scene and he painted it – not the scene so much as his excitement, breathlessly, using great slashing, zigzag strokes – blue, scarlet and yellow – for the angles of the building and even the sky."[35] Duncan Phillips also addressed Marin's cityscapes, writing that his "explosions of line and colour, especially in the Manhattan street scenes, was dedicated to the theme of energy."[36] Including Marin's nature paintings along with his pictures of urban life, Phillips wrote: "It is true that he aspired to the abstract condition of music, that he wished to makes his art as structural and sequential as Bach. ... Marin was not only an expressionist but a virtuoso in love with water-colour, his favorite instrument."[37]

The power of a virtuoso to make his or her audience respond with great emotion fills concert halls. On the walls of The Phillips Collection, Marin accomplishes a similar feat through his provocations to use the mind's eye. "The imagination must be able to enter a composition and move about there freely, cramped neither for space nor for air," wrote Guy Eglington in a 1924 article about Marin.[38] *Mt. Chocurua – White Mountains* was not painted until 1926, but it is just such a composition. The watercolor and graphite pencil on paper, purchased by the Phillipses in 1928, at first brings to mind Paul Cézanne's paintings of Mont Sainte-Victoire. Cézanne, esteemed by other artists for breaking rules of perspective, painted the mountain of Provence many times, bringing pleasure to visitors of art museums throughout the world. Marin manages to surpass the French master in both emotional intensity and accessibility with *Mt. Chocurua.* His rendition of the New Hampshire outdoor treasure all but demands viewers to enter and imagine themselves before the chartreuse meadow - deciding whether to stop at the tree-line, walk further to the foothills, or hike all the way onto the mountain's trails.

To Duncan Phillips, it made sense that Marin's works could be interpreted in so many different ways. For visitors to a London exhibition of Marin's works, Phillips wrote that the painter was "independent of all isms and his impetuosity was that of a poet-painter."[39] Lewis Mumford shared Phillips's regard for Marin's independence. "John Marin is not a second anything," Mumford wrote. "He is simply a first Marin, and in visual awareness, sensitiveness, and shear creative volume we have not witnessed his like before in American painting."[40] Prominent art critic Clement Greenberg agreed that Marin was an original. Like Phillips, Greenberg did not hesitate to mention the names of other artists in order to more fully communicate to readers. "Marin has taken cubism, married it to fauvist color and a bit of Winslow Homer, and of this made a personal instrument which has been surpassed on the score of sensitivity only by that of Klee among modern painters," Greenberg wrote.[41] The Phillipses collected works by Paul Klee and created a unit of the Swiss artist's bold abstractions. Greenberg continued his 1948 review for *The Nation* with an affirmation that Marin's work "registers sensations or emotions of an evanescence which has escaped contemporary art elsewhere."[42]

When Lewis Mumford wrote that Marin demonstrated America's possibilities, it was because his art can lead viewers to what Greenberg called an evanescence. The transitory mist comes from, as Duncan Phillips put it, Marin blowing through the world of modern art like a strong and bracing wind. It is in *Grey Sea,* one of Marin's most abstract works, that possibilities confront the viewer head-on. He completed the watercolor with black chalk in 1924, and it remains daunting to even the most thoughtful onlooker. "As powerful as a Homer - as rare in its reserve of tone as a Whistler – and more intense, more shaggy and elemental than either"[43] is how Phillips referred to the 1926 acquisition. Phillips felt the picture was so crucial to America's art vocabulary that he included it in the 1944 exhibit *American Paintings of The Phillips Collection* and he shipped it to Great Britain's Tate Gallery for their American art show of 1946. *Grey Sea* feels like nature itself, energy unbridled. The greys are somehow warm, not cool. The browns stabilize the picture, which is marked by an almost straight horizon line. Throughout the scene, there is an eerie interplay of movement and calm. A viewer might register the picture as overly simple or extremely complex. Marin executed the seascape long before the Phillipses collected works by Mark Rothko, yet, like Rothko's post-World-War-II paintings, *Grey Sea* calls for personal exploration.

Modernist John Marin's artistic descendants include Abstract Expressionists besides Rothko. Marin is the "single most important bridge between American modernism and the New York School,"[44] according to art historian Barbara Rose, who wrote that Marin was "a hero to the young artists of the emerging New York school such as Jackson Pollock and Willem de Kooning."[45] In addition to respect for another generation's art, there are stronger connections between Marin and two of the most renowned Abstract Expressionists – Pollock and Rothko. With Pollock, it is the immense energy immitted through the act of painting that makes its way into his pictures. With Rothko the bond to Marin can affect viewers even more overtly. Guy Eglington captured it in his 1924 article on Marin, even though the writing predates Rothko's era. When Eglington distilled Marin's importance to viewers, he wrote: "Consciously, or perhaps by instinct, he has always been mindful that a picture, in so far as it aspires to be more than a mere *tour de main*, is a house for the human spirit."[46]

For Duncan and Marjorie Phillips, works by their friend John Marin would serve as a house for the human spirit for themselves and visitors to their museum. Marin's originality, his "strong and bracing wind" as Duncan put it, would guide them.

Notes

[1] Duncan Phillips, *A Bulletin of The Phillips Collection*, Phillips Memorial Gallery, Washington, 1927.

[2] D. Phillips, "Trowbridge Memorial Lecture: The Artist Sees Differently," (Yale University, March 20, 1931), The Phillips Collection Archives, Washington, D.C., 12.

[3] D. Phillips, A Bulletin of The Phillips Collection, 1927.

[4] John Marin, *The Forum Exhibition of Modern American Painters* (New York: Anderson Galleries, 1916).

[5] Marin, "Letter to Stieglitz, Written in 1923," *Philadelphia Museum Bulletin*, XL (1945).

[6] Marsden Hartley, "As to John Marin and His Ideas," *John Marin: Watercolors, Oil Paintings, Etchings* (New York: Museum of Modern Art, 1936), 18.
[7] D. Phillips to Alfred Barr Jr., 15 January 1927, The Phillips Collection Archives, Washington, D.C.
[8] D. Phillips, "Original American Painting of Today," *Formes*, January 1932, 198.
[9] Edward Alden Jewell, "The Rise of John Marin," *New York Times*, October 23, 1933.
[10] Lewis Mumford, *Mumford on Modern Art in the 1930s*, ed. Robert Wojtowicz (Berkeley: University of California Press, 2007), 101.
[11] Ibid.
[12] Herbert J. Seligmann, *Alfred Stieglitz Talking* (New Haven: Yale University Press, 1966), 133.
[13] Thornton Wilder, *American Characteristics and Other Essays* (New York: Harper & Row, 1979), 239.
[14] Marin to Alfred Stieglitz, 14 September 1920, John Marin Family Papers, National Gallery of Art Library, Washington, D.C.
[15] Marin to Louis Kalonyme, 2 July 1945, John Marin Family Papers, National Gallery of Art Library, Washington, D.C.
[16] Marin to Duncan and Marjorie Phillips, 11 June 1945, John Marin Family Papers, National Gallery of Art Library, Washington, D.C.
[17] Alice Graeme, "Phillips Gallery to Show Work of Picasso, Marin," *Washington Post*, April 3, 1938.
[18] D. Phillips, "Picasso and Marin: An Exhibition April 10-May 1" (Washington, D.C.: The Phillips Gallery, 1938).
[19] Ibid.
[20] Marjorie Phillips, oral history interview by Paul Cummings for the Archives of American Art, 27 June 1974, Archives of American Art, Washington, D.C., 31.
[21] M. Phillips, *Duncan Phillips and His Collection* (New York: W.W. Norton, 1982), 101.
[22] Florence S. Berryman, "Noted Painter Here," *Washington Evening Star*, June 6, 1948.
[23] M. Phillips, *Duncan Phillips and His Collection*, 101.
[24] Marin to Herbert Seligmann, 8 January 1945, John Marin Family Papers, National Gallery of Art Library, Washington, D.C.
[25] Marin to Louis Kalonyme, 2 July 1945, John Marin Family Papers, National Gallery of Art Library, Washington, D.C.
[26] Ibid.
[27] M. Phillips to John Marin, 2 April 1938, John Marin Family Papers, National Gallery of Art Library, Washington, D.C.
[28] D. Phillips to John Marin, 6 January 1946, John Marin Family Papers, National Gallery of Art Library, Washington, D.C.
[29] D. Phillips to John Marin, 11 March 1947, John Marin Family Papers, National Gallery of Art Library, Washington, D.C.
[30] Marin to Duncan and Marjorie Phillips, 18 February 1937, John Marin Family Papers, National Gallery of Art Library, Washington, D.C.
[31] Marin to Duncan and Marjorie Phillips, 12 July 1948, John Marin Family Papers, National Gallery of Art Library, Washington, D.C.
[32] D. Phillips to John Marin, 6 January 1946, John Marin Family Papers, National Gallery of Art Library, Washington, D.C.

[33] Marin to Elizabeth S. Navas, Elizabeth S. Navas Papers, Archives of American Art, Washington, D.C.
[34] Beaumont Newhall, "On Painting: A Day with John Marin," *Art in America*, 49, no. 2 (1961): 55.
[35] Alfred H. Barr Jr., *What is Modern Painting?* (New York: Museum of Modern Art, 1943), 19.
[36] Phillips, "Introduction," *John Marin: Paintings, Water-Colours, Drawings and Etchings, 22 Sept. – 20 Oct.* (London: Arts Council Gallery, 1956).
[37] Ibid.
[38] Guy Eglington, "John Marin, Colorist and Painter of Sea Moods," *Arts & Decoration*, August 1924, 65.
[39] Phillips, "Introduction," 1956.
[40] Mumford, 101.
[41] Clement Greenberg, *Clement Greenberg – the Collected Essays and Criticism: Arrogant Purpose, 1945-1949*. Vol 2. 4 vols., ed. John O'Brian (Chicago: University of Chicago Press, 1986), 269.
[42] Ibid.
[43] D. Phillips, *A Bulletin of The Phillips Collection*, 1927.
[44] Barbara Rose, *John Marin: The 291 Years* (New York: Richard York Gallery, 1998), 34.
[45] Rose, 29.
[46] Eglington, 14.

Chapter 9

Jacob Lawrence: Despair, Hope, Relevance

Green, blue, orange, yellow, brown, and black.
Movement, always movement.
Not oil on canvas, but poster paint on panel.

Jacob Lawrence completed *The Migration Series* the year the United States entered World War II. Within months, Duncan and Marjorie Phillips bought half of the paintings in the sixty-panel series. A masterpiece of twentieth-century art, its relevance has increased – through its poignancy and its teachings.

Lawrence always intended for *The Migration Series* to be a vehicle for human learning. Education formed one building block for his own life; community provided another.

Harlem's renaissance had given way to the Depression by the time Lawrence's family moved there when he was thirteen. But the sense of community remained vibrant. "As a boy in Harlem I heard a lot of talk about black heroes. There were history clubs at which discussions about them took place, and you'd also hear it from street corner speakers," Lawrence told Grace Glueck of the *New York Times*. "I began to do paintings about them but found I couldn't pack everything into one picture. So I developed the idea of doing works in series."[1] Before beginning *The Migration Series* at age twenty-two, Lawrence had already completed three other multi-panel works, including a series on the life of Frederick Douglass and another about Harriet Tubman.

The Migration Series consists of board panels that measure 12 x 18 inches each. Through the art and accompanying captions, Lawrence tells the story of African Americans leaving their homes in southern states for opportunities in the North. It is a story of despair, hope, disappointment, and occasional triumph. The even-numbered panels were secured by MoMA, and the odd-numbered ones sold to the Phillips Memorial Gallery. Originally titled *Migration of the Negro*, the entire series made its D.C. debut in February 1942. Reviewing it, *Washington Post* art critic Ada Rainey wrote that Lawrence "has done a saga in paint that will provide thought for the student of sociology for years to come. Executed in tempera, these paintings are small in size, but big in content."[2] Prior to painting *The Migration Series,* Lawrence attended the American Artists School, known for encouraging its students to infuse social consciousness into their works.

More than Rainey could have imagined, the "saga in paint" has been a springboard to thought for adults and children of all races. A half-century after its creation, Lawrence's friend and fellow artist Lou Stovall wrote that he believed he knew why. Stovall, a painter and printmaker who collaborated with Lawrence on silkscreens many years after the creation of *The Migration Series,* wrote: "Jacob and I shared a common feeling that making art was a splendid way to teach tolerance and acceptance through the lessons of history."[3]

When Lawrence applied for a Julius Rosenwald Fellowship to work on *The Migration Series,* he envisioned that "the significance of a project such as this rests, I think, on its educational value. It is important as a part of the evolution of America."[4] On his application, Lawrence explained in convincing detail why he believed his idea was worthy of a grant: "I feel that my project would lay before the Negroes themselves a little of what part they have played in the History of the United States. In addition, the whole of America might learn some of the History of this particular minority group, of which they know very little."[5]

Philanthropist Julius Rosenwald, best known for building thousands of "Rosenwald Schools" for African American children, had been chairman of the board of Sears, Roebuck, and Company. From 1928 to 1948, the Rosenwald Fund awarded grants to African American artists, writers, scholars, and educators. In April 1940, Jacob Lawrence received a Rosenwald grant of $1,500, which was renewed twice. The money enabled him to rent his own studio on 125th Street, a main thoroughfare of Harlem. Various profiles on Lawrence point out that the studio, where he both lived and worked during the duration of painting *The Migration Series,* was in a run-down building with no heat or hot water. But Lawrence focused on the positive. When Elizabeth McCausland interviewed him for a piece in the November 1945 issue of *Magazine of Art,* he credited the fellowship with giving him "a chance to work, organizedly and uninterruptedly."[6]

Organization was paramount to Lawrence's method of working. When he painted *The Migration Series,* or any of his series, he would distribute all the blank panels across a room and apply one color at a time to each of them. He would paint all the blues, for instance, before moving on to the next color. Another Lawrence characteristic was to thoroughly research his topic prior to the preliminary drawings that preceded his paintings. In future years, he would become a college professor, but even as a young man, he valued history, and the truth it provided. In the Plan of Work for his first Rosenwald grant, Lawrence estimated he would need six months to conduct research for *The Migration*

Series. Most of it, he wrote, "would be carried out at the Negro History division of the Schomburg Library, West 135th Street in New York City."[7] The hours he spent there were rewarding ones. Years later, in an oral history interview, Lawrence said the Schomburg Library "had become a favorite place of mine to go and work and do research."[8]

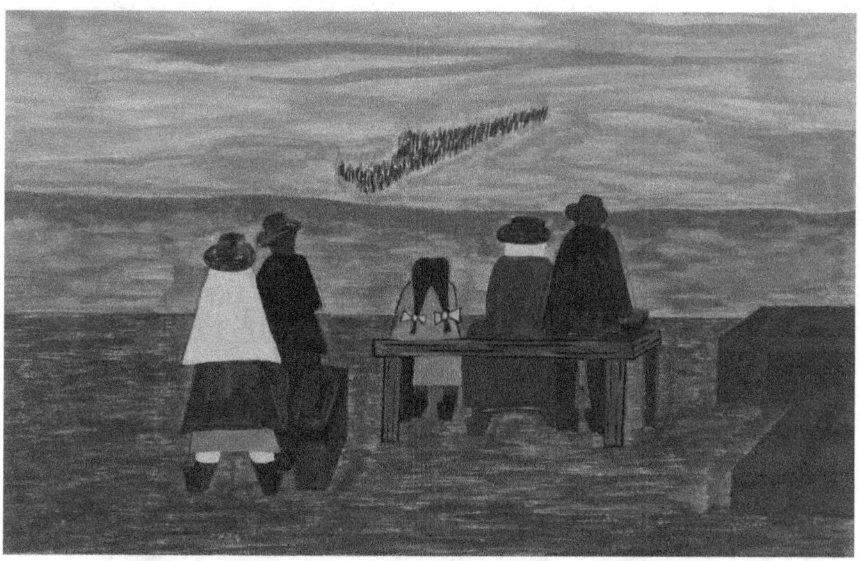

Image 9. 1. Jacob Lawrence, *The Migration Series, Panel no. 21: Families arrived at the station very early. They did not wish to miss their trains north.*, between 1940 and 1941, Casein tempera on hardboard 12 x 18 in.; 30.48 x 45.72 cm. The Phillips Collection: Acquired 1942; © 2016 The Jacob and Gwendolyn Knight Lawrence Foundation, Seattle / Artists Rights Society (ARS), New York. Paintings, 1162, American.

On his first Rosenwald application, Lawrence wrote that his intent was to paint the Great Migration by addressing: the causes of the migration; what stimulated it; how it spread; efforts to stop it; public opinion at the time of the migration, which he considered mainly the World War I years; and its effects on the South and the North. Lawrence saw the causes of the migration as: crop damage from the cotton boll weevil, especially in the summers of 1915 and 1916; low wages paid to African Americans in the South; the treatment of African Americans in the southern courts; and "the prevalence of mob violence."[9] He felt that African Americans were rallied to move North by editorials, speeches, and word-of-mouth. Through formal and informal channels of communication, they heard about higher wages, educational opportunities, and better housing conditions. His research showed that migration out of the South was heaviest in Texas, Louisiana, Mississippi, Alabama, Georgia, and Florida. Additionally, he wrote on his grant application that he intended to portray the migration's effects on African Americans "mentally, economically, and socially."[10]

Harlem and Beyond

Jacob Lawrence did not grow up in the South, but his parents had been part of the exodus. They met in New Jersey, where his father was a cook in Atlantic City and later on the railroad. His mother, a domestic worker, struggled to care for Jacob and his little brother and sister after the couple split. The children were in foster care in Philadelphia for three years before Rosa Lee Lawrence brought her son Jacob and his siblings to live with her in Harlem. She promptly enrolled him in classes at Utopia Children's House, where one of his teachers was muralist Charles Alston.

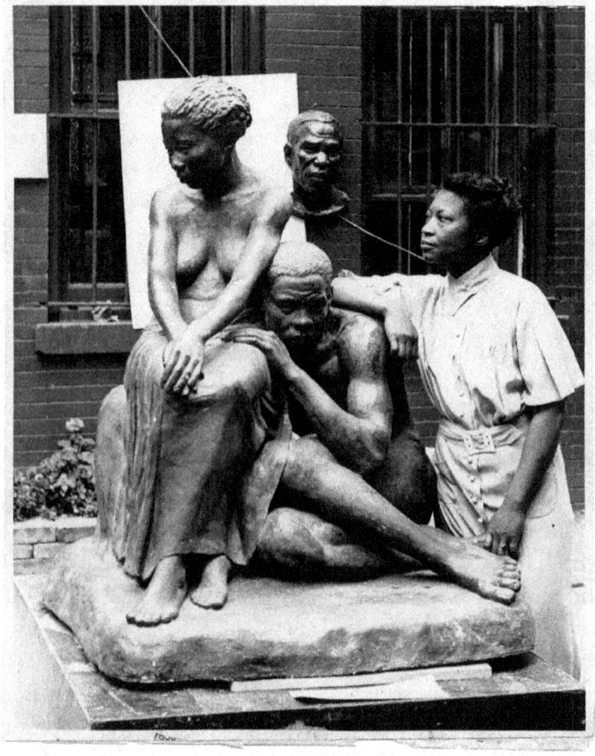

Image 9. 2. Augusta Savage with her sculpture *Realization,* ca. 1938.
Savage was one of Lawrence's teachers. She befriended him and his wife, artist Gwendolyn Knight, when the young couple lived in Harlem. Photo by Andrew Herman, Federal Art Project, Photographic Division collection, ca. 1920-1965. Archives of American Art, Smithsonian Institution.

Although Lawrence dropped out of high school at sixteen, the future college professor took additional classes from Alston at the Harlem Arts Workshop and from sculptor Augusta Savage, the first director of the Harlem Community Arts Center. Along the way, he found jobs at a laundry and a printing plant, and for a time, was employed by the Civilian Conservation Corps building a dam in upstate New York. But Savage wanted him working as a professional artist and her involvement helped him secure employment through the Federal Arts Project (FAP), part of the Works Progress Administration (WPA).

It was in one of Savage's classes that Lawrence met his future wife, painter Gwendolyn Knight. A fine arts student at Howard University from 1931 to 1933, she was unable to finish her degree due to financial hardship, a common situation during the Great Depression. After leaving Howard, Knight worked as Alston's assistant. Jacob shared with more than one reporter that Gwen topped the list of artists whose work he respected. As art critic Holland Cotter put it, he relied on her "evaluating eye"[11] through the fifty-nine years of their marriage.

During Lawrence's life – he died in 2000 at age eighty-two – he gave numerous interviews to journalists and scholars. Questions about who influenced his art were invariably asked. In a 1945 interview, Lawrence began his answer by saying "Perhaps I can explain best by telling whom I like," then named José Clemente Orozco, Honoré Daumier, and Francisco Goya. "They're forceful. Simple. Human. In your own work, the human subject is the most important thing. Then I like Arthur Dove."[12] More than twenty years later, in 1968, Lawrence said that his influences included German Expressionist Kathe Kollwitz and "many of the Chinese artists who are doing big woodblocks."[13] He mentioned Orozco again when he referred to "the Mexican School as the big school then [the 1930s] in the social consciousness school of painting" and included Diego Rivera and David Alfaro Siqueiros as part of that art movement.[14] Then in 1992, Lawrence opened up to Dr. Henry Louis Gates Jr. in a special interview commissioned by The Phillips Collection. Gates is the Harvard professor who produces and hosts the PBS series *Finding Your Roots.* Lawrence told Gates how he had been asked in the past if anyone in his family was artistically inclined, and confessed he was ashamed that in those interviews he always replied "no." It was only in retrospect, Lawrence told Gates, that he realized his mother and her friends were artistic in their everyday lives. "We lived in a deep Depression, not only my mother but the poor people in general. In order to add something to their lives, they decorated their tenements and their homes in all these colors."[15] He added that he thought the bonhomie in the neighborhood of his youth also affected his art. "You'd walk through Harlem and go to the Apollo Theater and the jokes that were being told and the pathos: People would laugh, but it was comedy on a very profound, deep level, philosophical level."[16]

Harlem luminaries took the young Lawrence under their wings. There was Alain Locke, a philosopher and Howard University professor, who was known by many as the dean of the Harlem Renaissance. Locke was pivotal to the young painter's success by providing a crucial connection to Duncan and Marjorie Phillips's purchase of half of *The Migration Series.* In Lawrence's interviews, he talked about two other prominent Harlem citizens who believed in him in his lean years. Lawrence said that one was his teacher Savage and the other was poet Claude McKay. Savage did more than assist Lawrence obtain a WPA paycheck. She promulgated artistic sensibilities heightened by her own Julius Rosenwald Fellowship in Paris. Augusta Savage showed her work at the Grand Palais there and trained with sculptor Charles Despiau – whose link to Lawrence manifests itself in the paring down of detail for emotional effect. Savage's fame as an artist would increase with a commission to create a sculpture for the 1939 World's Fair. As for McKay, he had long been a celebrated poet by the time he and Lawrence became friends. McKay "took a great deal of interest in my work and this was very meaningful because he was a much older man," Lawrence said. He explained that McKay influenced his painting, even though it was through the written word. "The inspiration is not always direct," Lawrence said when he spoke of his literary mentor from 125th Street.[17] He talked about a poem McKay wrote on marrying his past life in his native Jamaica with his new life in Harlem. "He mixes the experience of riding the subway and smelling the mangoes," Lawrence said.[18] Likely, Lawrence was remembering two of McKay's poems, "Subway Wind" and "The Tropics in New York." In reading them both, it is easy to understand how the established poet inspired the young visual artist.

In "Subway Wind" McKay paints a picture with words.

Subway Wind by Claude McKay

Far down, down through the city's great gaunt gut
The gray train rushing bears the weary wind;
In the packed cars the fans the crowds' breath cut,
Leaving the sick and heavy air behind.
And pale-cheeked children seek the upper door
To give their summer jackets to the breeze;
Their laugh is swallowed in the deafening roar
Of captive wind that moans for fields and seas.
Seas cooling warm where native schooners drift
Through sleepy waters, while gulls wheel and sweep,
Waiting for windy waves the keels to lift
Lightly among the island of the deep;
Islands of lofty palm trees blooming white
That led their perfume to the tropic sea,

Where fields lie idle in the dew-drenched night,
And the Trades float above them fresh and free. (1921)

With "The Tropics in New York," the rhythm in the poem bears a remarkable likeness to that in Lawrence's *Migration Series.*

The Tropics in New York by Claude McKay

Bananas ripe and green, and ginger-root,
Cocoa in pods and alligator pears,
And tangerine and mangoes and grape fruit,
Fit for the highest prize at parish fairs.

Set in the window, bringing memories
Of fruit-trees laden by low-singing rills,
And dewy dawns, and mystical skies
In benediction over nun-like hills.

My eyes grew dim, and I could no more gaze;
A wave of longing through my body swept,
And hungry for the old, familiar ways,
I turned aside and bowed my head and wept. (1920)

New York City beyond Harlem also affected the art of Jacob Armstead Lawrence. Several years before his interview with Gates, Lawrence agreed to speak with Avis Berman for her *ARTNews* piece "Jacob Lawrence and the Making of Americans." He told Berman that from the time he was a teenager, he would visit the Metropolitan Museum of Art and study what he considered "the magic" of the Italian masters. "I was especially fascinated by the works from the Early Renaissance," Lawrence said. "Although I didn't realize it at the time, I was responding to the architectonic structure, the economy of color, the flatness of the picture plane and, above all, the strong linear element."[19]

Lawrence would go on, of course, to create his own magic.

One art critic wrote of *The Migration Series,* "The drawn line skips, darts, pounces. … The picture sequences are the work of a poet, a man of fire and daring."[20] Another described Lawrence's art in general as a "Cubist-inflected style that held abstraction and representation in perfect balance."[21] While still in his twenties, Lawrence proclaimed: "My work is abstract in the sense of having been designed and composed, but it is not abstract in the sense of having no human content. An abstract style is simply your way of speaking. As far as you yourself are concerned, you want to communicate. I want the idea to strike right away."[22]

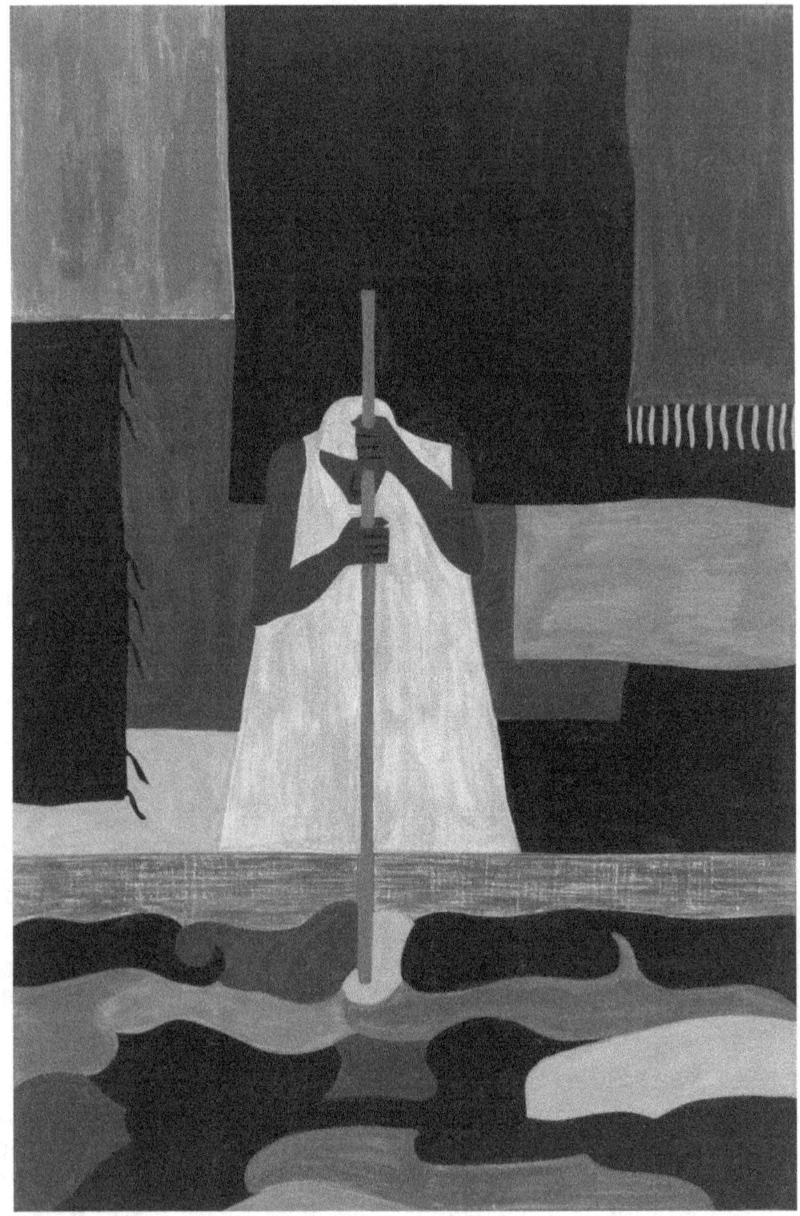

Image 9. 3. Jacob Lawrence, *The Migration Series, Panel no. 57: The female workers were the last to arrive north.*, between 1940 and 1941, Casein tempera on hardboard 18 x 12 in.; 45.72 x 30.48 cm. The Phillips Collection: Acquired 1942; © 2016 The Jacob and Gwendolyn Knight Lawrence Foundation, Seattle / Artists Rights Society (ARS), New York. Paintings, 1180, American.

Strike he did.

The sounds of bearing down can almost be heard as the woman hunches over a long pole. Her form, in a plain white dress and headscarf, occupies the bulk of Panel 57 of *The Migration Series*. When Lawrence first wrote the caption, in 1941, it read: *The female worker was also one of the last groups to leave the South*. In 1993, Lawrence rewrote many of the captions. Most of the alterations were minor. Notably, for Panel 57, he reversed his emphasis on the geographical regions, and he used the plural "workers" rather than the singular "worker." After Lawrence's changes, it reads: *The female workers were the last to arrive north*. In the painting, a viewer cannot be sure what kind of labor the woman is performing. The pole she grasps could represent a mop, or it could be a tool in a factory. While Lawrence leaves her exact job open to viewer interpretation, there is no ambiguity about the woman's physical pain. Her shoulders hurt. Her back aches.

For Panel 21, Lawrence changed only a couple of words, but his rewrite uses the verb "wish," a significant choice for people moving to what they hope is a better life. His 1941 caption read: *Families arrived at the station very early in order not to miss their train North*. His 1993 version reads: *Families arrived at the station very early. They did not wish to miss their trains north*. In the foreground of Panel 21, four adults and one child wait. Their suitcases are at the ready. Standing and seated, the figures are shown only from the back, yet Lawrence reveals much more. He shows onlookers of the painting what the five figures see. He does not settle for what they literally see, but what they imagine for themselves. In front of the train station, in front of the five figures, far into the distance, Lawrence has used his brushstrokes to paint a formation of people who traveled ahead of the current migrants. The sky over his horizon line is a cheerful blue but contains streaks of gray.

"Superbly Shown in Washington"

When Lou Stovall reminisced about his friend Jacob Lawrence, Stovall stated that the directors of The Phillips Collection and MoMA had a special place "in both our hearts" because of bringing *The Migration Series* to their permanent collections so early in Lawrence's career.[23] In Lawrence's interview with Henry Louis Gates Jr. he made a comment about the sale of *The Migration Series* being divided between the two art institutions and Gates pressed him to say more about his feelings on the series not being kept whole. Lawrence explained: "When I say broken up, I think we're inclined to think of selling one here, one there ... but I don't consider it broken, no."[24] Lawrence emphasized that he considered The Phillips Collection and MoMA to be "two very prestigious places."[25] Stovall concurred when he wrote that Washington D.C.'s Duncan Phillips and New York City's Alfred Barr recognized Lawrence's genius. "They believed, as I believe, that there is genius in every community," Stovall wrote. "I revere the courage of these two men to exhibit the paintings of a youth from Harlem, an unknown Black American, a prodigy."[26]

Past and present curators at the Phillips have researched the circumstances of the split sale. The sequence of events began when Alain Locke published his book *The Negro in Art* in 1940. The following year, Edith Halpert, owner of The Downtown Gallery, was planning an art exhibition based on Dr. Locke's book. It would include works by several African American artists, Horace Pippin among them. Elizabeth Hutton Turner, former senior curator at the Phillips, wrote that Locke brought Lawrence's *Migration Series* panels to the Harlem Community Center to show them to Halpert. Dr. Locke's gesture of promoting Lawrence's work succeeded. Not only did Halpert decide to include the panels in her exhibit, but she made them known to the editors of *Fortune* magazine, which published twenty-six of the sixty in their November 1941 issue.[27] The national exposure for Lawrence was perfectly timed to reap overall publicity for Halpert's exhibit, which she titled "American Negro Art." According to Phillips senior curator Elsa Smithgall, Duncan Phillips wrote to Halpert about visiting her gallery while the show was still up.[28] In her essay "One Series, Two Places," Smithgall wrote that it "seems most likely that it was Halpert who devised the idea of dividing the series into two groups of thirty as a sensible alternative to selling off the panels individually."[29] Smithgall added that "by splitting the series between even-and-odd numbered panels rather than dividing down the middle, Barr and Phillips had arrived at a solution that allowed each museum to maintain the integrity of the south-to-north progression of the narrative."[30]

Halpert became Lawrence's art dealer. "I was extremely fortunate that Edith Halpert invited me to join her," Lawrence told Avis Berman. "I didn't realize she had one of the top galleries in the country with Stuart Davis, Charles Sheeler, and Ben Shahn. They were artists I admired, and I later got to know them through the gallery."[31] Halpert sent a letter to Lawrence about the finalization of Phillips's purchase of half of the *Migration Series*; the bill of sale is dated February 21, 1942. She informed Lawrence that all sixty works were still on exhibition at the Phillips Gallery "and will be circuited by the Modern Museum as a unit in the near future."[32] Halpert added that she had heard from Locke about how the series was being received during its debut at the Phillips. "Dr. Locke reported that they are being superbly shown in Washington," Halpert wrote to her new client, "and that there is a great deal of interest in the collection."[33]

American involvement in World War II was well underway when Edith Halpert, Alfred Barr, and Duncan Phillips had agreed that the entire series would travel to a number of museums across the country before settling in New York and the District of Columbia. Phillips was justifiably proud of his part in sharing the works with Americans who might not have the luxury of viewing the series at one or both of its permanent East Coast homes. He made a point of highlighting *The Migration Series* tour when writing about American paintings of the Phillips

Memorial Gallery in the spring of 1944. "It should be noted," he wrote, "that our Jacob Lawrence panels are on a nation-wide circuit."[34]

No Protection from Racism

Unfortunately, systemic racism clouded Lawrence's life despite earning national acclaim for his art. While his *Migration Series* was on tour, Lawrence had been drafted into the U.S. Coast Guard. He was among 5,000 African Americans forced into one of three Coast Guard designations during World War II: mess attendants, who served meals to the crew; officer's stewards, who provided what the Coast Guard referred to as domestic services for officers; and steward's mates, who assisted with cleaning, stocking, and serving meals to officers. Lawrence was a steward's mate for nearly a year of his twenty-six months in the Coast Guard. When the service began to integrate, Lawrence was assigned as the ship's artist. However, the job change came with two demotions in rank. According to the Coast Guard Historian's Office, it was established policy that service members who switched occupations drop in rank; the theory being that individuals cannot contribute as much to the organization when they are learning anew. It seems no attempt was made by Lawrence's chain of command to request a waiver for the renowned artist to keep the rank he had earned cleaning and serving meals to officers.

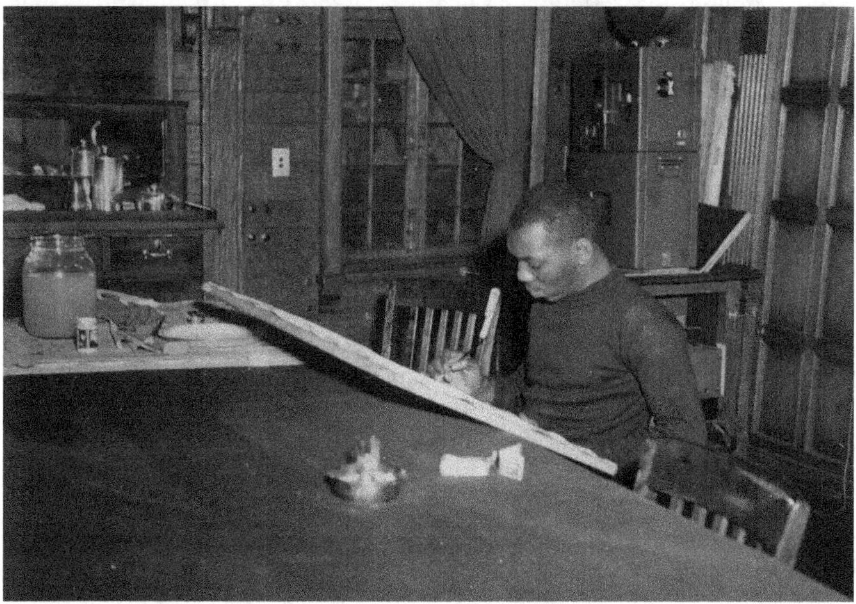

Image 9. 4. Jacob Lawrence aboard the USS *Sea Cloud* during World War II. Photograph from the Joseph C. Jenkins scrapbook, U.S. Coast Guard Heritage Asset Collection.

Long-standing Relationship with The Phillips Collection

Jacob Lawrence and Gwendolyn Knight had a long-standing relationship with the Phillips. Although immersed in their respective painting in the decades after World War II, they remained engaged with the museum and returned numerous times. In 1972, Marjorie Phillips accompanied them around the collection. After that visit, Jacob sent Marjorie a letter on behalf of himself and Gwen. He wrote: "Having your comments on the various works was, for us, most stimulating and rewarding. It was an experience that we shall always remember. I am honored to have thirty works of the Migration series a part of such a great Collection. We also enjoyed seeing your work … and hope your painting is progressing to your satisfaction."[35] Marjorie wrote him back two days later with news that MoMA had agreed to lend their thirty *Migration Series* panels that autumn, "for all of Washington to see the whole series together."[36] (The two museums have reunited the series for exhibitions in Washington, D.C., New York City, and sometimes, other locations, approximately every ten years.) In her letter to Lawrence, Marjorie also wrote that she "thoroughly enjoyed going around the gallery with you and your wife. It is always a great joy to see paintings with such knowledgeable, sensitive people."[37]

During his many years of involvement with The Phillips Collection, Lawrence taught art to college-level students. His affiliations as an educator include: North Carolina's Black Mountain College; New York City's Art Students League, Pratt Institute, and New School for Social Research; and his ultimate academic home, the University of Washington in Seattle. In 1970, he was invited to teach at the University of Washington on a visiting professorship and was made a full professor in 1971. He taught there until 1985, when he became professor emeritus.

It was during his University of Washington tenure that Suzanne Wright, for many years the director of education and community engagement at the Phillips, witnessed Lawrence interacting with students at a Washington, D.C. elementary school. Coordinating with Lawrence in advance, Phillips Collection staff had arranged with teachers for the students' artwork to be displayed around the school's cafeteria. One of the things that impressed Wright about Lawrence was how he valued children's perception. Recalling the school visit, Wright said: "He didn't speak down to them, he spoke to them about their art as artwork."[38] Before talking about the art on the walls, Lawrence told the schoolchildren that their very gathering had become a work of art. As the children settled in to listen to Jacob Lawrence, he looked over the assembly and spoke of how they formed painterly patterns. "He's at the front of the cafeteria expressing his joy and love of color and shape," Wright said.[39] The man who had himself become a Harlem luminary was continuing to educate and to contribute to community well-being. The Phillips Collection benefits still from his talent and his wisdom.

Green, blue, orange, yellow, brown, and black.

Movement, always movement.

Notes

1 Grace Glueck, "Sharing Success Pleases Jacob Lawrence," *New York Times*, June 3, 1974.
2 Ada Rainey, "Phillips Gallery Shows Jacob Lawrence Works," *Washington Post*, February 22, 1942.
3 Lou Stovall, *Working with Jacob Lawrence*, essay written for The Phillips Collection, The Phillips Collection Archives, Washington, D.C., undated.
4 Jacob Lawrence, in the Plan of Work for a Julius Rosenwald Fellowship application, 1940.
5 Ibid.
6 Elizabeth McCausland, "Jacob Lawrence," *Magazine of Art*, November 1945, 253.
7 Lawrence, Plan of Work for Rosenwald Fellowship.
8 Lawrence, interview by Carroll Greene, 1968, Archives of American Art, Washington, D.C., 35.
9 Ibid.
10 Ibid.
11 Holland Cotter, "Jacob Lawrence is Dead at 82: Vivid Painter Who Chronicled Odyssey of Black Americans," *New York Times*, June 10, 2000.
12 McCausland, 254.
13 Lawrence, interview by Carroll Greene, 42.
14 Ibid.
15 Lawrence, interview by Henry Louis Gates Jr., 1992, The Phillips Collection Archives, Washington, D.C., 11.
16 Ibid., 10.
17 Ibid., 11.
18 Ibid.
19 Avis Berman, "Jacob Lawrence and the Making of Americans," *ARTNews*, February 1984, 83.
20 John Russell, "The Epic of a People Writ Large on Canvas," *New York Times*, October 11, 1987.
21 Roberta Smith, "The Migration from the South in 60 Images," *New York Times*, January 13, 1995.
22 McCausland, 251.
23 Stovall, *The Art of Silkscreen Printmaking* (Washington, D.C.: Howard University Gallery of Art, 2001), 33.
24 Lawrence, interview by Henry Louis Gates Jr., 24.
25 Ibid.
26 Stovall, *The Art of Silkscreen Printmaking*, 33.
27 Elizabeth Hutton Turner, "Introduction," *Jacob Lawrence: The Migration Series* (Rappahannock Press, 1993), 14.

[28] Elsa Smithgall, "One Series, Two Places," *Jacob Lawrence: The Migration Series* by Leah Dickerman and Elsa Smithgall (The Museum of Modern Art and The Phillips Collection, 2015), 41.
[29] Ibid.
[30] Ibid., 42.
[31] Berman, 84.
[32] Edith Gregor Halpert to Jacob Lawrence, 12 March 1942, Downtown Gallery records, Archives of American Art, Washington, D.C.
[33] Ibid.
[34] Duncan Phillips, "Foreword," *The American Paintings of The Phillips Collection: April 9 to May 30 1944,* The Phillips Collection Archives, Washington, D.C.
[35] Jacob Lawrence to Marjorie Phillips, 21 August 1972, The Phillips Collection Archives, Washington, D.C.
[36] Marjorie Phillips to Jacob Lawrence, 23 August 1972, The Phillips Collection Archives, Washington, D.C.
[37] Ibid.
[38] Suzanne Wright, phone interview with author, May 2020.
[39] Ibid.

Chapter 10

Mark Rothko: A Catalyst for Introspection

Duncan Phillips was winding down four decades of collecting when he first saw the color-saturated canvases of Mark Rothko. Phillips was so enthralled with Rothko's art that in 1960, he and Marjorie Phillips built a special room at The Phillips Collection for three, and subsequently four, of Rothko's signature-style stacked rectangle paintings. It had long been Rothko's dream to have his paintings shown apart from works by other artists. To Duncan, the wall-size pictures in the Rothko Room would serve as a catalyst for viewer introspection. He was confident that some visitors would be up to the challenge.

Simpatico in their respect for viewers of art, Duncan Phillips and Mark Rothko each wrote and spoke about believing that viewers should experience paintings as individuals, taking from a work of art what they will. To boost a viewer's thoughtful pursuit of art, the two men independently put deep consideration into how works of art should be displayed. Related to their shared positions regarding the viewer, Rothko embraced what he saw as the dual responsibilities of an artist: "The function of art is to express," he wrote, "and to move."[1]

Marjorie Phillips wrote that she and Duncan regarded Rothko as "one of the greatest contemporary artists" and that they "felt him to have a deeply emotional and intellectual approach."[2] The couple was proud to present Rothko's paintings in a dedicated space and were unmoved by any whisperings of artist vanity. Their employee Arthur Hall Smith said he "could see a reason" for Rothko's desire for the solitary showing of his works "that is not ego." Smith, an abstract artist who interacted with Rothko during the early days of the Rothko Room and who witnessed innumerable visitor encounters with the paintings, said that they "demand a certain concentration."[3]

Part of what makes Mark Rothko so compelling as an artist is what he does not give the viewer in his paintings. He does not offer the lush landscapes of a Frederic Edwin Church or the rooftop creatures of a Marc Chagall or even the pulsating drips of a Jackson Pollock. What Rothko does provide is light reminiscent of the peerless Johannes Vermeer, and color that takes its cue from

Pierre Bonnard and Henri Matisse. Through his sublime use of color and light Rothko pulls the viewer in.

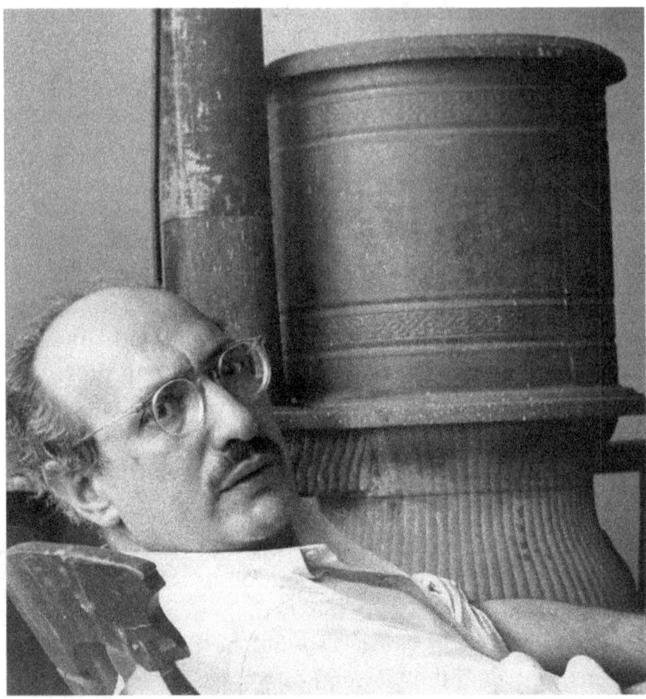

Image 10. 1. Henry Elkan. *Mark Rothko*, 1954. Rudi Blesh papers, circa 1900-1983. Archives of American Art, Smithsonian Institution.

Marcus Rothkowitz was born in 1903 in the section of the Russian Empire now known as Latvia and had been pushed into Talmudic studies as a boy. He was ten years old when his family immigrated to the United States, then journeyed from New York to Portland, Oregon, where relatives had settled. Artist Sean Scully imagined Rothko as "a small boy on the train, speaking no English, traveling across the great expanse of America."[4] As a young man, Rothko received a scholarship to Yale but only stayed for two years, moving on to study painting with Modernist Max Weber at the Art Students League of New York. Weber taught his students not to shy away from emotions and spiritualism in their art, and Rothko embraced the advice.

Another artist of influence in Rothko's life was Milton Avery, whose work Duncan Phillips collected with enough depth to be considered a unit at The Phillips Collection. One of the museum's most prominent works by Avery is *Girl Writing*, a 1941 oil-on-canvas of his daughter March on a wooden seat at an almost floating desk. One of her elbows is pressed onto the desk's slanted surface, anchoring March to the task before her. Avery chose not to paint his child's facial features. Instead, he reveals her concentration through the pressure of the elbow; bow of her head; angle of the writing instrument; and the winding of her legs, crossed first at the knees and again at the ankles. The painting is softly abstract. Were it a work of literature, it would be called magical realism. Anyone looking for a visual connection between Avery and Rothko can see it in the red socks on March's shoe-free feet.

Rothko spoke of Avery as possessing "an inner power in which gentleness and silence proved more audible and poignant" than artists who relied on "a show of power."[5] Through the older Avery, Rothko met many of his own contemporaries, some who – along with Rothko would be grouped together by various art critics as the New York School, the Abstract Expressionists, or the Irascibles. There were those among them, such as Pollock and Willem de Kooning who did indeed rely on a "show of power." Although Rothko would make New York City his home, he was not one of the hard-charging Cedar Tavern regulars like action painters Pollock or de Kooning. The more introverted Rothko avoided Pollock's notoriety, but respected his art. Betty Parsons, who served as an art dealer for both Rothko and Pollock, said in an oral history interview that she knew Rothko admired Pollock very much.[6] Rothko himself wrote of Pollock's "stature as a great artist" in a condolence letter to Lee Krasner, Pollock's widow, following Pollock's death in an automobile crash. When he wrote to Krasner, Rothko lamented that he never told Jackson how he felt. "Whatever it may have meant to him, it would have meant a lot to me to say so, especially now that I realize I can never do it."[7]

Duncan and Marjorie Phillips purchased a single work by Pollock, but it was not one of the drip paintings for which he became renowned. Rather, Duncan chose the relatively modest-sized *Collage and Oil*, created circa 1951 and acquired after Pollock's death. *Life* magazine had asked in 1949 if Jackson Pollock were the greatest living painter in the United States, but the hoopla that the question generated did not sway Phillips. The contemplative works of Rothko spoke to Phillips in more compelling ways – as an individual human being spending time absorbing a particular work, and as a collector driven to affect the lives of visitors to his and Marjorie's museum.

Rothko was also driven with a concern for how his work affected viewers. "I want pure response in terms of human need," he said to art historian William Seitz during an interview. In his notes, Seitz typed the line "insists that I write this down as a direct quote" followed by these words from Rothko: "One does not paint for design students or historians but for human beings, and the reaction in human terms is the only thing that is really satisfactory to the artist."[8] In a famous letter to the *New York Times*, Rothko and his fellow New York School artist Adolph Gottlieb advocated that "explanation must come out of a consummated experience between picture and onlooker."[9] "A painting doesn't need anybody to explain what it is about," Rothko later said. "If it is any good, it speaks for itself."[10] Rothko took the concept further when he addressed his expectations for works of art after making them available for viewing. "The instant one is completed, [the creator] is an outsider," he wrote. "The picture must be for him, as for anyone experiencing it later, a revelation, an unexpected and unprecedented resolution of an eternally familiar need."[11] Like Rothko, Duncan Phillips described viewer interaction with art with an Existentialist bent. In a 1963 unpublished essay specifically on seeing works by Rothko, Phillips proffered that "what we recall are not memories but states of mind weighted with relationships, disturbed or resolved."[12] A year later, in his second unpublished essay about looking at Rothko's paintings, Phillips wrote: "our minds are challenged by the relativities."[13] Marjorie Phillips chose some of Duncan's writing about Rothko's works for her memoir about her husband: "They not only pervade our consciousness but inspire contemplation. ... There is never a conflict, not even a dissonance, rather a duality, some evanescent difference, some sudden awareness of the complexity of existence."[14] Other art critics were attuned to the kind of metaphysical thoughts Phillips expressed for Rothko's works. In a 1998 *New Yorker* article, Calvin Tomkins advised his readers on encountering work by Rothko: "Rather than an object on the wall, each of his mature paintings is a place to be."[15] Virgil Barker, who served on the editorial boards of several influential art periodicals, preceded Tomkins's advice by forty years. In a book based upon humanities lectures he gave in 1958, Barker wrote: "Before a Rothko painting ... the pronouncing word is: to be."[16] Leslie Judd Portner, who wrote the "Art in Washington" column for the *Washington Post*, elaborated on internalizing viewing experiences with Rothko paintings. Before the Rothko Room was built, The Phillips Collection featured some of his works in a 1957 exhibition and Portner covered the event. "He does not consider himself a colorist," she wrote of Rothko, "because he uses color only as a means of arriving at luminosity." She was struck nonetheless by "color seeming to pulsate," concluding that Rothko's paintings "are simply and purely studies in light whose force and power is meant to be felt rather than analyzed."[17]

Minimal Guidance Aids Personal Reflection

When he debuted the Rothko Room three years after Portner's newspaper review, Duncan Phillips was continuing his long pursuit of providing viewers optimal conditions for personal reflection. One of those contributing conditions for Phillips was to not dictate meaning to viewers. It was a mindset that Rothko shared. Today at The Phillips Collection, revealing only minimal information about the four works in the Rothko Room remains a point of pride. Very simply, an incoming visitor can pause at the entryway to the room for the titles and dates of when the pictures were painted and when they were purchased. *Green and Maroon,* painted in 1953, was the first Rothko acquired by Phillips; it came to the museum in 1957. Two more, *Green and Tangerine on Red,* painted in 1956, and *Orange and Red on Red,* painted in 1957, arrived in 1960. The final Rothko to be installed in the Rothko Room, *Ochre and Red on Red,* painted in 1954, came into the Phillipses' possession in 1964. Phillips and Rothko made a special arrangement for the last painting. "In a very generous moment, you asked me whether I would like to receive the picture and enjoy it right away," Duncan Phillips wrote to Rothko in a letter about an installment plan for the purchase of *Ochre and Red on Red.* "Because of my advanced age that is really an inducement." Phillips wrote the letter, dated February 17, 1964, two years before his death at age seventy-nine. Closing the letter on behalf of Marjorie and himself, Duncan emphasized to Rothko the camaraderie they felt from the time the three of them had spent together. "I cannot tell you how much we enjoyed your visit and our talks,"[18] Phillips wrote. Kate Rothko Prizel, Rothko's daughter, recalled that her father first met Duncan Phillips in the mid-1950s and "recognized him as an astute and sensitive collector."[19] Prizel reflected on the role the two men played in one another's lives in a letter to the editor coinciding with the re-creation of the original Rothko Room in the Sant Building, a 2006 addition to The Phillips Collection. In her letter to the *Washington Post,* she wrote that the room at the Phillips was "particularly loved" by her father, who "favored an intimate setting and a relatively small space in which the viewer would feel surrounded by the pictures."[20]

Christopher Rothko was only six years old when his father committed suicide; his sister Kate was nineteen at the time of the artist's death. Christopher, who became a clinical psychologist, has spent a significant portion of his adult life studying his father's art and philosophies. During opening remarks for a panel discussion at the Tate Modern in London, he said he did not think his father's paintings were about self-expression. Rather, "he always wanted a conversation with his audience." He wanted us to look at his paintings, Christopher Rothko said, "because he was hoping to engage the inner part of ourselves."[21] In his book *Mark Rothko: From the Inside Out,* Christopher wrote that his father "wanted an encounter that arose from the ether and perhaps finished there as well; a meeting colored only by what artist and viewer brought to the painting."[22] Or, as Phillips put it: "Rothko denies a desire to enchant, he only invites reflection."[23]

Rothko indicated it does not matter if viewers replicate his sensibilities when experiencing his art. In fact, he said he did not always know what he himself meant by a work of his own making. In explaining to William Seitz that he was not interested in color but rather "a new kind of unity," Rothko admitted to the future MoMA curator that "when the unity is successful, you can't tell how achieved – because I do not know myself."[24] After the revealing 1952 interview,

Seitz visited Rothko's studio and observed that Rothko's paintings do not tell the viewer what to think or how to react. "As one looks, the sense of sameness and difference is constantly being altered," Seitz wrote in his notes, adding, "the variability is within the spectator."[25] Truly, Rothko and Phillips marched to the same beat of a different drummer.

Image 10. 2. Mark Rothko, *Green and Maroon*, 1953, Oil on canvas 91 1/8 x 54 7/8 in.; 231.4575 x 139.3825 cm. The Phillips Collection: Acquired 1957; © 1998 Kate Rothko Prizel & Christopher Rothko/Artists Rights Society (ARS), New York. Paintings, 1664, American.

In 1954, Rothko again communicated that viewers need not replicate his sensibilities when he was corresponding with Katharine Kuh of the Art Institute of Chicago about his upcoming one-man show there. She suggested publishing their correspondence about the exhibit, which she was organizing, and making it available to visitors. He balked at the idea of sharing with viewers the insight he had provided Kuh for her work as curator of his exhibit. "While on the surface this may seem an obliging and helpful thing to do, the real result is the paralysis of the mind and the imagination," Rothko wrote to Kuh. Then, he went further still in discussing his respect for the viewer. In the same letter, Rothko wrote that if he must place his trust somewhere, he would "invest it in the psyche of sensitive observers ... I would have no apprehensions about the use they would make of these pictures for the needs of their own spirits."[26]

The frankness on Rothko's part of stating he did not always know what he meant by his own works of art did not translate to washing his hands of a painting when it left his studio. On the contrary, few artists have been so open about their desire for a deep involvement in how their work is presented to the public. When he wrote to Kuh about their Chicago collaboration, Rothko discussed how to hang the works. Each painting mounted should "give the observer a key to the ideal relationship between himself and the rest of the pictures,"[27] he told Kuh. Rothko included his modus operandi for displaying a group of his paintings: "I hang the pictures low rather than high, particularly in the case of the largest ones, and often as close to the floor as is feasible for that is the way they are painted."[28] It is somehow comforting to enter the Rothko Room at The Phillips Collection and stand in approximation to where Rothko would have stood in his studio when he created the four canvases. *Ochre and Red on Red*, for instance, offers a powerful connection to the artist partly because of how it is presented in the room. The painting has the same effect as sunshine. No clouds filter the rays. It is the sun coming at the audience as in a science fiction film.

A Paradox

Sally Avery, Milton Avery's wife, said Rothko would chide her husband for not being selective enough about where he let his paintings be hung. As Sally told it, when Milton would reply that he was not interested once he had painted them, "Rothko thought that was wrong."[29] In discussing Rothko's concerns about the installation of his works, Sally Avery offered an explanation of why he took particular pains with the lighting. "When his paintings are shown with too much light, it destroys that mysterious quality because the paint has sunk into this unsized canvas and the light bleeds whatever quality they have, bleeds it away."[30] Art historian Dore Ashton also commented on the lighting of Rothko's paintings. "There were a few lights in the studio (nothing very professional, just hanging lights) which Mark turned off so I could see better," she wrote of a visit in 1959. "This paradox of his – to dim the light the better to see – is never understood by those who install his works."[31] Not even Duncan Phillips understood. Arthur Hall Smith recounted the day he opened the museum early so Rothko could see the Rothko Room for the first time. The "Irascible" was in Washington at the invitation of John and Jacqueline Kennedy, to attend JFK's swearing-in, along with fellow cultural notables John Steinbeck, Ernest Hemingway, and Carl Sandburg. In addition to that January 1961 invitation, Rothko would dine at the Kennedy White House in May 1962. In an oral history commissioned by The Phillips Collection, Smith spoke of Rothko's memorable winter visit to the museum:

> They had a snowfall at the time of the Kennedy inauguration. … [Rothko] was wearing Wellington boots through the snow, which he removed. He looked at the room for a long time and then decided the lighting should be changed. We changed the lighting the way he wanted, and he left. Duncan Phillips came in some days later, looked at it and said, 'Interesting, fascinating,' turned around, and then he said, 'Put it back the way it was.'[32]

Artist Willem de Looper's tenure as a Phillips employee overlapped with Smith's. "The older staff was not particularly fond of those paintings," de Looper said of Phillip's acquisition of Rothko's works. "In some cases, they were actually rather against them."[33] The younger staff, such as Smith and de Looper, welcomed the arrival of what at the time was considered contemporary art. In remembering those days, Smith marveled at where his favorite Rothko was kept before the Rothko Room was built. "My memory of the *Green and Maroon* is that it was squarer in format than it is. I suppose in the basement it had the weight of the mansion on it!"

Green and Tangerine on Red is another of the four one-per-wall paintings in the Rothko Room. A very special moment transpired among Rothko and the Phillipses regarding the painting. Marjorie did not document exactly when the remarkable conversation occurred, but she implied it was at Rothko's New York studio when the artist offered insight into what the painting might signify. It is important to note Marjorie's use of the word *could*: "In describing our wonderful *Green and Tangerine on Red*, Rothko said that the striking tangerine tone of the lower section of the canvas could symbolize the normal, happier side of living; and in proportion, the dark blue-green, rectangular measure above it could stand for the black clouds or worries that always hang over us."[34] Marjorie may well have carried forward an emphasis by Rothko that his words that day conveyed a *possible* meaning, rather than a concrete statement. Not long after the Rothko Room opened, the Museum of Modern Art held a retrospective of Rothko's work. Curator Peter Selz wrote in the exhibition catalogue: "We no longer look at a painting as we did in the nineteenth century; we are meant to enter it, to sink into its atmosphere of mist and light or to draw it around us like a coat – or a skin."[35] Selz, who would become the founding director of the University of California's art museum at Berkeley, shared Duncan Phillips's belief that Rothko's works serve as a catalyst for viewer introspection. MoMA's press release announcing its 1961 show quoted Selz on how he thought Rothko's paintings invite participation, and more importantly, why participation matters. "These silent paintings with their enormous, beautiful, opaque surfaces are mirrors, reflecting what the viewer brings with him." Selz said. He invoked a combination of the writings of Mark Rothko and Duncan Phillips when he added "In this sense, they can even be said to deal directly with human emotions, desires, relationships, for they … serve as echoes of our experience.[36]

Notes

[1] Mark Rothko, *The Artist's Reality: Philosophies of Art,* Ed. by Christopher Rothko (New Haven, CT: Yale University Press, 2006), 129.
[2] Marjorie Phillips, *Duncan Phillips and His Collection* (New York: W.W. Norton, 1982), 288.
[3] Arthur Hall Smith, interview with the author, Paris, 2007.
[4] Sean Scully, "Bodies of Light," *Art in America* 87, no. 7 (1999).
[5] Rothko, *Writings on Art,* Ed. by Miguel Lopez-Remiro (New Haven, CT: Yale University Press, 2006), 149.
[6] Betty Parsons, oral history interview by Gerald Silk for the Mark Rothko and His Times oral history project, 11 June 1981, Archives of American Art, Washington, D.C., 3.
[7] Rothko to Lee Krasner, 16 August 1956, Jackson Pollock and Lee Krasner Papers, Archives of American Art, Washington, D.C.
[8] William Seitz, "Notes from Interview with Rothko," 1952. William C. Seitz Papers, Archives of American Art, Washington, D.C.
[9] Edward Alden Jewell, "Globalism Pops into View: Puzzling Pictures in the Show by the Federation of Modern Painters and Sculptors Exemplify the Artists' Approach," *New York Times,* June 13, 1943.
[10] Rothko, *Writings on Art,* 133.
[11] Rothko, "The Romantics Were Prompted," in *Readings in American Art since 1900: A Documentary Survey,* ed. Barbara Rose (New York: Frederick A. Praeger, 1968), 144.
[12] Duncan Phillips, "Mark Rothko," 1963, The Phillips Collection Archives, Washington, D.C.
[13] D. Phillips, "Mark Rothko," 1964, The Phillips Collection Archives, Washington, D.C.
[14] M. Phillips, *Duncan Phillips and His Collection,* 288.
[15] Calvin Tomkins, "The Escape Artist: A New Rothko Retrospective at the Whitney," *New Yorker,* September 28, 1998, 103.

[16] Virgil Barker, *From Realism to Reality in Recent American Painting* (Lincoln: University of Nebraska Press, 1959), 91.
[17] Leslie Judd Portner, "Art in Washington: Two Aspects of Contemporary Art," *Washington Post*, February 10, 1957.
[18] D. Phillips to Mark Rothko, 17 February 1964, The Phillips Collection Archives, Washington, D.C.
[19] Kate Rothko Prizel, "Letter to the Editor: Rothko's 'Special Destination,'" *Washington Post*, October 13, 2005.
[20] Ibid.
[21] Christopher Rothko, "Curating Rothko," (panel discussion for *Rothko: The Late Series*: Tate Modern, London, 2008).
[22] C. Rothko, *Mark Rothko: From the Inside Out* (New Haven, CT: Yale University Press, 2015), 163.
[23] M. Phillips, *Duncan Phillips and His Collection*, 288.
[24] Seitz, "Notes from Interview with Rothko," 1952.
[25] Seitz, "Notes from Visit to Rothko's Studio," 1953. William C. Seitz Papers, Archives of American Art, Washington, D.C.
[26] Rothko, *Writings on Art*, 91.
[27] Katharine Kuh, *My Love Affair with Modern Art: Behind the Scenes with a Legendary Curator*, ed. Avis Berman (New York: Arcadia Publishing, 2006), 148.
[28] Ibid.
[29] Sally Avery, oral history interview by Tom Wolf for the Mark Rothko and His Times oral history project, 19 February 1982, Archives of American Art, Washington D.C., 8.
[30] Ibid, 9.
[31] Dore Ashton, "Rothko's Passion," *Art International* (1979): 9.
[32] A. Hall Smith, oral history interview by Donita M. Moorhus for The Phillips Collection Oral History Project, 2005, The Phillips Collection Archives, Washington, D.C.
[33] Willem de Looper, oral history interview by Donita M. Moorhus for The Phillips Collection Oral History Project, 2005, The Phillips Collection Archives, Washington, D.C.
[34] M. Phillips, *Duncan Phillips and His Collection*, 288.
[35] Peter Selz, *Mark Rothko* (New York: Museum of Modern Art, 1961), 10.
[36] Museum of Modern Art (press release on Rothko retrospective, January 18, 1961), Museum of Modern Art, New York.

Conclusion - Return Inward: A Legacy Endures

No stiff upper lip for him. Duncan Phillips was unafraid to speak from the heart, and of the heart. Today he would be called a man in touch with his feelings. He took those feelings and used them to rally others to art. He wrote that "Art is a means of giving permanence to our moods and memories, of restoring to us something at least of the original charms of a thousand sensuous influences that have touched our lives in passing."[1] After Phillips's own passing, in May 1966, the *New York Times* published a reflection piece on what the museum co-founder meant to art, modern art especially. *Times* art critic Hilton Kramer included an appropriate focus on how Phillips lived by a code of independence, demanding it in himself and encouraging it in others. "His methods were the reverse of popularization." Kramer wrote. "It was the individual, rather than the crowd, to whom he always addressed his endeavors."[2] Duncan's success in providing optimal conditions for personal experiences with the art in his and Marjorie's collection remains readily apparent within the museum. It is a result of Duncan, then Marjorie, then employees – those who knew one or both of the co-founders, and those who came after – always striving to improve the quality of life for fellow human beings through relationships with art. Duncan Phillips believed it was important work, and many times he explained why. In 1929, he wrote: "I hold that what we need today is not less individual expression and not less cultivation of individual sensibility but more, to the end that the art of living will come back and with it the human joys of finding art to match our unique emotional experiences."[3] In the mid-1930s, when Duncan was coming to the end of a slide presentation, he wrote in his script: "Art for too long has been a well-built house but with no place in it for love. Art must be a home for the affections. Love must come back to its vacant dwelling."[4] Then at the very end of the typed script, he inked a note to himself, or perhaps to an assistant: *Lights on.*

Directors and staff at The Phillips Collection have kept the lights on in a metaphorical sense by following Duncan and Marjorie's practices of providing optimal conditions for personal exploration of art. Their legacy is nuanced and far-reaching, but it comes down to respect for independent thought. By continuing the celebration of modern art through their methods of encouraging individual viewing experiences, The Phillips Collection maintains its relevancy. As discussed throughout this book, Duncan Phillips documented his belief in the artist's and the viewer's "return inward" or as he explained it, "the driving need to invent his own unique method to be as identical as possible with himself."[5] He continued to commit to paper his ideas about looking within oneself for the richest possible connection to art. An unpublished essay handwritten by Phillips bears a date of 1945. Its title is "Some Omissions and Misconceptions at the Sources of Art History." In it, he offered techniques on how to interact with the visual arts. Memory, perception, intuition, and imagination figured prominently. He advised viewers of art to be prepared to "see with the eyes of the mind and of the understanding of the heart."[6] Some of those viewers include artists who, in their individual ways, extended the reach of the Dupont Circle museum. Washington, D.C. artists Gene Davis and Sam Gilliam are among them. It is unlikely that Davis ever read Duncan Phillips's unpublished essay from 1945, nor was he in attendance at the Depression-era slide presentation when Phillips spoke so openly about love. Yet Duncan Phillips's message about seeing with the understanding of the heart reached him. Davis was one of the artists who became known collectively as the Washington Color Painters or Washington Color School, and according to him, "most of us haunted the Gallery in the early Fifties and many of the lessons learned there undeniably were translated into later paintings."[7] In an essay he titled "A Rambling Love Note to the Phillips Gallery," Davis wrote that "The Phillips Collection has never received enough credit for the influential role it played in the development of the Washington Color Painters, including Ken Noland, Morris Louis, Tom Downing, Howard Mehring as well as myself."[8] Davis cited Bonnard, Dove, and O'Keeffe as having affected him and his circle from time spent at the Phillips.[9] Younger artist Gilliam discussed the impact of The Phillips Collection on the Washington Color Painters even more specifically: "Noland followed the Paul Klee paintings and drawings in the Phillips. It was obvious that Louis was involved with the Doves and O'Keeffes."[10] Gilliam also spoke about the influence of works by two particular artists in the permanent collection of the Phillips: "The rhythmic flatness of a Milton Avery or a Matisse was immediately in our hands."[11]

One of Duncan Phillips's main goals, revealing "the continuity of tradition," truly came to life with Gilliam, through the artist's own deep scholarship and through time spent with Duncan and Marjorie's art collection. Gilliam considers himself a member of the third generation of Washington Color Painters, whom he refers to as Color Field Painters. "Kenneth Noland and Morris Louis are first generation, Gene Davis and Tom Downing are second generation."[12] Beyond access to The Phillips Collection, the National Gallery of Art, and other Washington, D.C. galleries, Gilliam spoke about the benefit of Washington's proximity to New York City. He moved to D.C. in 1962, a year after earning a master's degree in painting from the University of Louisville, where he had been awarded a bachelor's degree in fine arts. Through the combination of visits to museums and galleries in New York and D.C., Gilliam refreshed his formal art education. He said that especially during his first years on the

Eastern corridor, he was able to make in-person observations about connections among artists throughout the centuries. For instance, he noticed that works by Richard Diebenkorn were similar to what was "being advanced by Rothko, by [Barnett] Newman ... and in a way, even the nineteenth-century Hudson River School, the sense of the painting – the scale of it. ... It was almost as if one had come 500 years or more in painting from Giotto to Pollock and Louis ... and you could appreciate each equally and mutually."[13] According to Gilliam, there was another connection between New York City and the District of Columbia besides driving or taking the train north to actually view works of art. It revolved around word-of-mouth. Gilliam talked about how Jacob Kainen, for one, would come back from "the city" with tales of progress. Kainen, the artist who disagreed with Duncan Phillips about Arthur Dove, knew what was happening in New York largely because of his association with artists Arshile Gorky and Willem de Kooning as well as art critic Clement Greenberg. Gilliam said that Kainen passed the information and his assessments to the "third wave" of Washington Color Painters.[14] Gilliam noted that there were also other Washington artists who stayed up-to date on New York, but Kainen was among the most accessible.

New York City had claimed prominence as the international capital of art well before the Washington Color Painters hit their strides. However, for Davis, renowned for his wall-size works featuring stripes, and Gilliam, a Guggenheim Foundation award recipient, The Phillips Collection became the place they loved. Part of their affection for the Phillips came from their admiration of people deeply involved with the museum. Davis wrote how the "artistic cathedral" was enhanced by his interactions with long-time Phillips employees Jim McLaughlin and John Gernand. McLaughlin was known among staff as able to handle any job at the museum and he eventually became a curator. Gernand, who served as registrar, is partly remembered by Phillips staff for feeding slices of ham to the cats every day at 1 p.m. Davis reminisced about how talking with the "amiable" McLaughlin and Gernand became a "weekend ritual."[15] Another Davis memory of the Phillips "came at the time of the opening of the Gallery's new wing [1960] ... It was on a Sunday afternoon and I decided to drop by for a visit. On entering the lobby of the strangely modern structure, I noted that both Mr. and Mrs. Phillips were personally greeting Gallery goers with a handshake and a few words of welcome."[16]

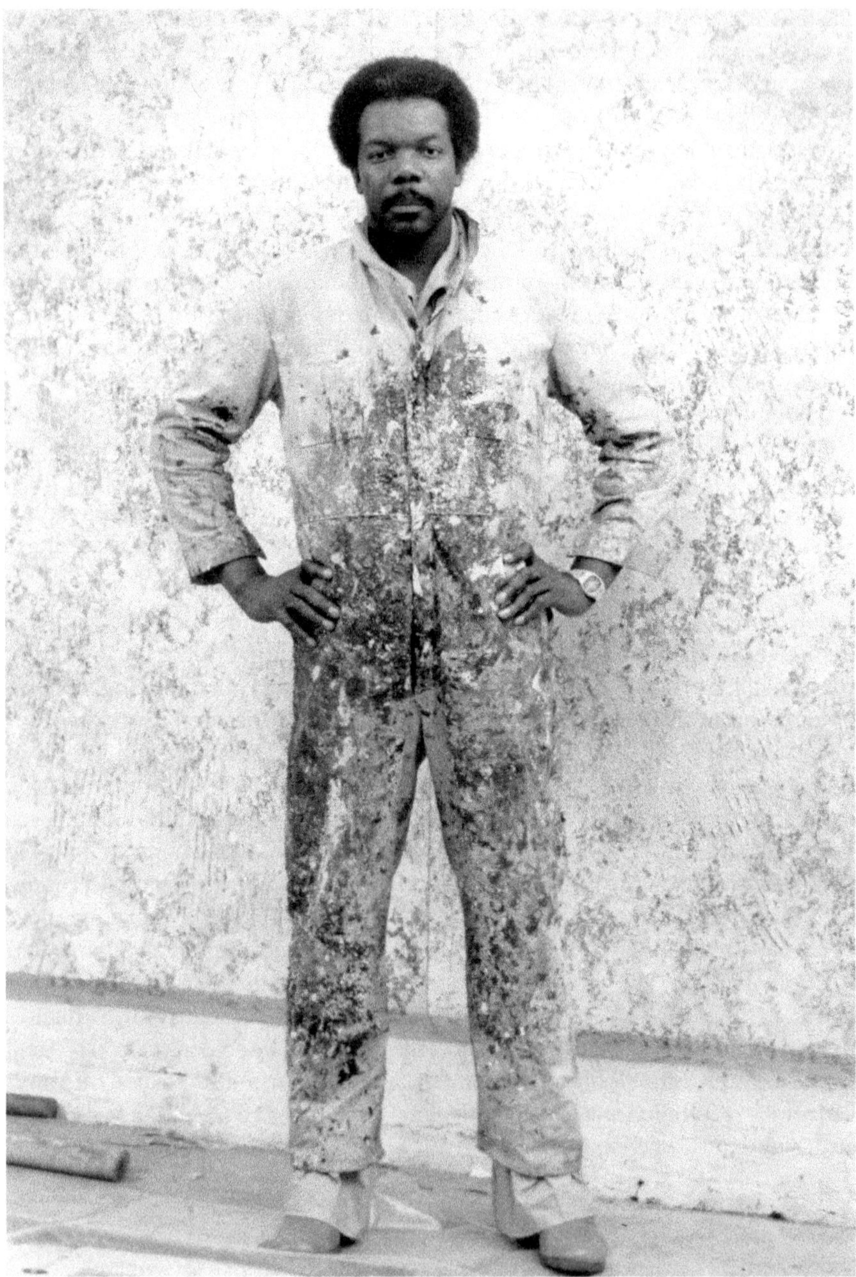

Image C. 1. *Portrait of Sam Gilliam,* 1969. Photo by Paul Feinberg ©. Courtesy of the David Kordansky Gallery, Los Angeles.

For Gilliam, Marjorie Phillips was the embodiment of The Phillips Collection. She had a direct and profound influence on his career, and was "a big part of giving Washington a significance in the art world."[17] In 1967, the year after Duncan died, Marjorie bought Gilliam's work *Red Petals* for The Phillips Collection. According to Katherine Grotto Revell, *Red Petals*, which measures roughly seven-by-eight feet, was among the first paintings in which Gilliam poured paint onto an unprimed canvas, folded the canvas onto itself, suspended it, and left the paint to settle overnight, subject to the force of gravity.[18] Revell explained that "the next day he would sponge, daub, fold or roll the canvas"[19] and in the case of *Red Petals*, he re-stretched the canvas.

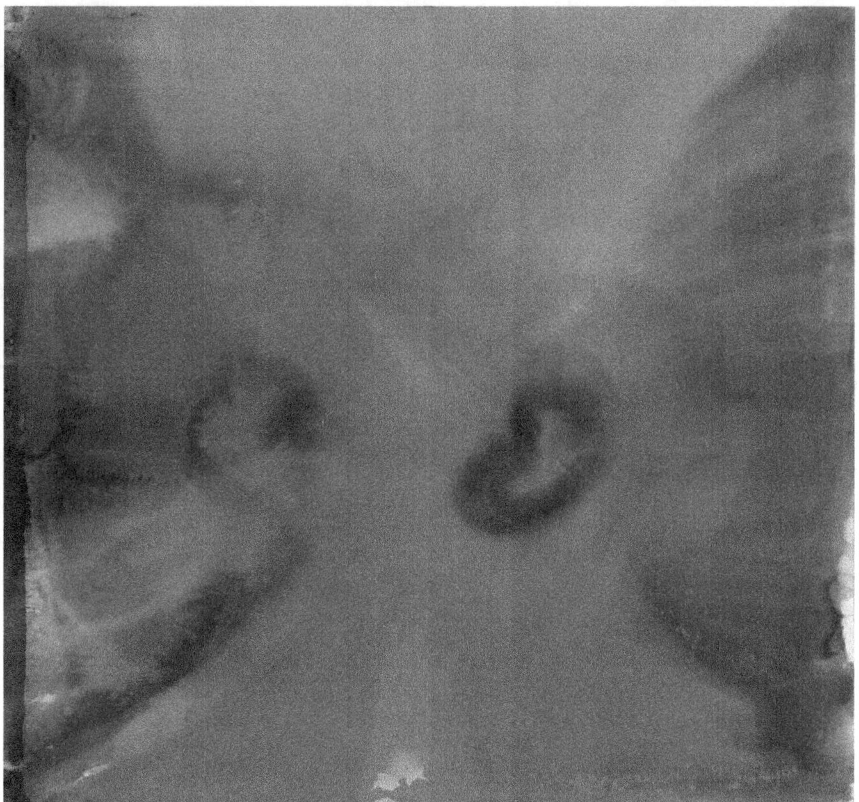

Image C. 2. Sam Gilliam, *Red Petals*, 1967, Acrylic on canvas 88 x 93 in.; 223.52 x 236.22 cm. The Phillips Collection: Acquired 1967. Paintings, 0789, American. Courtesy of the artist and the David Kordansky Gallery, Los Angeles.

In addition to purchasing Gilliam's innovative work, Marjorie Phillips gave him his first one-man show at a museum. What impressed Gilliam most about the co-founder was her "come as you are, up as you are"[20] credo; she did not want him to make new art for the 1967 show. He explained that he and other artists could be held back by the practice of many galleries insisting on all new works from an artist should a show be offered. Like her husband, Marjorie was happy installing exhibitions at the Phillips herself or with designated assistants. However, she told Gilliam that he could install his Phillips Collection show himself. Gilliam said that he respected Marjorie for many reasons. One was the fact that she painted. "Mrs. Phillips being attuned to the life of a painter was very important, it meant a lot to me and other artists."[21] Gilliam said that he will always be grateful to Marjorie Phillips for what she did for local artists. According to Gilliam, she stimulated the collecting of Washington artists in two main ways. The first was by virtue of showing their art at her museum. "The environment of The Phillips Collection with its Rothkos and Daumiers and Lawrence's *Migration Series* gave validity to local artists."[22] The second was that she never backed away from her ground-rule that artists need not create new works of art for a show at the Phillips. "Her purpose was to have us collected,"[23] Gilliam said of himself and fellow Washington painters. "Many of us who showed there went on to European markets."[24] Although Gilliam achieved both critical and financial success by making art, he also taught art at the Corcoran School of Art, the Maryland Institute College of Art, and Carnegie Mellon University. Gene Davis also taught at the Corcoran School of Art.

Washington painters were not the only ones influenced by The Phillips Collection, nor the only ones to share its influence with younger artists. Californian Richard Diebenkorn said that trips to the Phillips Memorial Gallery constituted a key point in his life when he was a Marine stationed at Quantico, Virginia, in 1944. "Here's a painter in the armed services during wartime. Here was Duncan Phillips's magnificent house which he opened to all comers," Diebenkorn said in an oral history interview. "And it wasn't like a museum, it was like a house, and you could sort of sprawl in the furniture." [25] Like Gilliam and Davis, Diebenkorn would succeed on an international level, and he, too, would teach throughout his career. "It was a refuge, it was a kind of sanctuary for me," Diebenkorn said of the Phillips. "I just absorbed everything on those walls. ... I absorbed something else, and that has to do with the incredible generosity that was there to take home with you."[26]

Did Duncan or Marjorie ever see the young Diebenkorn when he made his weekend excursions to their collection of art? There is no record of it. But it is safe to say they would not have minded him getting comfortable in one of the soft chairs they set out for that purpose. Diebenkorn seemed to innately understand what Duncan and Marjorie Phillips wanted for him, for other visiting artists, and for members of the viewing public. Come, make yourself at home. Enjoy the art. Think independently. Return inward.

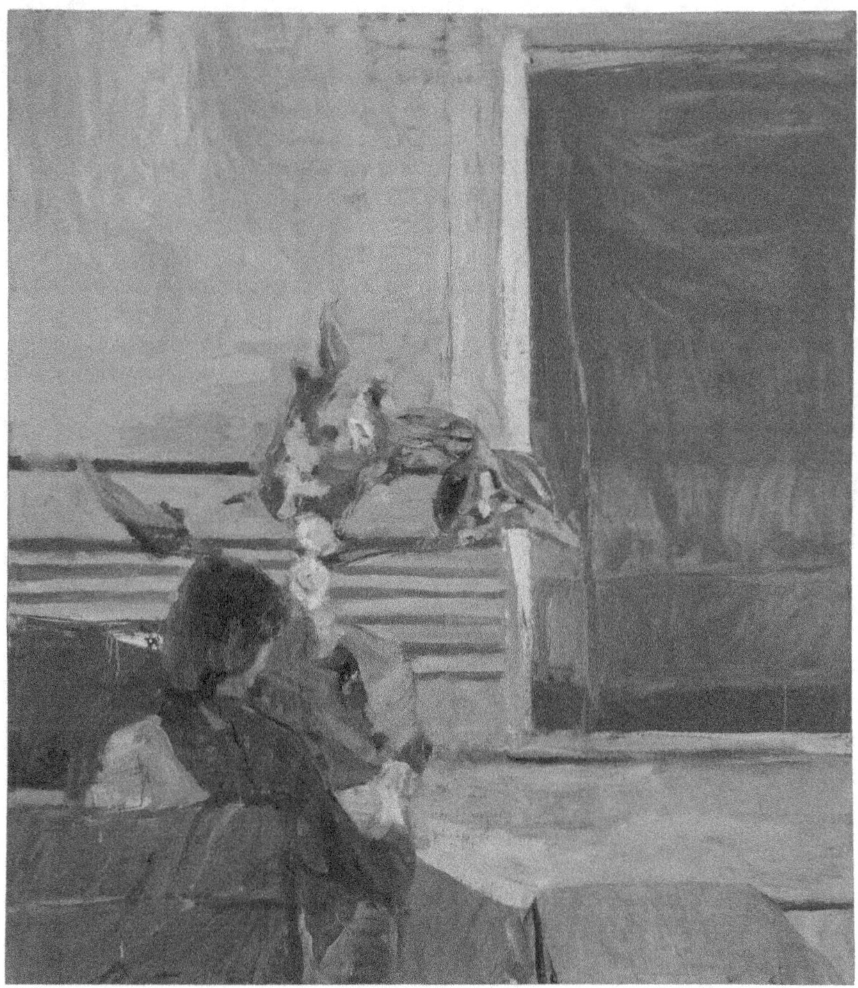

Image C. 3. Richard Diebenkorn, *Girl with Plant,* 1960, Oil on canvas 80 x 69 1/2 in.; 203.2 x 176.53 cm. The Phillips Collection: Acquired 1961; © Richard Diebenkorn Foundation. Paintings, 0519, American. Courtesy of Richard Diebenkorn Foundation.

Notes

[1] Duncan Phillips, *The Enchantment of Art: As Part of the Enchantment of Experience Fifteen Years Later* (Washington, D.C.: Phillips Publications, 1927), 17.
[2] Hilton Kramer, "The Phillips Gallery Reflects Integrity of a Gifted Man," *New York Times,* May 12, 1966.
[3] D. Phillips, "Art and Understanding," *Art and Understanding* 1 (November 1929): 12.

[4] D. Phillips, "Freshness of Vision," slide lecture circa 1935, The Phillips Collection Archives, Washington, D.C.
[5] D. Phillips, *A Bulletin of The Phillips Collection Relating to a Tri-Unit Exhibition of Paintings and Sculpture*, Phillips Memorial Gallery, Washington, D.C., 1927.
[6] D. Phillips, unpublished essay "Some Omissions and Misconceptions at the Sources of Art History," 1945, The Phillips Collection Archives, Washington, D.C.
[7] Gene Davis, "A Rambling Love Note to the Phillips Gallery," undated, The Phillips Collection Archives, Washington, D.C.
[8] Ibid.
[9] Davis, phone interview by Fritz Jellinghouse for "Artists on The Phillips Collection," 1982, The Phillips Collection Archives, Washington, D.C.
[10] Sam Gilliam, oral history interview by Donita M. Moorhus for The Phillips Collection Oral History Project, 28 October 2010, The Phillips Collection Archives, Washington, D.C.
[11] Ibid., 12.
[12] Gilliam, phone interview by the author, 20 December 2019.
[13] Gilliam, oral history by Kenneth Young for the Archives of American Art, 18 September 1984, Archives of American Art, Washington, D.C., 10.
[14] Ibid., 13.
[15] Davis, "A Rambling Love Note."
[16] Ibid.
[17] Gilliam, phone interview by the author.
[18] Katherine Grotto Revell, "Sam Gilliam," in *The Eye of Duncan Phillips, A Collection in the Making*, Ed. by Erika D. Passantino and David W. Scott (New Haven, CT: Yale University Press), 656.
[19] Ibid.
[20] Gilliam, phone interview by the author.
[21] Ibid.
[22] Ibid.
[23] Ibid.
[24] Ibid.
[25] Richard Diebenkorn, phone interview by Fritz Jellinghouse for "Artists on The Phillips Collection," 1982, The Phillips Collection Archives, Washington, D.C.
[26] Ibid.

Index

I

J

K

L

M

T

U

V

W

Y

www.ingramcontent.com/pod-product-compliance
Lightning Source LLC
LaVergne TN
LVHW050646100826
845148LV00011B/2004

* 9 7 8 1 6 4 8 8 9 3 2 7 8 *